DISEASES OF VEGETABLE CROPS

Dr. M. LAKSHMI NAGA NANDINI

ABOUT THE AUTHOR

Dr. M. Lakshmi Naga Nandini is working as Assistant Professor (Plant Pathology), in Department of Agriculture and Horticultural Sciences, School of Agriculture and Food Technology, Vignan's Foundation for Science, Technology and Research (Deemed to be University). She has completed her PG and Ph.D. from Dr.YSR Horticultural University, Venkataramannagudem, West Godavari, Andhra Pradesh. She received medals during her PG & Ph.D programmes and several meritorious awards in International and National conferences for her research contributions. A budding expert in Plant Pathology, she has published over 15 research articles in refereed journals, authored 2 books and contributed about 10 chapters to different books in National and International repute. She also served as a reviewer of editorial board in national journals and several international scientific societies. Her areas of specialization are Biological Control and Molecular Plant Pathology.

<u>**Preface**</u>

Plant pathology is one of the most vital branches of agricultural sciences. Plant diseases render a huge loss of agricultural produce every year in terms of both quality and quantity. The better diagnosis and detection of the pathogens in the early stages of infection are quite necessary for the effective management of these diseases. There has been a long-felt need by the student and teacher for a comprehensive book on diseases of vegetable crops, fruit crops, and plantation crops. Because of that, it has been my ambition to write a book on plant pathology for the benefit of students of botany and agriculture and which is devoted to covering, in general, certain basic aspects of knowledge on diagnostic symptoms, mode of the perpetuation of the pathogen and dissemination, favorable conditions for disease development, and latest management strategy seem. This volume has been produced to introduce the student to the basic and fundamental aspects of the subject before he attempts to learn about the diseases of vegetable crops. The selected bibliography given at the end of each chapter should help the student to acquire additional knowledge on the subject. In the last chapter, an attempt is made to critically review the present status of plant pathology in India and to assess the future needs so as to give perspective to young minds desirous of specializing in this branch of science.

It is sincerely hoped that this book would be extremely useful to students, teachers, and researchers. This book will also assist in various competitive examinations, such as those for plant protection officer, district horticulture officer, and other government jobs in agriculture, horticulture, and plant protection. Moreover, plant protection experts, vegetable specialists, horticultural officers, and extension workers may utilize this informative book as a ready reckon.

Dr. M. Lakshmi Naga Nandini

Contents

TOMATO

Introduction:

- Tomato (*Solanum lycopersicon* L.) is an important vegetable crop grown globally and consumed as salad, ketchups, sauce, soup, pickles etc.
- It is also cooked along with other vegetables to provide taste and is the basic need of the Indian kitchen. Ripened fruits are good source of ascorbic acid and minerals.
- The crop is generally grown during winter months (Oct-April) in the plains of India while in the hills it is mostly grown during summer and rainy season, thus fresh fruits are available round the year in the market.
- Prevalence of high humidity and warm temperature not only favours the luxuriant growth of the crop but also favours the development of various fungal, bacterial and viral diseases.
- Under favourable environmental conditions, epiphytotics of certain diseases have often reduced the yield considerably in certain years.
- Some of the important fungal, bacterial and viral disease problems are described in this lecture.

Diseases:

S. No.	Disease Name	Causal Organism
Fungal diseases		
1.	Early blight	*Alternaria solani*
2.	Damping off	*Pythium aphanidermatum*
3.	Stemphylium leaf spot	*Stemphylium lycopersici*
4.	Cercospora leaf spot	*Cercospora solani*
5.	Septoria leaf spot	*Septoria lycopersici*
6.	Anthracnose	*Colletotrichum gloeosporioides*
7.	Gray mould	*Botrytis cinerea*
8.	Buckeye rot	*P. nicotianae var. Parasitica*
9.	Fusarium wilt	*Fusarium oxysporum* f. sp. *Lycopersici*
10.	Verticillium wilt	*Verticillium alboatrum*
11.	Phoma Rot	*Phoma destructive*
Bacterial diseases		
12.	Bacterial leaf spot	*Xanthomonas campestris pv. Vesicatoria*
13.	Bacterial fruit canker	*Clavibacter michiganense sub sp. Michiganense*
14.	Bacterial wilt	*Burkholderia solanacearum*
15.	Bacterial soft rot and Hollow stem	*Erwinia carotovora pv. carotovora*
Viral diseases		
16.	Mosaic	Tomato mosaic virus, Cucumber mosaic virus
17.	Tomato spotted wilt	Tomato Spotted Wilt Virus (TSWV), Groundnut bud necrosis virus
18.	Leaf curl	Tomato leaf curl virus (ToLCV)

Physiological Disorders		
19.	Blossom End Rot	
20.	Catface	
21.	Fruit Cracking	
22.	Sunscald	
23.	Puffiness	
24.	Blotchy ripening	
25.	Gold Fleck	

1. Damping off

Causal Organism: *Pythium aphanidermatam, P. debaryanum, P. ultimum, Fusarium* and *Rhizoctonia*

Economic Importance:

- Damping-off, a disease of germinating seeds and seedlings, generally refers to sudden plant death in the seedling stage.
- It is fatal to young seedlings and becomes colonized resulting in plant losses and delayed planting.

Symptoms:

- Damping off of tomato occurs in two stages, *i.e.* the pre-emergence and the post emergence phase.
- In the pre-emergence the phase the seedlings are killed just before they reach the soil surface.
- The young radical and the plumule are killed and there is complete rotting of the seedlings. The post-emergence phase is characterized by the infection of the young, juvenile tissues of the collar at the ground level.
- The infected tissues become soft and water soaked. The seedlings topple over or collapse.

Mode of spread and survival:

- All the causal organisms are soil inhabitants and they build up in soil with the available hosts. Generally these pathogens have wide host range.
- P.I: Oospores in soil or plant debris.
- S.I: Zoospores through irrigation water.

Management:

- Use raised seed bed.

- Provide light, but frequent irrigation for better drainage. Drench with Copper oxychloride (Blitox) 0.2% or Bordeaux mixture 1%.
- Seed treatment with fungal culture *Trichoderma viride* (4 g/kg of seed) or Thiram (3 g/kg of seed) is the only preventive measure to control the pre-emergence damping off.
- Spray 0.2% Metalaxyl when there is cloudy weather.

2. Fusarium Wilt

Causal Organism: *Fusarium oxysporum* f. sp. *lycopersici*, *Fusarium solani*

Symptoms:

- The first symptom of the disease is clearing of the veinlets and chlorosis of the leaves.
- The younger leaves may die in succession and the entire may wilt and die in a course of few days.
- Soon the petiole and the leaves droop and wilt. In young plants, symptom consists of clearing of vein let and dropping of petioles.
- In field, yellowing of the lower leaves first and affected leaflets wilt and die. The symptoms continue in subsequent leaves.
- At later stage, browning of vascular system occurs. Plants become stunted and die.

Pathogen:

- Mycelium is septate and hyaline. It produces macro and micro conidia.
- Micro conidia are one celled, hyaline, and ovoid to ellipsoid. Two races of pathogen have been identified.

Mode of spread and survival:

- The fungus is seed borne and soil borne.
- The fungus survives in the soil as chlamydospores or as saprophytically growing mycelium in infected crop debris for more than 10 years.
- One of the chief methods of its distribution is by seedlings raised in infected soil.
- Wind borne conidia, surface drainage water and agricultural implements also help in distribution of the pathogen from field to field.

Management:

- The affected plants should be removed and destroyed.
- Crop rotation with a non-host crop such as cereals. Soil application of Phorate (Thimet) @1g/plant on 10th day of transplanting for nematode management.
- Soil drench with Carbendazim (Bavistin) @0.1% or COC@0.25%. Repeat soil drenching after 3-4 weeks.

- Use resistance varieties like Roza, Columbia, Roma, HS-110, Sel-28, and Ace varieties of tomato are resistant against fusarium wilt.

3. Septoria Leaf Spot

Causal Organism: *Septoria lycopersici*

Economic Importance:

- Septoria leaf spot is one of the most common and destructive diseases of tomato.
- The disease causes rapid defoliation in warm and moist weather.
- It is of worldwide occurrence, its severity and extent of damage depend on crop and environmental conditions.

Symptoms:

- The plant may be attacked at any stage of its growth. Less vigorous plants are usually affected.
- The disease is characterized by small, round to irregular spots with a **grey center** and dark margin on leaves.
- Spots usually start on lower leaves and gradually advance upwards. Complete defoliation of affected leaves.
- Stems and flowers are sometimes attacked. Fruits are rarely attacked.

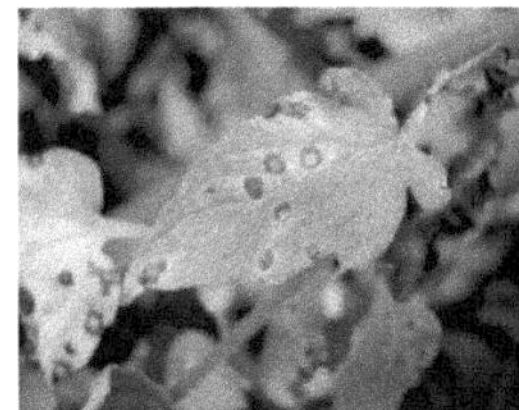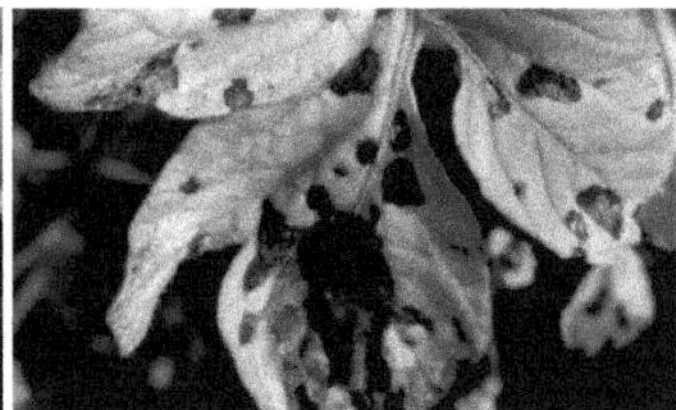

Pathogen:

- Mycelium is septate, branched, and hyaline when young and darkens with age.
- Pycnidia are erumpent. Pycnidiospores are filiform, hyaline and septate.

Mode of spread and survival:

- The pathogen is spread by wind and rain splashes, insects and on the hands and clothings of tomato pickers.
- It survives from one season to the next on infested crop debris and also on solanaceous weeds.
- The fungus also survives on or in the seed. Seed stocks contaminated with spores produce infected seedlings.
- P.I: Mycelium or conidia in infected plant debris
- S.I: Air borne conidia

Favourable conditions:

- High humidity or persistent dew at 25^0 C.
- Moist weather with intermittent showers.

Management:

- Removal and destruction of the affected plant parts.

- Crop rotation with non hosts.
- Seed treatment with Thiram or Mancozeb (Dithane M-45) (2 g/kg seed) is useful in checking seed borne infection.
- In the field spraying with Mancozeb or Zineb 0.2 % at 10 days interval effectively controls the disease.
- Tomato line **PI 422397** is resistant (Fullelove *et al.,* 1998).

4. Early blight

Causal Organism: *Alternaria solani*

Economic Importance:

- It is a very common disease of tomato.
- The disease can occur over a wide range of climatic conditions and can be very destructive if left uncontrolled, often resulting in complete defoliation of plants.
- The disease is equally serious on the hills as well as in the plains.

Symptoms:

- This is a common disease of tomato occurring on the foliage at any stage of the growth.
- The fungus attacks the foliage causing characteristic leaf spots and blight.
- Early blight is first observed on the plants as small, black lesions mostly on the older foliage.
- Spots enlarge, and by the time they are one-fourth inch in diameter or larger, concentric rings in a bull's eye pattern can be seen in the center of the diseased area.
- Tissue surrounding the spots may turn yellow. If high temperature and humidity occur at this time, much of the foliage is killed.
- Lesions on the stems are similar to those on leaves, sometimes girdling the plant if they occur near the soil line.
- The fungus also infects the fruit, generally through the calyx or stem attachment.
- Lesions attain considerable size, usually involving nearly the entire fruit; concentric rings are also present on the fruit.

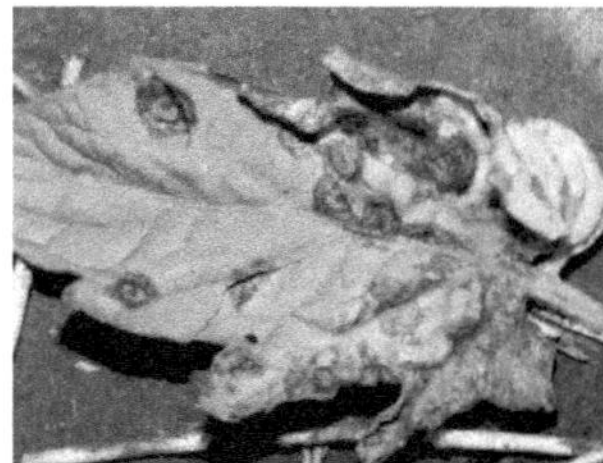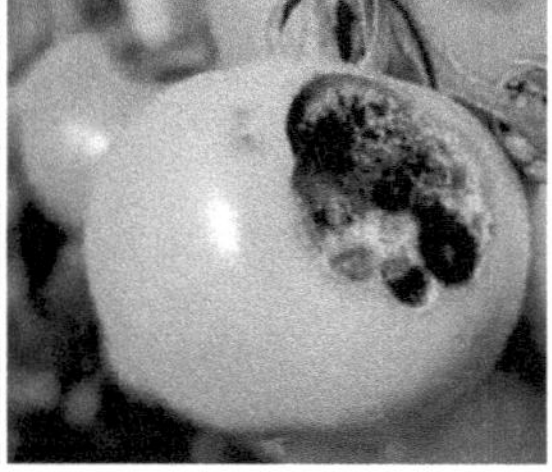

Pathogen:

- Mycelium is septate, branched, light brown which become darker with age.
- Conidiophores are dark coloured. Conidia are beaked, muriform, dark coloured and borne singly.

Mode of spread and survival:

- The pathogen is spread by wind and rain splashes. Under dry conditions it survives in infected plant debris in the soil for upto three years and is also seed borne.

- P.I: Mycelium or conidia in infected plant debris.
- S.I: Conidia dispersed by wind, water or rain splashes.

Epidemiology:
- Dry warm weather alternating with the intermittent rains. Reduction in plant vigour and senescence favours the disease.

Management:
- Removal and destruction of crop debris.
- Maintain proper vigour of the plant.
- Use of disease free seed.
- Practicing crop rotation helps to minimize the disease incidence.
- Spray the crop with Mancozeb@0.25% or chlorothalonil (Kavach) @0.2% or Zineb@ 0.25% at weekly intervals for effective disease control.
- Use pathogen-free seeds and resistant cultivars like **Arka Rakshak, Arka samara** and **DARL-30.**

5. **Stemphylium leaf spot**

Causal Organism: *Stemphylium lycopersici*

Symptoms:
- Small brownish **black specks** on the underside of leaves.
- Later these specks develop on both leaf surfaces into grayish brown, glazed lesions of 3 mm or less in size.
- On older leaves lesions dry up, crack and the centers drop out leaving a shot hole appearance.
- Yellowing of the leaf occurs followed by defoliation of the plant.

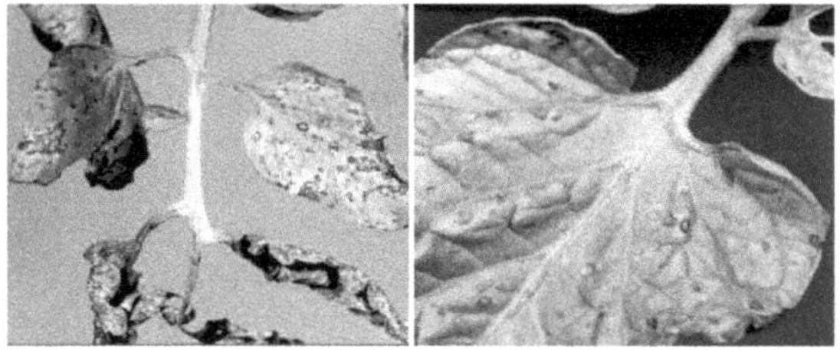

Disease cycle:
- P.I: Mycelium or conidia in infected plant debris
- S.I: Air borne conidia

Favourable conditions:
- Warm, moist weather favours the disease.

Management:
- Rouging and burning of infected plant debris. Foliar application of mancozeb@0.25% (Jones *et al.,* 1991).

6. **Gray Mould**

Causal Organism: *Botrytis cinerea*

Symptoms:

- Lesion is a watery area with a light brown or tan coloured central region. Converted into a soft, watery mass within a few days.
- Skin is broken; the grayish mycelium and spore clusters develop within a few hours.
- Halo forms around the point of entry small whitish rings approximately develop on young green fruit.
- "Ghost spots" are usually single rings but may be solid white spots; the center of which contains dark brown specks.

Pathogen:
- Mycelium is septate and branched, hyaline but become dark in colour upon age.
- Conidiophores are branched and bear conidia at the apex. Conidia are continuous or one septate, oblong and dark.

Mode of spread and survival:
- High relative humidities are necessary for prolific spore production.
- Optimum temperatures for infection are between 65° and 75° F (18° and 24° C), and infection can occur within 5 hours. High temperatures, above 82° F (28° C), suppress growth and spore production.

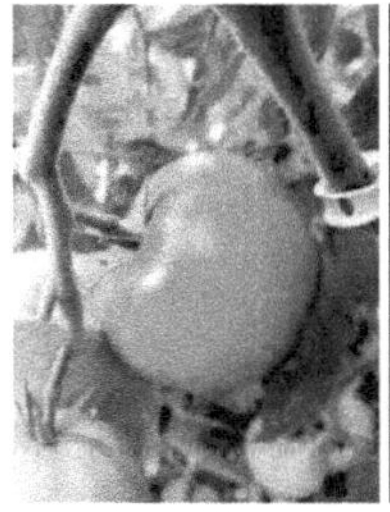
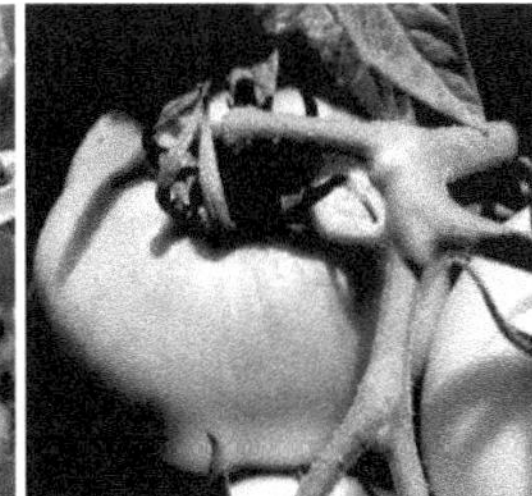

Management:
- Spraying with Bordeaux mixture 1.0 % or mancozeb 0.2% is helpful in reducing the disease.
- Resistant varieties like **Vetomold** may be grown in areas where disease appears in an endemic form. Eurocross varities like **Antincold, LMRI** and **Sapsford's No.1** are resistant.

7. **Phoma Rot**

Causal Organism: *Phoma destructive*

Symptoms:
- Distinguished from other rots by the black color of this spot. Small, black, pimple-like eruptions. Specks are the pycnidia or fruiting bodies of the fungus.

Pathogen:
- The ascospores are irregularly arranged in two series. They are ellipsoid with obtuse ends, hyaline and guttulate.
- Pycnidia are solitary to gregarious and dark brown. Conidia typically biguttulate, straight and irregular.

Mode of spread:
- The pathogen is seed borne.

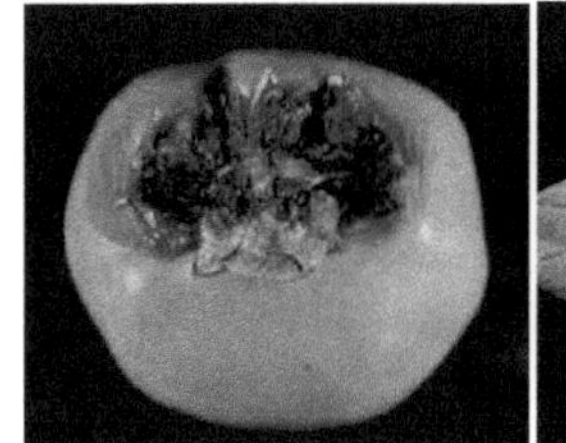

Management:

- Seed treatment with organomercurial and spraying the crop with zineb 0.2% gives adequate protection against the disease.

8. Buckeye rot

Causal Organism: *Phytophthora nicotianae var. parasitica*

Symptoms:

- Immature fruits (green colour) irrespective of their development stages are susceptible.
- Water soaked light brown discoloured spots appear which increase readily showing concentric dark brown rings slightly resembling the markings as a buckeye.
- The lesions rapidly enlarge and within 3-4 days, whole of the fruit surface turns dark brown and feels soft to touch.
- In warm and humid weather, white flocculent superficial growth of the fungus consisting of sporangia and sporangiophpores also develops on the diseased fruits. Later, these fruits may drop off from the plant.

Pathogen:

- The mycelium of the pathogen is hyaline and coenocytic with branching typically at right angles.
- The sporangiophores arise from hyphal threads and produce sporangia.The sporangia are broadly ovoid to globose in shape having one hemispherical papilla at the tip.
- Chlamydospores are smooth, globose, and slightly yellowish with thick brown walls, produced abundantly in culture and germinate by producing zoospores or germ tubes.
- Antheridia are amphigynous, spherical or oval and oogonia are rough, thick walled and yellowish brown in colour.
- Oospores are aplerotic, 18 to 20 μm in diameter with 2 μm thick wall.

Disease cycle:

- The fungus overwinters in the soil in the form of oospores or chlamydospores and can remain active in soil for at least one year without the support of a susceptible host.
- With the onset of monsoon rains, in the presence of high soil moisture and moderate temperatures (20-25°C), the chlamydospores and oospores start germinating by producing mycelium and sporangia.
- The sporangia in turn produce biflagellate zoospores, which are splashed by rain to the fruits.

- The symptoms develop on fruits after 3-4 day of infection. Infected fruit become mummified and fall down on the ground. The sporangia produced on infected fruits, liberate zoospores which are again splashed by rain and cause secondary infection.

Epidemiology:
- Maximum fruit infection under field conditions occurs at a temperature range of 20-25°C, RH > 80 per cent and high rainfall conditions.
- Higher doses of N resulted in higher fruit rot while higher levels of P resulted in more yield of healthy fruits and less fruit rot.

Forecasting:
- Based on weekly temperature and cumulative rainfall, short term forecasting of the disease can be done. June 20 is considered as the zero date.
- The disease is not expected to occur at temperatures at or below 20°C, though at temperatures of 22.5°C or above even a slight rainfall (10 mm) will result in disease appearance, which is expected to appear after 4 days of infection.

Management:
- Stake the plants erect and remove foliage and fruit up to a height of 15-20 cm to avoid moist and stagnant air conditions.
- Collect and destroy the affected fruits regularly. Apply pine needle/grass mulch on the field floor to create a barrier between the host and soil borne inoculum.
- With the onset of monsoon rains, spray the crop with metalaxyl + mancozeb (Ridomil MZ) (0.25%) followed by sprays of either mancozeb (0.25%) or copper oxychloride (0.3%) or Bordeaux mixture (4:4:50) and repeat at 7-10 days interval.

9. Anthracnose:

Causal Organism: *Colletotrichum gloeosporioide, Colletotrichum phomoides*

Symptoms:
- Green and ripe tomatoes can be infected, but symptoms are expressed on ripe fruits. As the fungus colonizes the fruit, a semisoft decay occurs.
- Anthracnose lesions often merge and result in large rotted areas, which render the fruit unfit for processing.
- Although symptoms do not appear until the fruit is ripening, the infection occurs when fruits are small and green.
- Symptoms of anthracnose appear first as small, circular, slightly sunken lesions on the surface of ripening fruits.

- The spots quickly enlarge, become bruise like depressions, and develop a water-soaked appearance directly beneath the skin (epidermis) of the fruit.
- As these spots expand, they develop dark centers or concentric rings of dark specks.
- The rings consist of numerous small spore-producing bodies of the fungus (microsclerotia and acervuli).
- In moist weather these bodies exude large numbers of spores, giving diseased areas a cream to salmon pink colour.

Favourable conditions:
- Excessive moisture.
- Older leaves and mature fruits are more susceptible.

Mode of spread and survival:
- P.I: Incipient infection carried by fruits from the field.
- S.I: Conidia by wind and rain splash.

Management:
- Harvest fruit as soon as possible after ripening.
- Avoid excessive overhead irrigation or use drip irrigation to reduce moisture levels on fruit and humidity in the plant canopy.
- A three-year rotation may also reduce chances for infection.
- Foliar spray, twice, with carbendazim @0.1% at 15 days interval or chlorothalonil (Kavach) @0.2% at 10-15 days interval.
- Last spray to be given 10 days before harvest ¾ Fumigation of fruits with benzylisothiocyanate and coating with groundnut oil controls post harvest spots and rots.

10. Bacterial wilt

Causal Organism: *Burkholderia solanacearum*

Economic Importance:
- Bacterial wilt/brown rot is one of the most destructive diseases of tomatoes, causing extensive damage to the crop.

Symptoms:
- This is one of the most serious diseases of tomato crop. Relatively high soil moisture and soil temperature favour disease development.
- Characteristic symptoms of bacterial wilt are the rapid and complete wilting of normal grown up plants. Lower leaves may drop before wilting.
- Pathogen is mostly confined to vascular region; in advantage cases, it may invade the cortex and pith and cause yellow brown discolouration of tissues.

- Infected plant parts when cut and immersed in clear water, a white streak of bacterial ooze is seen coming out from cut ends.

Pathogen:
- The bacterium is gram negative, rod shaped often occurs in pairs, motile with 1-4 flagella. The optimum temperature for growth is 30-37˚C.

Mode of spread and survival:
- The bacterium survives in soil and they spread through irrigation water and by transplanting of infected seedlings.
- The bacterium survives for 3 years in fallow and for a unlimited period in cultivated land.
- Chilli, egg plant, grount nut, potato and tobacco are alternative hosts which help it to survive between tomato crops.

Management:
- Avoid damage to seedling while transplanting.
- Apply bleaching powder @ 10kg/ha.
- Crop rotations, *viz.,* cowpea-maize-cabbage, okra-cowpea-maize, maize- cowpea-maize and finger millet-egg plant are reported effective in reducing bacterial wilt of tomato.
- Use resistant variety like **Shakti, Arka Rakshak** and **Arka Samrat** or tolerant variety like **NS 501** and **538** etc.

11. Bacterial Leaf Spot

Causal Organism: *Xanthomonas campestris* pv. *vesicatoria*

Economic Importance:
- It is a serious problem in tropical and subtropical regions of high humidity and rainfall.

Symptoms:
- Moist weather and splattering rains are conducive to disease development.
- Most outbreaks of the disease can be traced back to heavy rainstorms that occur in the area.
- Infected leaves show small, brown, water soaked, circular spots surrounded with yellowish halo.
- On older plants the leaflet infection is mostly on older leaves and may cause serious defoliation.

- The most striking symptoms are on the green fruit. Small, water-soaked spots first appear which later become raised and enlarge until they are one-eighth to one-fourth inch in diameter.
- Centers of these lesions become irregular, light brown and slightly sunken with a rough, scabby surface.
- Ripe fruits are not susceptible to the disease.
- Surface of the seed becomes contaminated with the bacteria, remaining on the seed surface for some time.
- The organism survives in alternate hosts, on volunteer tomato plants and on infected plant debris.

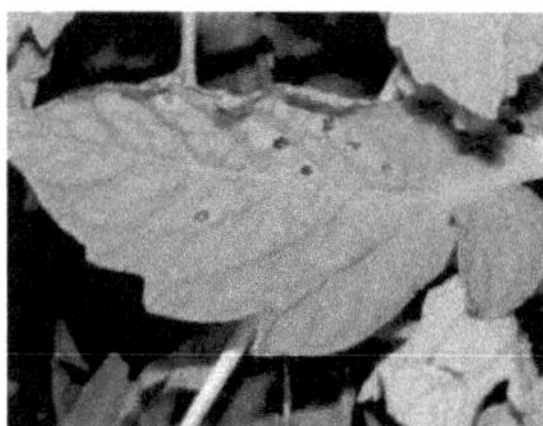

Pathogen:
- The bacterium is gram negative, short rod shaped and has a single, polar flagellum.
- Capsules are formed.

Mode of spread and survival:
- The pathogen survives in the diseased plant debris, volunteer plants. It is seed borne.
- The bacterium enters through stomata or injuries and lenticels.
- Secondary spread through rain splashes. Disease spreads to new areas through infected seeds and diseased transplants.

Management:
- Disease-free seed and seedlings should always be used and the crop should be rotated with non-host crops so as to avoid last year's crop residue.
- Seed treatment with mercuric chloride (1:1000) is also recommended for control of disease.
- Spraying with a combination of copper and organic fungicides in a regular preventative spray program at 5 to 10 day intervals or Spraying with Agrimycin-100 (100 ppm) thrice at 10 days intervals effectively controls the disease (Roberts *et al.,* 1999).

12. Bacterial Soft Rot and Hollow Stem

Causal Organism: *Erwinia carotovora* pv. *carotovora*

Symptoms:
- Soft watery decay of fruit, starting at one or more points, as very small spots on the fruit.
- These spots enlarge very rapidly until the entire fruit as soft watery mass.
- Pathogen liquefies fruit tissue by breaking down the pectate "glue" that holds plant cells together.
- Leakage of internal collapse resembling a shriveled water balloon (Naika *et al.,* 2005).

Pathogen:
- Bacteria are single-celled, rapidly multiply and spread in water.
- During wet weather and High humidity, Heavy rain fall or irrigation and warm temperatures in the 73 - 95 F range favours disease.

13. Bacterial fruit canker

Causal Organism: *Clavibacter michiganense subsp. Michiganense*

Economic Importance:
- Bacterial canker is a destructive disease of tomato present throughout the tomato growing regions of the world and cause serious losses in tomato crop.

Symptoms:
- Disease appears as **spots** on leaves, stems and fruits and as **wilting** of leaves and shoots.
- White blister like spots in the margins of leaves. Spots become brown with age and coalesce, but do not fall off.
- Leaves wilt and curl upward. Light coloured streaks on stems and petioles at the joints. Cracks develop in streaks and form cankers.
- Slimy bacterial ooze through the cracks in humid weather. Small, shallow, water soaked, white spots on fruits.
- The centers of white spots become slightly raised, tan coloured and rough.
- **Birds eye** like appearance of spots, which have brownish centers and white halos.
- Vascular discolouration is seen. Large cavities in pith and cortex which extend to outer surface of stem and cause cankers.

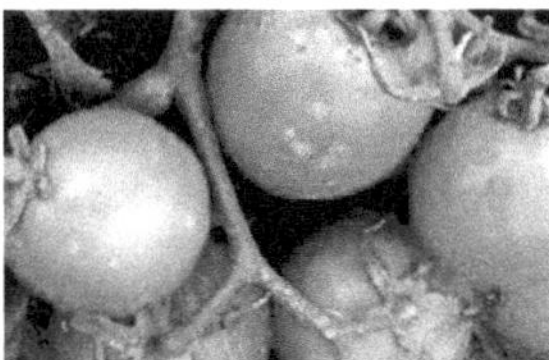

Mode of spread and survival:
- Survive in or on seeds and on plant debris in soil.
- Spreads through the seed and Solanaceous weeds such as *Solanum nigrum.*

Epidemiology:
- Soil temperature of 28^0 C and humid weather favours the disease.

Management:
- Extraction of seed through fermentation of pulp at room temperature for 72 hours eradicates the bacterium from the seed.
- Hot water treatment of seed at 52^0 C.
- Three year crop rotation.

- Protective sprays with COC and streptomycin sulphate.
- Soil solarization.

14. Root knot nematode

Causal Organism: *Meloidogyne* sp.

- Root knot is the most important group of phytonematodes and was first recorded in green house vegetables in England in the year 1855.
- Of the four predominant species of *Meloidogyne*, *M. incognita* and *M. javanica* are commonly found in the tropics, whereas *M. arenaria* is more common in the sub-tropics.
- *M. hapla* is common in the temperate region and can occasionally found in the cooler uplands of tropics.

Symptoms:

- Formation of galls on host root system is the primary symptom.
- Roots branch profusely starting from the gall tissue causing a '**beard root**' symptom.
- In severely infected plants the root system is reduced and the rootlets are almost completely absent.
- The roots are seriously hampered in their function of uptake and transport of water and nutrients.
- Plants wilt during the hot part of day, especially under dry conditions and are often stunted.
- Seedlings infected in nursery do not normally survive transplanting and those surviving have reduced flowering and fruit production.

Mode of spread and Survival:

- Juveniles and eggs survive periods of moisture stress in a state of anhydrobiosis.
- Irrigation water and soil adhering to animal feet and implements help in dissemination of juveniles and eggs of nematodes.

Management:

- Crop rotation with graminaceous hosts. Inclusion of non-preferred hosts like mustard, sesame, maize, wheat, etc., in the cropping system.
- Intercropping of marigold with tomato reduces nematode population.
- Nursery should be raised in nematode free sites or fumigated beds.
- Deep ploughing of infested fields during summer. Three summer ploughings at 10 days interval reduces juvenile population.
- Flooding the field for prolonged periods.
- Use of biocontrol agents like *Paecilomyces lilacinus* (egg parasite). Nursery bed treatment with metham sodium (Vapam)@25ml/m2 or Carbofuran (Furadan)@0.39g a.i/m2.
- Bare root dip treatment in EC formulation of systemic pesticides like Dimethoate (Rogor) or Profenophos (Curacron) for 6-8 hours before transplantation.
- Grow resistant varieties like **Hissar Lalit** and **PNR-7**.

15. Tomato spotted wilt

Causal Organism: Tomato Spotted Wilt Virus (TSWV), Groundnut bud necrosis virus

Symptoms:

- Symptoms vary among hosts and in a single host species.
- **Stunting** is a common symptom of TSWV infection. It causes streaking of the leaves, stems and fruits.
- **Chlorotic or necrotic rings** form on the leaves of many infected hosts.
- Fruits show numerous spots about one-half inch in diameter with concentric, circular markings.
- **Pale red or yellow areas with concentric circular marking** in the normal red skin of ripe tomato are formed.
- Discoloration of seed. Thickening of veins and **bronzing** of young leaves.
- Growing tips may die-back and terminal branches may be streaked.
- Affected plants may have a one sided growth habit or may be entirely stunted and have drooping leaves.

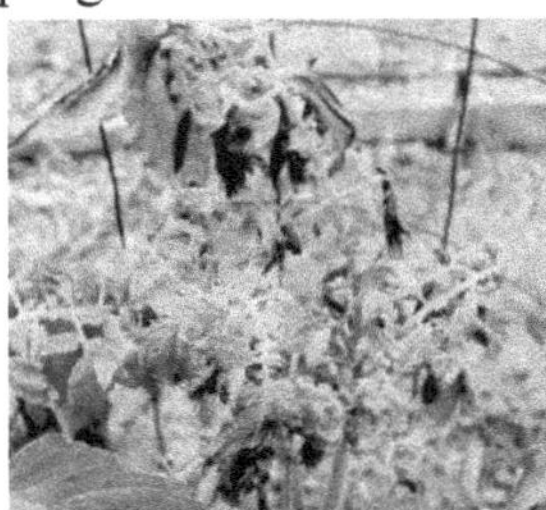

Pathogen:

- It is isometric particles of 70 – 90nm diameter. Thermal inactivation point is 40°C.

Mode of spread and Survival:

- The spotted wilt virus is transmitted through thrips, *Frankliniella schultzii, Scirtothrips dorsalis, F. Occidentalis* and *Thrips tabaci*).
- Adult thrips transmit the disease, only when the larvae acquire the virus from infected plants.

Collateral hosts: *Acanthospermum hispidum, Aster sp., Boerhaavia diffusa, Chrysanthemum sp., Cleome gynandra*, cowpea, *Dahlia variabilis*, egg plant, French bean, Gerbera sp., groundnut, *Lagasca mollis*, lettuce, marigold, pea, pepper, pineapple, potato, *Trianthema portulacastrum*, water melon and *Zinnia elegans*.

Management:

- Removal and destruction of infected plants & weed hosts.
- Vector control with dimethoate (Rogor) or methyl demeton at 10 days interval.
- Growing *Crotolaria juncea* as a barrier crop reduces vector migration.
- Spraying of sorghum or coconut leaf extract.

16. Tomato Mosaic

Causal Organism: *Tomato mosaic virus*

Symptoms:

- The disease is characterized by light and dark green mottling on the leaves often accompanied by wilting of young leaves in sunny days when plants first become infected.
- The leaflets of affected leaves are usually distorted, puckered and smaller than normal.
- Sometimes the leaflets become indented resulting in "fern leaf" symptoms.
- The affected plant appears stunted, pale green and spindly.
- The symptoms vary depending on the strain of the virus. Some strains cause yellowing or leaf mottling which may also affect the fruit.
- Some other strains produce **streak symptoms** consisting of longitudinal necrotic streaks on stem or petioles.
- Such diseased plants are killed **Necrotic sunken lesions also appear on fruits** and sometimes internal necrosis or browning of mature fruit occurs.
- The virus is spread by contact with clothes, hand of working labour, touching of infected plants with healthy ones, plant debris and implements.

Pathogen:

- Virus paricles are rod shaped, not enveloped, usually straight and thermal inactivation point is 85 - 90°C.

Mode of spread and survival:

- The virus is seed borne and upto 94% of seeds may contain the virus.
- The virus infection occurs during transplanting. It is readily sap transmissible.
- Many solanaceous plants are susceptible to tomato mosaic virus.
- The virus is spread easily by man and implements in cultural operations or by animals and by leaf contact. Infection is through roots.

Collateral hosts: *Capsicum annuum, C. frutescens, Chenopodium armanticolor, C. murale, C. quinoa, Cucumis melo, C. sativus, Cucurbita pepo, Datura metel, Lycopersicon pimpinellifolium, Nicotiana benthamiana, N. clevelandii, N. glutinosa, N. megalosiphon, N. rustica, N.tabacum, Petunia hybrida, Physalis floridana, P. peruviana, Vigna ungiculata*, brinjal, cowpea and French bean.

Management:

- Seeds from disease free healthy plants should be selected for sowing.
- Soaking of the seeds in a solution of Tri-sodium orthohosphate (90 g/litre of water) for 15 to 20 minutes prior to sowing helps to reduce the disease incidence. The seeds should be thoroughly rinsed and dried in shade.

- In the nursery all the infected plants should be removed carefully and destroyed.
- Seedlings with infected with the viral disease should not be used for transplanting.
- Crop rotation with crops other than tobacco, potato, chilli, capsicum, brinjal, etc. should be undertaken.
- All collateral hosts in the vicinity should be destroyed before planting new crop.
- Heat treatment for 2-4 days at 70°C.
- Cross protection of tomato seedlings by inoculating with mild strains (Zitter, 1991).
- Field workers should avoid using tobacco products while working in the field.

17. Leaf curl

Causal Organism: *Tomato leaf curl virus* (ToLCV)

Symptom:

- Leaf curl disease is characterized by severe stunting of the plants with downward rolling and crinkling of the leaves.
- The newly emerging leaves exhibit slight yellow colouration and later they also show curling symptoms.
- Older leaves become leathery and brittle. The nodes and internodes are significantly reduced in size.
- The infected plants look pale and produce more lateral branches giving a bushy appearance. The infected plants remain stunted.

Pathogen:

- The virus particles are 80nm in diameter.

Mode of spread and survival:

- It is neither seed nor sap transmissible.
- But seeds from fresh fruits having infection may have the virus on the seed coat.
- The virus is transmitted by white fly, *Bemisia tabaci* and grafting. Even a single viruliferous insect is able to transmit the virus.

Management:

- Keep yellow sticky traps @ 12/ha to monitor the white fly.
- Raise barrier crops-cereals around the field.
- Removal of weed host.
- Protected nursery in net house or green house.
- Spray Imidachloprid (Gaucho) 0.05 % or Dimethoate (Rogor) 0.05% @ 15, 25, 45 days after transplanting to control vector (Panagopoulos, 2000).

- Use resistant variety *Lycopersicon perurvianum,* **Akara Ananya, Akara Rakshak, Akara Samrat.**

Physiological Disorders of Tomato:

- Physiological disorders are abnormalities in fruit colour or appearance that are abiotic in origin.
- These disorders are distinguished from deficiencies of a single nutrient and physical-chemical or herbicide injury.

1. Blossom End Rot:

- Blossom-end rot is a serious disorder of tomato; it can be very damaging, and severe losses may occur if preventive control measures are not undertaken.

Symptoms:

- Blossom end rot is a very common problem on green and ripe tomatoes.
- It begins with light tan, water-soaked lesion, which then enlarges, turn black and leathery.
- Although blossom end rot itself causes only local injury, secondary organisms frequently invade the lesion and cause complete rot of the fruit.
- It often occurs in rapidly developing fruit during periods of hot, dry weather and tends to have the greatest impact on the earliest maturing fruit (Sherf *et al.,* 1986).

Cause:

- A localized calcium deficiency in the distal end of the fruit results in blossom-end rot because calcium is not a highly mobile element, a deficiency can occur with a fluctuation in water supply, even for a short period of time.
- Thus, moisture extremes promote the likelihood of the disorder.

Management:

- It can be managed by proper fertilization, water management, and planting cultivars tolerant to blossom-end rot.
- Soil testing is recommended to determine if there is a shortage of calcium. Liming with high-calcium limestone 2-4 months before planting can alleviate blossom-end rot.
- If calcium deficiency occurs, foliar spray of anhydrous calcium chloride may be helpful.

2. Catface:

Symptoms:

- Catface tomatoes are misshapen, with enlarged scars and holes in the blossom end of the fruit.

Cause:

- Cold weather at the time of blossom set distorts and kills certain cells that should develop into fruit, resulting in the deformities.
- The disorder is most often observed among first-formed fruit.

Management:
- Catface can be controlled by planting cultivars not subject to this damage.
- In greenhouse, heating to avoid low temperatures can reduce catfacing. This includes temperature control for the growing of transplants for field planting.

3. Fruit Cracking:

Symptoms:
- Two types of cracking occur in tomato fruit.
- Concentric cracking is a splitting of the epidermis in circular patterns around the stem scar.
- Radial cracking is a splitting that radiates toward the blossom end from the stem scar.
- Cracks occur on tomatoes as they near maturity, depending on the cultivar.
- Less susceptible cultivars do not crack until the breaker stage; more tolerant cultivars do not crack until they are red ripe; resistant cultivars rarely crack at all.

Cause:
- Cracking is associated with rapid fruit development and wide fluctuations in water availability to the plant.
- Fruit that has reached the ripening stage during dry weather may show considerable cracking if the dry period is followed by heavy rains and high temperatures.

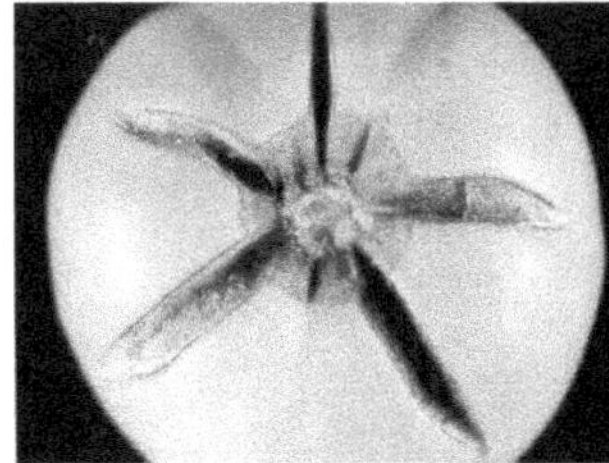 

Management:
- Growth cracking could be minimized by planting cultivars tolerant to cracking, proper water management, practicing good nutritional program to prevent overly succulent plants, and preventing defoliation due to foliar diseases to limit fruit exposure.

4. Sunscald:

Symptoms:
- Sunscald occurs on green tomato fruit exposed to the sun.

- The initial symptom is a whitish, shiny area that appears blistered.
- The killed, bleached tissues gradually collapse, forming a slightly sunken area that may become pale yellowish and wrinkled as the fruit ripens.
- The killed tissue is quickly invaded by secondary organisms and the fruit decays.

Cause:

- Fruit most subject to sunscald are those that have been exposed suddenly to the sun because of pruning, natural spreading of the plant caused by a heavy fruit load, or loss of foliage from diseases.
- The extent of the injury is more serious during periods of abnormally high temperatures.

Management:

- Sunscald can be managed by careful pruning and harvesting, good foliar disease control, and planting cultivars with good foliage cover that does not break open and expose the fruit (Singh, 2005).

5. Puffiness:

Symptoms:

- The outer wall of the fruit is normal, but the tomato is hollow inside. One of the seed cavities is usually empty.

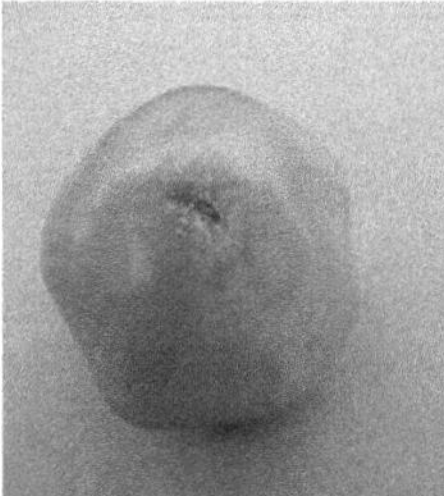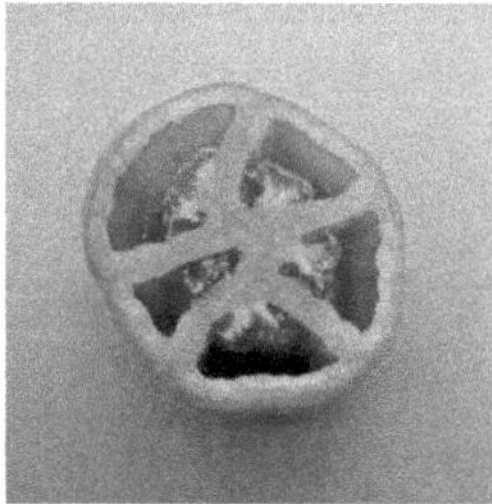

Cause:

- Extreme high or low temperatures, excessive nitrogen fertilization, and heavy rains may interfere with normal pollination, resulting in puffy fruit.
- Puffiness occurs most frequently on early fruit.

Management:

- No effective controls.
- Puffiness should decline later in the summer.

6. Blotchy ripening:

Symptoms:

- In this case greenish yellow and whitish patches appear on ripened fruit, particular on the stem end portion sometimes white or brown tissues are present in blotched area.

Cause:

- These disorders mainly due to imbalance of nitrogen and potasic nutrient in soil, water deficiency in the excessive transpiration.

7. Gold Fleck:

Symptoms:

- Around the calyx and fruit shoulder, small irregular shaped green spots develop at random on surface immature fruit, which become gold in colour as fruit ripens.
- These tiny yellow spots called gold flecks.

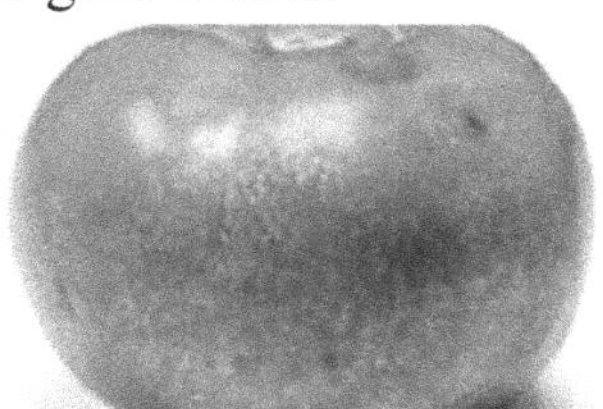

Cause:

- These gold flecks appear due to deposition of calcium oxalate.
- With high incidence, fruits become unattractive and their shelf life also gets reduced.

Management:

- Summer shading lowers the incidence of this disorder.

References:

Agrios, G. N., (2005). *Plant Pathology* (p. 902). Academic Press, San Diego, CA. Anonymous (2015). *National Horticulture Board Database* (pp. 177–185). NHB Publication. New Delhi.

Fullelove, G., Wright, R., Meurant, N., Barnes, J., O'Brien, R. and Lovatt, J., (1998). *Tomato Information kit: Agrilink, Your Growing Guide to Better Farming.* Department of Primary Industries, Queensland Horticulture Institute: Brisbane.

Jones, J. B., Jones, J. P., Stall, R. E. and Zitter, T. A., (1991). *Compendium of Tomato Diseases (p. 73).* APS Press, St. Paul.

Naika, S., Jeude, J. V. L. D., Goffau, M. D., Hilmi, M. and Dam, B. V., (2005). Agrodok 17. *Cultivation of Tomato Production, Processing and Marketing* (p. 6). Digigrafi, Wageningen, Netherlands.

Panagopoulos, C. G., (2000). *Diseases of vegetable crops.* In: Vegetable Disease (pp. 15–189). Stamoulis, Athens.

Persley, D., Cooke, T. and House, S., (2010). *Diseases of Vegetable Crops in Australia.* CSIRO Publishing: Collingwood, Victoria.

Roberts, P. D., Murphy, J. F., and Goldberg, N. P., (1999). Fungal and bacterial diseases. In: Albajes, R., Gullino, M. L., Van Lenteren, J. C. and Elad, Y., (eds.), *Integrated Pest and Disease Management in Greenhouse Crops* (pp. 40–47). Kluwer Academic Publishers, Norwell, USA.

Sherf, A. F. and MacNab, A. A., (1986). *Vegetable Diseases and Their Control* (2nd edn., p. 728). John Wiley & Sons, NY.

Singh, R. S., (2005). *Plant Diseases* (p. 720). Oxford and IBH Publishing Co. Pvt Ltd., New Delhi.

Zitter, T. A., (1991). Tomato mosaic and Tobacco mosaic. In: Jones, J. B., Jones, J. P., Stall, R. E., & Zitter, T. A., (eds.), *Compendium of Tomato Diseases* (p. 39). APS Press.

BRINJAL

Introduction:

- Brinjal (*Solanum melongena* L.) also known as egg-plant, aubergine, Guinea squash, is one of the important vegetable crops grown almost worldwide.
- It is native to India, where it has been cultivated since remote antiquity for its fleshy fruits.
- Eggplant fruits were a common food in China as long as 600 BC, when it was called Malayan purple melon. Now, it is extensively grown in eastern and southern Asia, including India, USA and other countries (Raabe *et al.,* 1981).
- The raw vegetables contains only 15 calories/ 100 g but its caloric value rises sharply when it is fried.
- Africans following folk medicine have long used brinjals to treat epilepsy and convulsions. In Southeast Asia, it is still used to treat measles and stomach cancer.
- During cultivation, crop is affected by several diseases of fungal, bacterial and phytoplasma nature, which inflict heavy losses in its production.
- A detailed account of various diseases affecting this crop and their management are described in this lecture.

Diseases:

S. No.	Disease Name	Causal Organism
Fungal diseases		
1.	Damping off	*Pythium aphanidermatum*
2.	Cercospora leaf spot	*Cercospora solani*
3.	Alternaria leaf spot	*Alternaria solani, A. melongenae*
4.	Collar rot	*Sclerotium rolfsii*
5.	Verticillium wilt	*Verticillium dahliae*
6.	Phomopsis blight and fruit rot	*Phomopsis vexans*
Bacterial diseases		
7.	Bacterial wilt	*Burkholderia solanacearum*
8.	Little leaf	Phytoplasma

1. **Phomopsis fruit rot or blight**

Causal Organism: *Phomopsis vexans (P.S: Diaporthe vexans)*

Economic Importance:

- It is a serious disease of brinjal infecting the foliage and the fruits caused by fungal pathogens.
- This disease was reported for the first time from Belgaon district of Bombay, India (Uppal *et al.,* 1935; Pawar and Patel, 1957).
- Damage the fruits partly or completely in the field as well as during transit.
- The disease is favored by warm, wet weather and is spread by splashing water. Yield loss is 10–20% due to fruit rot.

Symptoms:

- The plants are attacked at all stages of growth, producing damping-off symptoms in nurseries and collar rot on young plants.
- On leaves, circular to irregular, clearly defined grayish brown spots having light centers appear.
- The diseased leaves become yellowish in colour and may drop off. **Several black pycnidia** can be seen on older spots.
- The lesions on stem are dark brown, round to oval and have grayish centers where pycnidia develop.
- At the base of the stem, the fungus causes characteristic constrictions leading to canker development and toppling of plants.
- On fruits, small pale sunken spots appear which on enlargement cover entire fruit surface. These spots become watery leading to soft rot phase of the disease.
- A large number of dot like pycnidia also develop on such spots.
- The infection of fruit through calyx leads to development of dry rot and fruits appear black and mummified.

Pathogen:

- The mycelium of the pathogen is septate and hyaline becoming dark with age.
- Pycnidia are submerged and later becoming erumpent with a prominent ostiole.
- Conidia are produced on simple to branched conidiophores and are of 2 types.
- Alpha conidia, which are sub cylindrical and beta conidia, which are filiform and curved.
- Role of beta-conidia in the epidemiology of the disease is not very clear.

- The perfect stage produces perithecia in which asci with 8 hyaline, bicelled, ellipsoid-fusoid ascospores are produced which are usually contricted at septum.

Mode of survival and spread:
- P.I: Pathogen is seed borne and also survives in plant debris as mycelium and pycnidia.
- S.I: Conidia dispersed through rain splashes, irrigation water, agricultural tools and insects.

Favourable conditions:
- High relative humidity coupled with higher temperatures favour disease development.
- Maximum disease development takes place at about 26^0C under wet weather conditions with 55% R.H.

Management:
- Removal and destruction of diseased crop debris.
- Practicing crop rotation and summer ploughings helps in reducing initial inoculum.
- Use of disease free seed.
- Hot water treatment of seed at 50^0C for 30 minutes.
- Seed treatment with thiophanate methyl at 1g/kg seed.
- Spray twice with thiophanate methyl or carbendazim@0.1% at 20 days interval.

2. Cercospora Leaf Spot

Causal Organism: *Cercospora melongenae, Cercospora solani*

Symptoms:
- The leaf spots are characterized by chlorotic lesions, angular to irregular in shape, later turn grayish-brown with profuse sporulation at the centre of the spot.
- Severely infected leaves drop off prematurely, resulting in reduced fruit yield.

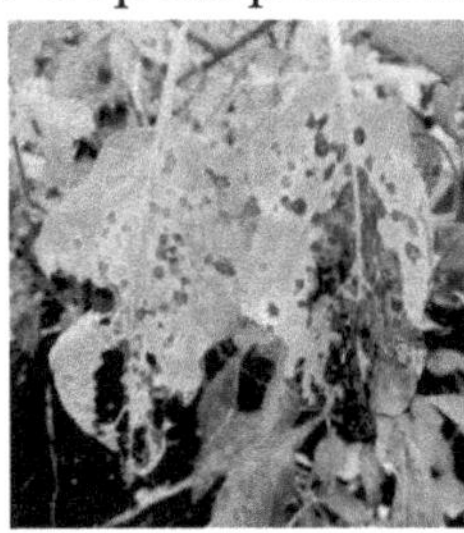

Pathogen:
- The fungus produces stromata which are globular.
- Conidiophores in mass are medium dark and slightly olivaceous brown in colour and paler towards the tip.
- Conidia are sub hyaline to pale olivaceous.

Mode of spread and survival:
- The disease is spread by air borne conidia.

Management:
- **Pant Samrat** variety is resistant to both the leaf spots.

- Diseases can be managed by growing resistant varieties like **Pusa purple cluster, Black round** and **H-4.**
- Spraying 1 per cent Bordeaux mixture or 2 g Copper oxychloride or 2.5 g Zineb per litre of water effectively controls leaf spots.

3. Alternaria leaf Spot

Causal Organism: *Alternaria melongenae, Alternaria Solani*

Economic Importance:
- Alternaria leaf spots also known as early blight. Early blight is more commonly known as a leaf spotting or foliar blight disease.
- Early blight can cause serious defoliation of tomato crops. It is often associated with septoria leaf spot, and these two fungal diseases, either separately or together, are responsible for most of the defoliation caused by diseases in field tomato crops in Canada.
- The pathogen also infects potato and solanaceous weeds. Pepper and eggplant are rarely affected.
- This disease is responsible for damaging the leaves and fruit.

Symptoms:
- Cracks appearing in leaf spot.
- The two species of *Alternaria* occur commonly, causing the characteristic leaf spots with concentric rings.
- The spots are mostly irregular, 4-8 mm in diameter and may coalesce to cover large areas of the leaf blade.
- Severely affected leaves may drop off. *A. melongenae* also infects the fruits causing large deep-seated spots.
- The infected fruits turn yellow and drop off prematurely.

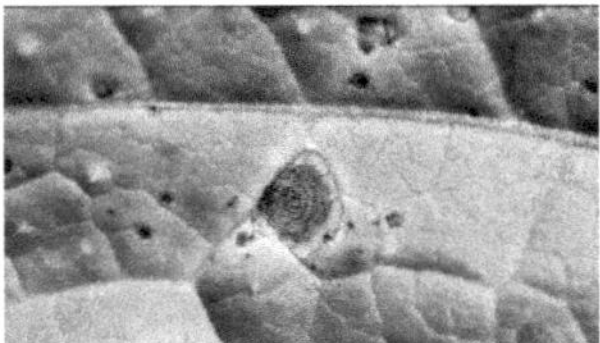

Pathogen:
- Mycelium is septate, branched, light brown to dark brown. It is inter and intra cellular.
- Conidiophores emerge through stomata and dark colored.
- Conidia are single celled, muriform, beaked and produced in chains.
- The conidia are with 5-10 transverse septa and a few longitudinal or oblique septa.

Mode of spread and survival:
- The disease is spread by wind borne conidia.

Management:
- Infected plant debries should be collected and burnt.

- The infected plants should be sprayed with Zineb or Mancozeb (Dithane M-45) or 0.1% Carbendazim is effective in controlling the disease.

4. Damping off

Causal Organism: *Pythium aphanidermatum, Pythium indicum, P. debaryanum, P. ultimum, Phytophthora parasitica, Rhizoctonia solani* and *Sclerotium rolfsii.*

Economic importance:

- Damping-off is a term often given to the sudden death of seedlings.
- It is an important disease of solanaceous crops. It is usually associated with the fungi Pythium, Rhizoctonia, or Phytophthora.
- The disease causes severe damage to the nursery. Damping-off generally occurs under cold, wet conditions.
- High soil moisture and moderate temperature, along with high humidity, especially in the rainy season, leads to the development of the disease.

Symptoms:

- Sudden collapsing of the seed lings occur in the seed bed.
- The seedlings are attacked at the collar region and the attacked seedlings are toppled down.
- The disease spreads through fungi present in the soil. The disease spreads through fungi present in the soil.

Management:

- Avoid nursery sowing in the same bed year after year with frequent heavy irrigation.
- Soil should be solarizing for 30 days.
- Healthy seed should be selected for sowing.
- Application of native bio-control agent Trichodermaviride in soil @ 1.2 kg/ha is also found effective to control damping-off to a considerable extent.
- The topsoil of the nursery should be treated with Thiram @ 5g/m2 area of the soil, and nursery should be drenched with the same chemical @ 2 g/liter of water at the fortnightly interval.
- The disease can be controlled by seed treatment with agrosan or ceresin @2gm/kg of seed.

5. Collar rot:

Causal Organism: *Sclerotium rolfsii*

Symptoms:

- The disease occasionally occurs in serious form.
- The lower portion of the stem is affected from the soil borne inoculum (sclerotia).

- **Decortications** are the main symptom.
- Exposure and necrosis of underlying tissues may lead to collapse of the plant.
- Near the ground surface on the stem may be seen the mycelia and sclerotia.
  - Lack of plant vigour, accumulation of water around the stem, and mechanical injuries help in development of this disease.

Management:
- Collection and destruction of diseased parts and portions of the plant.
- Seed treatment with 4 g of *Trichoderma viride* formulation per kg seed will help in reducing the disease.
- Spraying with Mancozeb @ 2g/Litre of water.

6. Verticillium Wilt

Causal Organism: *Verticilium dahliae*

Symptoms:
- The disease attacks the young plants as well as mature plants.
- The infected young plants show dwarfing and stunting due to the shortening of the internodes. Such plants do not flower and fruit.
- Infection after the flowering stage results in development of distorted floral buds and fruits. The affected fruits finally drop off.
- The infected leaves show the presence of irregularly scattered necrotic pale yellow spots over the leaf lamina.
- Later on, these spots coalesce resulting in complete wilting of the leaves.
- The roots of the affected plants are split open longitudinally, a characteristic dark brown discoloration if the xylem vessels is observed.

Disease Cycle:
- **P.I.:** Through soil borne spores
- **S.I.:** Through air borne conidia/ Irrigation water

Management:

- Crop rotation with bhendi, tomato, potato should be avoided.
- Soil application and foliar application with Benomyl (Benlate) (0.1%) is effective in reducing the wilt disease.

7. Little leaf

Causal Organism: Phytoplasma

Economic Importance:

- This disease of brinjal was reported from India in 1938 and as far as known it occurs only in India and Sri Lanka.
- In almost all the states of the country it has become a serious problem facing brinjal cultivation.
- The yield and growth of the plants are highly affected when plants are infected during early growth stage, i.e., before 35 and 55 days after sowing. (Thomas and Krishnaswamy, 1939).

Symptoms:

- The characteristic symptom is the smallness of the leaves.
- The petioles are so short and the leaves appear to be sticking to be stem. Such leaves are narrow, soft, smooth and yellow.
- Newly formed leaves are much more shorterer. The internodes of the stem are also shortened.
- Axillary buds get enlarged but their petioles and leaves remain shortened. This gives the plant a bushy appearance.
- Mostly, there is no flowering but if flowers are formed they remain green.
- Fruiting is rare, if any fruit is formed, it becomes hard, tough and fails to mature.
- Young fruit turns necrotic, get mummified and cling to the plant.

Pathogen:

- Little leaf was first considered a disease caused by a virus. In 1969 it was attributed to a mycoplasma-like organism, closely related to aster-yellows and curly top.
- It is a sap transmissible disease.
- The organism has been transmitted to Datura, tomato and tobacco.
- It occurs in nature on *Datura fastuosa* and *Vinca rosea.*
- Natural transmission is through a vector, ***Cestius phycytis*** (***Eutettix phycytis***) while ***Empoasca devastans*** is a less effective vector.
- Perennation of the organism is through its weed hosts.

- The disease is caused by phytoplasma having ovoid to spherical body which is concentrated in the phloem sieve tubes.

Mode of spread and survival:
- The disease is transmitted by leaf hoppers, *Hishimonas phycitis* and *Empoasca devastans* and grafting.
- *E. devastans* is less effective vector. Perennation of virus is through weed host.
- This disease has a very wide host range. The varieties pusa purple long and selection T are highly susceptible.
- **Collateral hosts: *Datura fastuosa, D. stramonium, Vinca rosea, Argemone mexicana,* chilli, tomato and tobacco.**

Management:
- The severity of the disease can be reduced by destruction of affected plants and spraying of insecticides.
- New crop should be planted only when diseased plants in the field and its neighbourhood have been removed.
- Methyldemeton (Metasystox) 25 EC 2 ml / litre Dimethoate 30 EC 2 ml/ litre Malathion (Cythion)50 EC 3 ml/litre has been recommended for vector control.
- Although mycoplasmas are reported to be suppressed by tetracyclines field application of this method has not yet been recommended.
- Seed dip in teracyclines (10-50ppm).
- Varietal resistance has not been systematically studied.
- Cultivars such as **Pusa Purple Cluster, Arka Sheel, Aushy, Manjari Gota** and **Banaras Giant** show moderate resistance to resistance in the field.
- Other cultivars found tolerant to the disease are **Black Beauty, Brinjal Round** and **Surati.**

8. **Bacterial wilt**

Causal Organism: *Ralstonia solanacearum*

Symptoms:
- Sudden wilting and death of infected plants is the characteristic symptom.
- The petiole of older leaves droop down and the leaves show epinasty symptoms accompanied by yellowing and stunting of whole plant.
- Typical browning of vascular tissues of roots and stems can be seen.
- From cross sections of infected plants whitish bacterial exudate comes out.

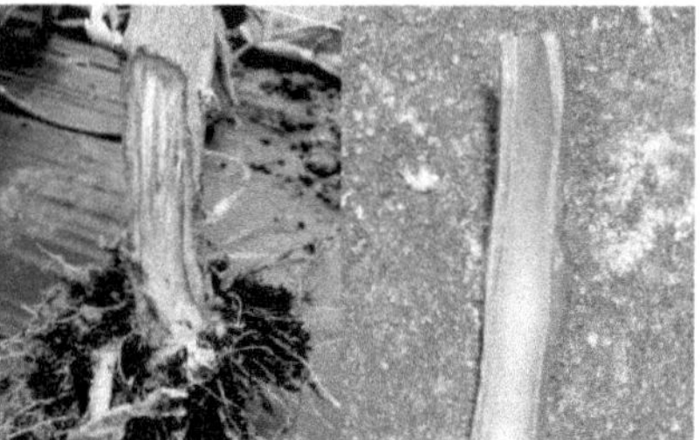

Pathogen:

- The bacterium is Gram negative, motile, rod shape having rounded ends with 1-4 polar flagella.
- Race 1 of *R. solanacearum* affects solanaceous plants such as tomato, egg plant and many other non-solanaceous plants also.

Mode of survival and spread:

- The bacterium is both soil and seed borne in nature and overwinters in infected plant parts, in wild host plants and weeds.
- Spread through irrigation water or infested soil and agricultural implements. Presence of root knot nematode, *Meloidogyne javanica* increases the wilt incidence.

Favourable conditions:

- Relatively high soil moisture and soil temperature favour the disease development.

Management:

- Grow resistant varieties like **Pant Samrat, Arka Nidhi, Arkas Kashav, Arka Neelakantha, Surya** and **BB 1, 44 & 49**.
- Crop rotation with non solanaceous hosts.
- Green manuring with ***Brassica*** species (Biofumigation).
- Soil solarization with a transparent polyethylene sheet (125 μm thick) for 8-10 weeks during March-June.
- Biological control with *Pseudomonas fluorescens, P. glumae, P. cepacia, Bacillus sp. & Erwinia sp.*
- Spray Copper fungicides to control the disease (2% Bordeaux mixture).
- The disease is more prevalent in the presence of root knot Nematodes, so control of these nematodes will suppress the disease spread.

References:

Akhtar, M., (1997). Biological control of plant parasitic nematodes by neem products in agricultural soils. *Applied Soil Ecology, 7*, 219–223.

Anonymous, (2011). *Small Fruit and Vegetable IPM Advisory–Integrated Pest Management.* Utah State University Cooperative Extension Web portal.

Chupp, C., (1953). *A Monograph of the Fungus Genus Cercospora.* Cornell Univ., Ithaca, New York.

Dhawan, S. C. and Sethi, C. L., (1977). Inter-relationship between root-knot nematode, *Meloidogyne incognita* and little leaf of Brinjal. *Indian Phytopathology,* 30, 55–63. Farr, D. F., Bills, G. F., Chamuris, G. P., & Rossman, A. Y., (1989). *Fungi on Plants and Plant Products in the United States.* APS Press, St. Paul, Minnesota.

Gonsalves, A. K., & Ferreira, S., (1994). *Cercospora primer.* http://www.extento.hawaii.edu/ kbase/crop/Type/cer_prim.htm-DISEASES (Accessed on 18 November 2019).

Jatala, P., (1985). Biological control of nematodes. In: Sasser, J. N., & Carter, C. C., (eds.), *An Advanced Treatise on Meloidogyne: Biology and Control* (pp. 303–308). North Carolina State University Graphics.

Kranz, J. S., & Werner, K., (1978). *Diseases, Pests and Weeds in Tropical Crops* (pp. 194–195). Wiley Publications.

Pawar, V. H., & Patel, M. K., (1957). Phomopsis blight and fruit rot of Brinjal. *Indian Phytopath.,* 10(2), 115–120.

Raabe, R. D., Conners, I. L., & Martinez, A. P., (1981). *Checklist of Plant Diseases in Hawaii.* Hawaii Institute of Agriculture and Human Resources, College of Tropical Agriculture and Human Resources, University of Hawaii.

Uppal, B. N., Patel, M. K., & Kamat, M. N., (1935). *The Fungi of Bombay Bull.,* 178, 56. Varma, A., Chenulu, V. V., Raychaudhuri, S. P., Prakash, N., & Rao, P. S., (1969). Mycoplasma like bodies in tissue infected with sandal spike and brinjal little leaf. *Indian Phytopath.,* 22, 289–291.

Zareena, S. K., & Vanita Das, V. V., (2014). Root knot disease and its management in brinjal. *Global Journal of Bio-Science and Biotechnology,* 3(1), 126–127.

CHILLI

Introduction:

- Bell pepper (*Capsicum annuum* L.) and Chilli (*Capsicum frutescens* L.) popularly known as Shimla Mirch" and 'Lal Mirch", respectively, are important solanaceous crops grown throughout the world.
- The fruits are a good source of vitamin A and ascorbic acid.
- These are native of Mexico with secondary centre of origin in Guatemala and Portuguese explorer introduced it to Asia.
- In India, these are grown in most of the states of the country. During cultivation these crops are affected by various diseases which reduce the potential yields drastically.
- In this lecture, a detailed account of the diseases has been given.

Diseases:

S. No.	Disease Name	Causal Organism
Fungal diseases		
1.	Damping off	*Pythium aphanidermatum*
2.	Anthracnose/ Die back and fruit rot	*Colletotrichum capsici*
3.	Powdery mildew	*Leveillula taurica*

4.	Cercospora leaf spot or Frog eye leaf spot	*Cercospora capsici*
5.	Alternaria leaf spot/ blight/ fruit rot	*Alternaria solani*
6.	Sclerotial wilt	*Sclerotium rolfsii*
7.	Verticillium wilt	*Verticillum* sp.
8.	Fusarium wilt	*Fusarium oxysporum f.sp. capsici*
9.	Choanephora blight /Wet Rot	*Choanephora cucurbitarum*
Bacterial diseases		
10.	Bacterial Leaf spot	*Xanthomonas campestris pv. vesicatoria*
Viral diseases		
11.	Leaf curl	*Chilli leaf curl virus*
12.	Mosaic complex	*Chilli mosaic virus, Potato Virus Y, Cucumber Mosaic Virus (CMV), Tobacco Mosaic Virus (TMV)* and *Tomato spotted wilt virus*
Physiological Disorders		
13.	Blossom End Rot (BER)	
14.	Sunscald	
15.	Misshapen fruit	

1. Damping off

Causal Organism: *Pythium aphanidermatum*

Economic importance:

- The disease causes severe damage in the nursery.
- High soil, moisture and moderate temperature along with high humidity especially in the rainy season leads to the development of the disease.
- Disease of nursery beds and young seedlings resulting in reduced (25-75% loss) seed germination and poor stand of seedlings.

Symptoms:

- Two types of symptoms are observed.

Pre-emergence damping off:

- Seedlings disintegrate before they come out of soil surface.
- This is known as pre-emergence damping-off which results in poor field emergence/ poor seed germination.

Post-emergence damping off:

- It is characterised by development of disease after seedlings have emerged out of soil surface but before the stems are lignified.
- Lesion formation at collar region. Infected areas appear brown and water soaked.
- Plants shrivel and collapse as a result of softening of tissues.
- Infected stems become hard, thin (Wire stem symptoms) and infected seedlings topple.

- Disease appears in patches both in nursery and field beds.

Disease cycle:
- P.I: Oospores in soil or plant debris
- S.I: Zoospores through irrigation water

Favourable conditions:
- Heavy rainfall.
- Excessive and frequent irrigation.
- Poorly drained soil and close spacing.
- High soil moisture with temp around 25-30^0 C.
- *P. aphanidermatum*, prefer temp above 20^0 C.
- *P. debaryanum, P. ultimum*, prefer cool temp ($<20^0$ C).

Management:
- Raise nursery in light soil with proper drainage.
- Burning farm trash on the surface of the beds. Sowing seed on raised beds of 6-8" high (15cm).
- **Using low seed rate of 650 g/cent.**
- Seed dressing with Argosan or ceresan or Thiram or captan @ 2-3 g/Kg. Soil drenching with 1% Bordeaux mixture or COC@ 0.3% or **metalaxyl@0.2%.**
- Biocontrol with *Trichoderma viride* and *Trichoderma harzianum*.

2. **Dieback and fruit rot**

Causal Organism: *Colletotrichum capsici, C. gloeosporioides, C. coccodes,* and *C. acutatum* (Telomorph: *Glomerella cingulata)*

Economic importance:
- It was first reported from South India on ripening fruits and young twigs of chillies by **Mc Ray in 1914.**
- In A.P. it is a most common disease especially in Guntur and Krishna districts.

Symptoms:
- Symptoms are appeared from **December to October** in transplanted crop.
- Small, circular to irregular, brownish black scattered spots appear on leaves.
- Severely infected leaves defoliate.
- Infection of growing tips leads to necrosis of branches from tip backwards.
- Necrotic tissues appear grayish white with black dot like acervuli in the center.
- Shedding of flowers due to the infection at pedicel and tips of branches.

Fruit symptoms:

- Ripe fruits are more liable for attack than the green ones.
- Small, circular, yellowish to **pinkish sunken spots** appear on fruits. Spots increase along fruit length attaining elliptical shape.
- Severe infection result in the shrivelling and drying of fruits. Such fruits become white or greyish in colour and lose their pungency.
- On the surface of the lesions minute black dot like fruiting bodies called '**acervuli**' develop in **concentric rings** and fruits appear straw coloured.
- The affected fruits may fall off subsequently.
- The seeds produced in severely infected fruits are discoloured and covered with mycelial mat (Ahmed, 1982).

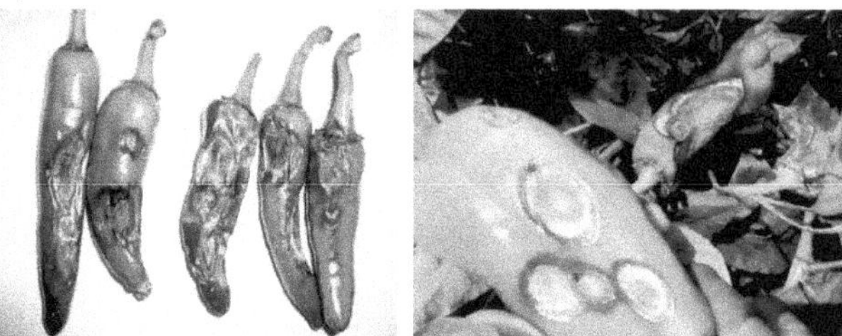

Pathogen:

- The mycelium is septate and grows both inter and intracellularly in the host tissue.
- The asexual fruiting bodies, acervuli contain many rigid, brown coloured, 1-5 septate setae.
- A large number of conidia are borne on conidiophores in each acervulus which are falcate, unicellular, hyaline having a normally truncated base.

Mode of spread and survival:

- The fungus is seed borne and the secondary infection is by air borne conidia and also by rain (Alam *et al,* 2002).
- The disease spreads rapidly by wind blown rains during rainy season. Flies and other insects are found responsible for dissemination of the spores from one fruit to another.
- The fungus may not survive long in soil, but may survive on the dead twigs stored under dry conditions.
- Seeds from badly diseased fruits may also carry the primary inoculums.

Management:

- Collect and destroy all infected plant parts.
- Collect seeds only form fruits without infection.
- Removal and destruction of solanaceous weed hosts and infected plant debris.
- Seed treatment with captan or thiram 3-4g/kg. Spray thrice with captan@1.5% or mancozeb@0.25% just before flowering, at fruit formation stage and 15 days after second spray.
- Resistant varieties are **G3, G4, B61, Lorai, etc.**

3. Choanephora blight /Wet Rot

Causal Organism: *Choanephora cucurbitarum*

Symptoms*:*

- The pathogen attacks flowers, buds and tender young shoots.
- This disease produces blossom blight as well as a fruit rot stage and occasionally leaf blight.
- Blossoms exhibit a lack of turgidity as petals begin to wilt.
- Luxuriant growth of the pathogen is seen on infected portion which appears as black pin heads or Stiff whisker-like strands of the causal fungus, topped with black heads (sporangia) grow off the infected blossoms causing a blossom drop.
- Young fruit may become infected, soften and abort with the black fungal growth apparent on the fruit.

Management:

- Adopt recommended spacing to maintain adequate air circulation.
- Select the seeds from healthy fruits and treat the seed with captan or thiram@3g/kg seed (Ushakiran, 2006).
- Spray Mancozeb@0.25% or Copper oxy chloride@0.3%.
- Grow resistant varieties like **Seoul hot, Liachi-2, AT-Good,** etc.

4. **Powdery mildew**

Causal Organism: *Leveillula taurica*

Economic importance:

- It usually occurs during cooler parts of the year *i.e.* from December to February.

Symptoms:

- White powdery coating appears mostly on the lower surface.
- Sometimes the powdery coating can also be seen on the upper surface. Correspondingly on the upper surface yellow patches are seen.
- Severe infection results in the drying and shedding of affected leaves.
- Powdery growth can also be seen on young fruits, and branches.
- Diseased fruits do not grow further and may drop down.

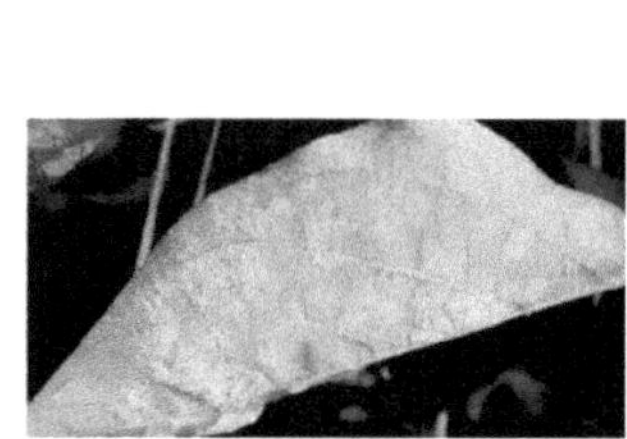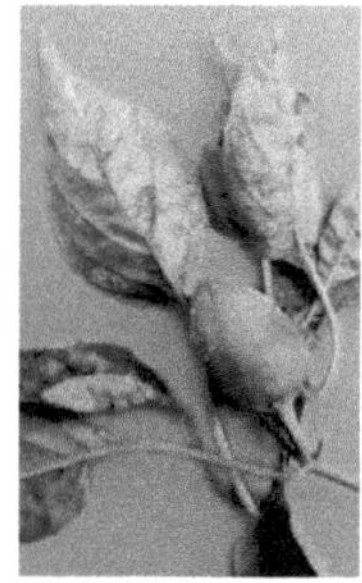

Disease cycle:
- The powdery mildew disease cycle (life cycle) starts when spores (known as conidia) land on a chilli leaf.
- Spores germinate much like a seed and begin to grow into the leaf.
- Chilli powdery mildew parasitizes the plant using it as a food source. The fungus initially grows unseen within the leaf for a latency period of 18-21 days.
- Then the fungus grows out of the breathing pores (stomatoes) on the under surface of the leaf, producing spores which are borne singly on numerous, fine strands or stalks (conidiophores).
- These fungal strands become visible as white patches or mildew colonies on the underside of the leaf.
- Repeated cycles of powdery mildew can lead to severe outbreaks of powdery mildew that economically damage the crop.
- P.I: Dormant mycelium in the infected crop debris.
- S.I: Air-borne conidia.

Favourable conditions:
- Cool dry weather favours conidial germination.
- High RH favours disease development.

Management:
- Spraying wettable Sulphur (Sulfex) @0.3% or Dinocap (Karathane) or Carbendazim or Tridemorph (Calixin) 0.1%.

5. Cercospora leaf spot:

Causal Organism: *Cercospora capsici, C. melongenae*
- It usually occurs in October - November and continues up to February.

Symptoms:
- Circular spots with brown margins appear on leaves.
- The spots enlarge and coalesce with others.
- The central portion of the spot becomes white and the leaves turn yellow and defoliate.
- Sometimes central portion of spot drops off.
- Spots also appear on stems and twigs as dark brown, irregular lesions with whitish centers.
- In severe cases die-back of twigs occurs.

Pathogen:

- Stromata are well developed.
- Conidiophores are 30- 60 x 4.5 – 5.5 micron meter.
- Conidia are subhyaline to coloured, acicular to obculate.

Mode of spread and survival:

- Primary source of infection are infected seeds, volunteer plants and infected plant debris. Secondary spread is through air borne conidia.

Management:

- Mulch and furrow or drip irrigates to help reduce spread of the pathogen from splashing water.
- Seed Treatment with carbendazim @ 2g/kg seed.
- Spray carbendazim@0.1% or Difolaton (Foltaf) @0.3%, Mancozeb 0.25% or Chlorothalonil (Kavach) 0.1% at 15 days interval.

6. Alternaria rot

Causal Organism: *Alternaria solani, Alternaria alternata*

Symptoms:

- The fungus is reported to enter wounds (sunscald or punctures). Dusty black spores on fruit spots are characteristic.
- In most instances this disease follows blossom-end rot, but it also follows injuries, chilling, and other decays.
- On the fruit, large greenish-brown to brown lesions covered, with grayish-brown mould are produced.
- Similar lesions on the lower-part of the fruit are characteristic of Alternaria rot following blossom-end rot.
- The larger lesions may show alternating light and dark-brown concentric zones.
- Shipping peppers under standard refrigeration will check the development of this rot, but when the fruit is removed from refrigeration the decay will advance rapidly at moderate to warm temperatures.

Pathogen:

- Hyphae are septate, branched, light brown becoming darker with age and inter and intra cellular.
- Conidiophores emerge through stomata. Conidia are single and muriform.

Mode of spread and survival:

- Infected seeds, volunteer plants and infected plant debris are primary source of infection.

Management:

Pre storage dry heat:

- The effectiveness of a pre storage dry heat treatment and hot water dip in reducing storage rots of capsicum caused by *Alternaria alternata.*
- Treatment with hot air at 38°C for 48-72 h or hot water at 50°C to 53°C for 2 to 3 min, resulted in reduction in the pathogenicity and development of these pathogens in inoculate peppers (Prabhavathy *et al.,* 1995).

7. Fusarium wilt

Causal Organism: *Fusarium oxysporum* f.sp. *capsici*

Symptoms:

- Fusarium wilt is characterised by wilting of the plant and upward and inward rolling of the leaves. The leaves turn yellow and die.
- Generally appear localised areas of the field where a high percentage of the plants wilt and die, although scattered wilted plants may also occur.
- Disease symptoms are characterised by an initial slight yellowing of the foliage and wilting of the upper leaves that progress in a few days into a permanent wilt with the leaves still attached.
- By the time above ground symptoms are evident; the vascular system of the plant is discoloured, particularly in the lower stem and roots.

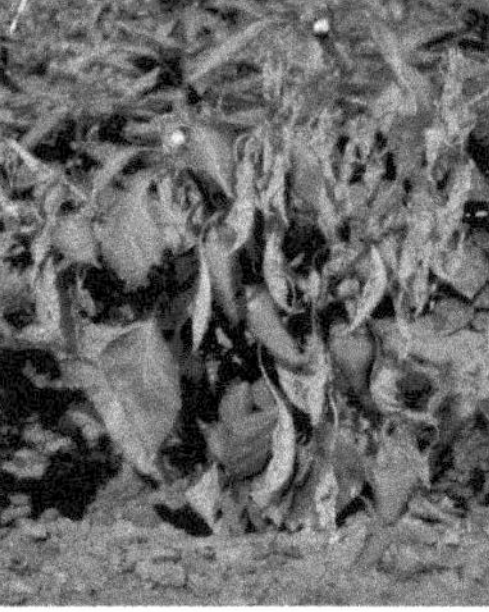

Pathogen:

- Mycelium is grayish white.
- Microconidia are formed singly, hyaline and cylindrical.
- Macro conidia are cylindrical to falcate.
- Chlamydospores are globose to oval and rough walled.

Management:

- Use of wilt resistant varieties.

- Drenching with 1% Bordeaux mixture or Blue copper or (COC) Fytolan 0.25% may give protection.
- Seed treatment with 4g *Trichoderma viride* formulation or 2g Carbendazim per kg seed is effective.
- Mix 2kg *T.viride* formulation mixed with 50kg FYM, sprinkle water and cover with a thin polythene sheet. When mycelia growth is visible on the heap after 15 days, apply the mixture in rows of chilli in an area of one acre.

8. Sclerotinia wilt

Causal Organism: *Sclerotinia sclerotiorum*

Economic Importance:
- The disease is more important in tarai area (foot hills of H.P and Uttrakhand) of the country where it causes considerable yield losses.

Symptoms:
- Circular to elongate water-soaked lesions closer to the inflorescence appear on the branches followed by watery soft rot.
- At the point of infection, a dry, discoloured spot develops.
- As a result of tissue necrosis, the portion of the plant beyond the point of infection wilts.
- If the infection is at the base of the main stem, the entire plant wilts and if only few branches are attacked than partial wilting of the plant may take place.
- In the advance stages under cool humid conditions, the mycelium emerges out and creamy coloured compact sclerotial initials as well as matured black sclerotia of varying sizes are evident on above ground parts.
- Fruits are also attacked. The rotting of the flesh takes place and in rotting tissue large number of sclerotia is seen.

Pathogen:
- Mycelium in culture as well as on host surface is hyaline, cottony, branched, consisting of closely septate hyphae, and filled with dense granular protoplasm.
- Fungus germinate by two means i.e. myceliogenic and carpogenic (forming apothecia).
- Primary infection occurs through ascospore whereas secondary infection takes place through mycelium.
- Microconidia (spermatia) are produced on short lateral branches of the vegetative mycelium in chains.

- When food supply is exhausted and the vegetative growth ceases, the hyphae with granular protoplasm collect in small dense masses and form sclerotia (Thind, 1985).

Disease cycle and epidemiology:

- The fungus survives in soil in the form of sclerotia.
- In the presence of proper humidity and light conditions, sclerotia germinate by forming apothecium which in turn forms asci and ascospores.
- The spores, upon escaping from the ascus, lodge on a susceptible host, and a new infection may originate.
- Mycelium from sclerotia is also capable of infecting eggplant.
- The pathogen can infect the susceptible host over a wide range of temperatures *i.e.* from 0 to 25°C with an optimum at 15 to 20°C.
- The fungus can tolerate wide pH range but is best adapted to an acidic substrate.
- Application of nitrogenous fertilizers enhances this disease.

Management:

- Collect and destroy the infected plant debris.
- Follow crop rotation with cereals i.e. paddy or maize.
- With the initiation of the disease, spray the crop with carbendazim (0.1%) or thiophanate methyl (Topsin M) (0.1%) or combination of mancozeb (0.25%) and carbendazim (0.05%) and repeat at 10 to 14 days interval.
- Fungi like *Trichoderma harzianum* and *T. viride* (40 g/ m2 at the time of field preparation) have also been reported as antagonistic to this fungus.

9. Bacterial leaf spot

Causal Organism: *Xanthomoas campestris pv. vesicatoria, X. vesicatoria, X. gardneri*

Symptoms:

- Leaves, fruits and stems are affected.
- Lesions on leaf begin as circular, water soaked spots.
- Spots become necrotic with brown center with chlorotic borders.
- Enlarged spots may develop straw coloured centres.
- Lesions are slightly raised on lower leaf surface.
- Severely spotted leaves turn yellow and drop.
- Raised brown lesions appear on fruits.
- Narrow elongated lesions or streaks may develop on stems.

Mode of survival and spread:

- The bacterium is seed borne. Spread by rain splash.

Management:

- Seeds should be collected from healthy fruits.
- Seed treatment with copper oxychloride 2g/kg seed. Spray twice with Agrimycin (100 ppm) or plantomycin (200ppm) along with 3g COC per litre of water at 15 days interval.

10. Mosaic complex

Causal Organism: Chilli mosaic virus, Potato Virus Y, Cucumber Mosaic Virus (CMV), Tobacco Mosaic Virus (TMV) and Tomato spotted wilt virus

Symptoms: Symptoms vary with the infected virus

TMV:

- Backward bending of petiole.
- Raised blisters and mottled areas of light and dark green areas on the foliage.
- Leaves point towards ground.
- Necrotic spots on stem.
- Fruit ripens unevenly and is reduced in size.

CMV:

- Downward curling along with midrib.
- Most plants exhibit some degree of "shoe stringing" (narrowing of the leaves) in addition to stunting, yellowing, and whitish spotting of the leaves.
- Fruit may be small and distorted.

PVY:

- Vein banding on the leaves. Small, crinkled leaves are formed.

Pathogen:

- Different viruses like *Potato virus Y* (PVY) and its strains, *cucumber mosaic virus* (CMV), *tobacco mosaic Virus* (TMV), *tobacco etch virus*, *pepper vein banding virus*, *pepper mottle virus* and *pepper sever mosaic virus* besides *chilli mosaic virus* are involved in producing mosaic symptoms in this crop.
- PVY virions are filamentous flexuous rods, non-enveloped and consist of single stranded RNA.
- CMV virions are isometric, non enveloped, 29 nm in dia. having single stranded RNA.
- TMV virions are rod shaped non-enveloped having ss RNA.
- Pepper mottle virus is filamentous flexuous having ss RNA.
- Pepper severe mosaic virus is also filamentous flexuous of 761 x 13 nm size consisting of ss RNA.

Spread:

- Sap transmissible (TMV)
- Aphids: *Myzus persicae, Aphis gossypii, A. Craccivora*

Tomato Spotted Wilt Virus:
- The disease affects late maturing pods, reducing the yields.
- This virus occurs throughout temperate and subtropical regions and infects a diverse group of plant species from tomatoes and peppers to peanuts, lettuce, pineapple and many ornamentals.
- The virus is transmitted from diseased to healthy plants by **thrips**.
- The virus overwinters in perennial weeds.

Symptoms:
- The disease is most commonly recognized by the symptoms on the fruit.
- Both green and red fruit can be infected. Infected green pods display small, off coloured spots.
- Red fruit exhibit patches of yellow that never turns red.
- Other fruit symptoms include **chlorotic and necrotic spotting, concentric ring patterns**, and distortion.
- Foliage symptoms include general mosaic, chlorotic ring spots, and deformation.
- In some cultivars, the **shoot terminals die** and leaves defoliate.
- When new growth develops, it is severely distorted.
- Plants infected at an early age are stunted severely.

Management:
- Select healthy seed for planting.
- Crop rotation with non-hosts.
- Control perennial weed hosts.
- Rogue out and destroy infected plants in early stages of infection.
- Grow disease tolerant varieties like **Bhagyalakshmi, Bhaskar** and **LCA 305.**
- Soak the seed in Trisodium orthophosphate (Na_3PO_4) solution (150g/lt) for 30 min prior to sowing.
- Growing barrier crops like sorghum or maize (2-3 rows) around chillies to reduce the disease incidence.
- Cover the seed bed with nylon net or paddy straw.
- Spray seedlings in nursery with monochrotophos (Nuvacron) @1.5ml/lt or dimethoate@2ml/lt before transplantation in the main field.
- Apply carbofuran granules@10-12kg/acre in the main field or spray with monochrotophos@1.5ml/lt or dimethoate@2ml/lt.

11. Leaf curl

Causal Organism: *Chilli leaf curl virus*

Economic Importance:

- It is an important disease of this crop and cause significant yield reductions if the vector is present in the area.

Symptoms:
- The symptom of the disease appears as curling of the leaves followed by reduction in their size which later turn pale yellow in colour.
- Severe curling, crinkling and distortion of leaves accompanied by **vein clearing** and **reduction of leaf lamina.**
- Leaf margins are rolled downward and inward in the form of **inverted cup.**
- Curled leaves have thickened veins.
- The older leaves become leathery and brittle.
- The affected plants become stunted.
- Fruits formation in susceptible cultivars is rudimentary and distorted.
- Diseased plants fail to flower or bear any fruits.
- In advanced stage, defoliation takes place and growth is arrested.

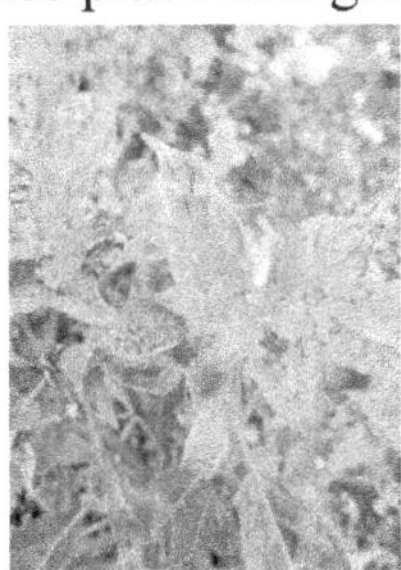

Pathogen:
- The disease is caused by *tobacco leaf curl virus* (TLCV), which belongs to Bigeminivirus group.
- The virus consists of geminate isometric particles measuring 18 to 20 nm in diameter.

Disease cycle and epidemiology:
- The virus survives from one season to another on various annual and perennial hosts and transmitted to pepper by the vector **white fly** named ***Bemisia tabaci.***
- The epidemic of the disease depends on the availability of the vector, sources of inoculum, vector activity and their population and prevailing environmental conditions.
- During wet weather, the spread of the disease becomes slow due to reduced activity of vector.

Management:
- Pepper varieties like **Punjab Lal, Perennial** and **Guhati Black** are resistant to mosaic viruses belonging to Poty and Cucumovirus groups.
- Planting of maize as barrier crop is also helpful in reducing the mosaic incidence.
- Combined use of yellow traps and insecticidal sprays reduces the population of vectors.

Physiological Disorders of Capsicum:

1. **Blossom End Rot (BER):**

Symptoms:

- Sunken, collapsed tissue near the blossom end of the pepper fruit.
- Often forms on or between lobes and can occur on sidewalls.
- Quickly invaded by bacteria and fungi that can lead to further decay.

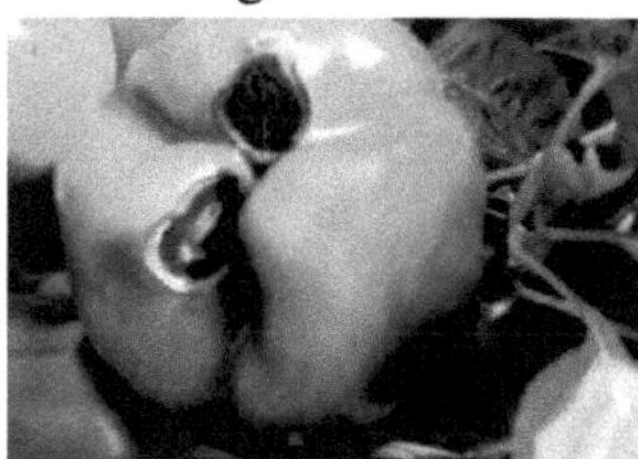

Causes:

- Lack of calcium in the soil has an important role in causing BER.
- It is most often associated with inadequate soil moisture content.

Management:

- Maintain adequate irrigation, especially during periods of hot, dry, and windy weather.
- Test soil for calcium levels before planting and if needed add lime or dolomite prior to preparing plant beds.
- Applying calcium products to the foliage probably won't help.

2. **Sunscald:**

Symptoms:

- Discoloured or bleached areas on fruit in areas directly exposed to the sun.
- Sunken, collapsed tissue.

Causes:

- Direct sunlight on the fruit.
- Inadequate foliage growth to cover and protect fruit.

Management:

- Provide adequate irrigation and fertilization to produce a strong plant with adequate foliage.
- Grow two rows of peppers about 12 inches apart.
- Rows will grow together and protect fruits.

3. Misshapen fruit:

Symptoms:

- Faulty pollination and fertilization cause abnormal shape of pepper fruits.
- The faulty pollination may be due to injury caused by insect, or low or high temperature to the stigmatic portion.

Causes:

- This condition generally occurs more when the crop is grown at a temperature lower than optimum required for normal pollination and fertilization.

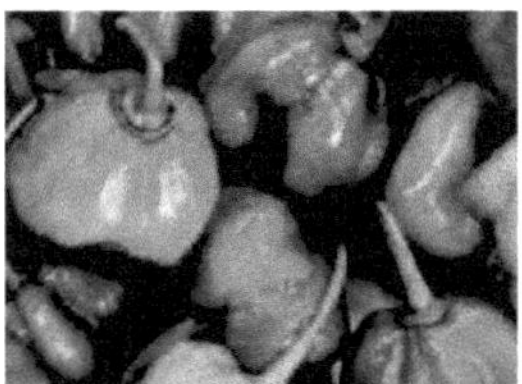

Management:

- Crop should not be grown at a temperature lower than optimum required for normal pollination and fertilization.

References:

Agrios, G. N., (2005). Plant Pathology (p. 902). Academic Press, San Diego, CA.

Ahmed, S. S., (1982). Studies on seed borne aspects of anthracnose of chilies caused by *Colletotrichum capsici* (Sydow.) Butler and Bisby. M.Sc. (Agri.) *Thesis, Univ. Agric. Sci.*, Bangalore.

Alam, S., Banu, M. S., Ali, M. F., Akhter, N., Islam, M. R., & Alam, M. S., (2002). In vitro inhibition of conidial germination of *Colletotrichum gloeosporioides* Penz. by fungicides, plant extracts and phytohormons. *Pakistan J. Biological Sciences,* 5, 303–306.

Anonymous, (2011). *India Horticultural Database–2011.* National Horticulture Board, Ministry of Agriculture, Govt. of India, Gurgaon.

Bagri, R. K., Choudhary, S. L., & Rai, P. K., (2004). Management of fruit rot of chili with different plant products. *Indian Phytopathology,* 57(1), 107–109.

Bailey, J. A., & Jeger, M. J., (1992). *Colletotrichum: Biology, Pathology and Control* (p. 388). Wallingford: Commonwealth Mycological Institute.

Khodke, S. W., & Gahukar, K. B., (1995). Fruit rot of chili caused by *Colletotrichum gloeosporioides* Penz. In Amravati district. *P. K. V. Research J.,* 19(1), 98–99.

Mesta, R. K., (1996). Studies on fruit rot of chili caused by *Colletotrichum capsici* (Sydow.) Butler and Bisby. *M.Sc. (Agri.) Thesis,* Univ. Agric. Sci., Dharwad.

Mishra, D., (1988). Fungicidal control of anthracnose and fruit root (*Colletotrichum capsici*) of chili (*Capsicum annuum*). *Indian J. Agricultural Science,* 58(2), 147–149.

Mridha, M. A. U., & Choudhary, M. A. H., (1990). Efficacy of some selected fungicides against seed borne infection of chili fruit rot fungi. *Seed Research,* 18(1), 98–99. Pakdeevaraporn, P., Wasee, S., Taylor, P. W. J., & Mongkolporn, O., (2005a). *Plant Breeding,* 124(2), 206–208.

Panagopoulos, C. G., (2000). Diseases of vegetable crops. *In: Vegetable Disease* (pp. 15–189). Stamoulis, Athens.

Persley, D., Cooke, T., & House, S., (2010). *Diseases of Vegetable Crops in Australia.* CSIRO Publishing: Collingwood, Victoria.

Prabhavathy, K. G., & Reddy, S. R., (1995). Post-harvest fungal disease of chili (*C. annuum*) from Andhra Pradesh. *Indian Phytopathology,* 48(4), 492.

Sherf, A. F., & MacNab, A. A., (1986). *Vegetable Diseases and Their Control* (2nd edn., p. 728). John Wiley & Sons, NY.

Singh, R. S., (2005). *Plant Diseases* (p. 720). Oxford and IBH Publishing Co. Pvt Ltd., New Delhi.

Than, P. P., Jeewon, R., Hyde, K. D., Pongsupasamit, S., Mongkolporn, O., & Taylor, P. W. J., (2008*). Plant Pathology,* 57(3), 562–572.

Thind, T. S., & Jhooty, J. S., (1985). Relative prevalence of fungal diseases of chili fruits in Punjab. *Indian J. Mycol. Pl. Path.,* 15, 305–307.

Ushakiran, L., Chetry, G. K. N., & Singh, N. I., (2006). Fruit rot disease of chili and their management in agro-climatic conditions of Manipur. *J. Mycopathol. Res.,* 44(2), 257–262.

BHENDI

Introduction:

- Bhendi (*Abelmoschus esculentus*) also known as 'okra' or 'lady's finger' is one of the important vegetables grown throughout the country both under open and protected structures.
- It is probably originated in Ethiopia and is widely spread all over tropical, subtropical and warm temperate regions of thw world.
- Okra plays an important role in the human diet by supplying fats, proteins, carbohydrates, minerals and vitamins. Moreover, its mucilage is suitable for certain medical and industrial applications.
- During cultivation, the crop is severely infected with various diseases, which not only reduce the quantity but also affect the quality of the fruits. This lecture deals with the fungal and viral diseases affecting this crop and their management.

Diseases:

S. No.	Disease Name	Causal Organism
Fungal diseases		
1.	Powdery mildew	*Erysiphe cichoracearum*
2.	Cercospora leaf spot	*Cercospora malayensis*
3.	Alternaria leaf spot	*Alternaria hibiscinum*

4.	Fusarium wilt	*Fusarium oxysporum* f.sp. *vasinfectum*
Viral diseases		
5.	Yellow vein mosaic	*Bhendi yellow vein mosaic virus*

1. Cercospora leaf spot

Causal Organism: *Cercospora malayensis, Cercospora abelmoschi*

Symptoms:

- In India, two species of Cercospora produce leaf spots in bhendi.
- *C. malayensis* causes brown, irregular spots and *C. abelmoschi* causes **sooty black, angular spots** on lower surface of leaves.
- Both the leaf spots cause severe defoliation and are common during humid season.

Pathogen:

- Conidiophores are pale to medium olivaceous brown, multiseptate, some times branched, geniculate and irregular.
- Conidia are obclavate to cylindric, olivaceous brown and straight to curved.

Mode of spread and survival:

- P.I: The fungi survive through conidia and stromata on crop refuse in soil.
- S.I: Air borne conidia.

Management:

- Spray mancozeb or zineb@0.2% or carbendazim@0.1% for disease control a month after sowing and repeat at fortnightly intervals based on disease incidence.

2. Powdery mildew

Causal Organism: *Erysiphe cichoracearum*

Symptoms:

- Powdery mildew is very severe on bhendi.
- Grayish powdery growth occurs on the under as well as on the upper surface of the leaf causing severe reduction in fruit yield (Sataraddi *et al.*, 2009).

Pathogen:

- Conidia are single celled, hyaline, barrel shaped and in long chains.
- Cleistothecia are globose and dark brown myceloid appendages.
- The asci are pedicellate, ovate or ellipsoid.
- The number of ascospores is usually 2 rarely 3 per ascus.
- The ascospores are single celled, hyaline and oval to sub cylindrical.

Management:
- Dust finely ground sulphur at 30 kg/ha or spray wettable sulphur@0.3% or Dinocap@0.1% three to four times at 15 days intervals.

3. Fusarium wilt

Causal Organism: *Fusarium oxysporum* f.sp. *vasinfectum*

Symptoms:
- The conspicuous symptom is a typical wilt, beginning with a yellowing and stunting of the plant, followed by wilting and rolling of the leaves as if the roots were unable to supply sufficient water.
- Finally, the plant dies.
- If a diseased stem is split lengthwise, the vascular bundles appear as dark streaks.
- When severely infected, nearly the whole stem is blackened (Suryanarayan and Bhombe, 1961).

Pathogen:
- Macroconidia are 3- 5 septate formed on sporodochia and pionnotes.
- In mass conidia appear buff or salmon orange in color.
- Macroconidia are fusiform and curved inward at both ends.
- The base is pedicellate.
- Microconidia are septate.
- Terminal and intercalary chlamydospores are broadly ovate.

Mode of spread and survival:
- The fungus is soil borne.

Management:
- Treat the seeds with Mancozeb @ 3g/kg seed.
- Drench the field with Copper oxy chloride @ 0.25%.

4. Yellow vein mosaic

Causal Organism: *Bhendi Yellow vein mosaic virus or bhendi vein clearing virus*

Economic Importance:

- The YVMD was first identified in India by Kulkarni (1924) and later studied by Capoor and Verma (1950) and Verma (1952).

Symptoms:
- Yellowing of the entire network of veins in the leaf blade (vein clearing) is the characteristic symptom.
- In severe infections the younger leaves turn yellow, become reduced in size and the plant is highly stunted.
- The veins of the leaves will be cleared by the virus and intervienal area becomes completely yellow or white.
- In a field, most of the plants may be diseased and the infection may start at any stage of plant growth.
- Infection restricts flowering and fruits are not formed, if formed, turns smaller, harder and rough.
- Loss in fruit yield ranges from 50-100% based on disease incidence.
- The affected plants produce fruits with yellow or white colour and they are not fit for marketing (Nath and Sakia 1992).

Pathogen:
- The virus particles are 16 – 18nm in diameter.

Mode of spread and survival:
- P.I: Infected plant parts
- S.I: The virus is transmitted by the whitefly, *Bemisia tabaci.*

Management:
- By selecting varieties resistant to yellow vein mosaic like **Parbhani Kranti, Arka Abhay, Arka Anamika,** and **Varsha Uphar,** the incidence of the disease can be minimised (Sanwal *et al.*, 2014a).
- **Janardhan** and **Haritha** can tolerate yellow vein mosaic.
- For sowing during the summer season, when the whitefly activity is high, the susceptible varieties should be avoided.
- Spraying monocrotophos 1.5 ml/litre of water can restrict the disease spread.
- Synthetic pyrethroids should not be used because it will aggravate the situation.
- It can be controlled by application of Chlorpyriphos (Dursban) 2.5 ml + neem oil 2 ml lit of water.

References:

Dutta O P. 1984. *Breeding okra for resistance to yellow vein mosaic virus and enation leaf curl virus.* Annual Report, IIHR, Bangalore (India).

Lana AF. (1976). Mosaic virus and leaf curl disease of okra in Nigeria. *Pest Articles and News Summaries, 22,* 474-478.

Khan MA and Mukhopadhyay. (1985). Studies on the effect of some alternative culture methods on the incidence of YVMV disease of okra. *Indian Journal of Virology,* 1(1), 69-72.

Sharma B R and Dhillon T S. 1983. Genetics of resistance to yellow vein mosaic virus in interspecific crosses of okra. *Genetics Agraria, 37*: 267–75.

POTATO

Introduction:

- Potato cultivation was too old as 2000 years ago from South America Andes.
- Potato (*Solanum tuberosum* L.) is from genus Solanum and only 8 species are cultivated worldwide.
- The edible potato has achieved a significant important among non-cereals food crop as it can provide 15 times more yield as compare to cereals.
- It provides essential amino acid (lysine) along with more energy and protein as compared to other single food crop.
- Potato crop is susceptible to many biotic and abiotic diseases.

Diseases:

S. No.	Disease Name	Causal Organism
Fungal diseases		
1.	Late blight	*Phytophthora infestans*
2.	Early blight	*Alternaria solani*
3.	Sclerotium rot	*Sclerotium rolfsii*
4.	Wart	*Synchytrium endobioticum*
5.	Dry rot	*Fusarium* sp.
6.	Black scurf	*Rhizoctonia solani*
Bacterial disease		
7.	Black leg and soft rot	*Erwinia caratovora subsp. Caratovora*
8.	Brown rot	*Ralstonia solanacearum*
9.	Common scab	*Streptomyces scabies*
10.	Wiches broom	*Phytoplasma*
Viral diseases		
11.	Leaf roll	*Potato leaf roll virus*
12.	Spindle tuber	*Viroid*
Physiological Disorders		
13.	Hollow heart	
14.	Black heart	

15.	Greening	
16.	Freezing injury	
17.	Growth cracks	
18.	Internal brown spot	
19.	Uneven sprouting	

1. Late blight

Causal Organism: *Phytophthora infestans*

Economic Importance:

- It is one of the serious diseases of potato wherever it is grown and caused the worst ever famine "The Irish famine" in 1845.
- Usually infection starts in **6 weeks** old plants.
- First reported from Andes Mountains of South America. In India, the disease was first reported in Darjeeling district in India (1880).

Symptoms:

- Initially starts from leaf tips or margins and spread inward.
- Small faded green patches on upper surface of leaf which turn into brown spots.
- Downy growth of the pathogen on subsequent lower surface.
- Progressive defoliation and collapse of plants under favourable conditions.
- Water soaked stripes on stem which becomes necrotic.
- Purplish brown spots appear on skin of tubers.
- On cutting, the affected tubers show rusty brown necrosis spreading from surface to the centre.
- Decay of plant parts under favourable weather which emits foul smell.

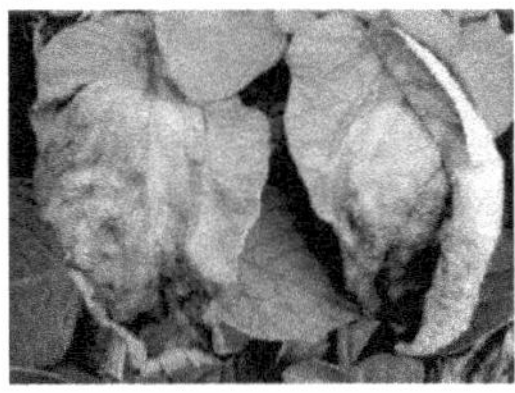
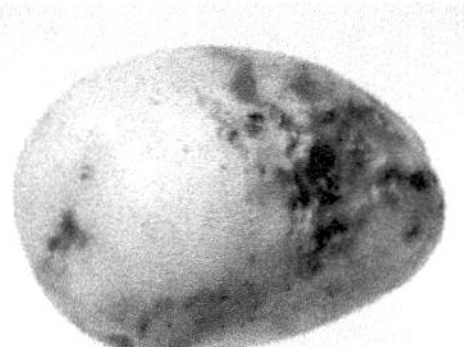

Pathogen:

- The mycelium is endophytic, coenocytic and hyaline which are intercellular with double club shaped haustoria type.
- Sporangiophores are hyaline, branched intermediate and thick walled.
- Sporangia are thin walled, hyaline, oval or pear shaped with a definite papilla at the apex.
- The sporangium may act as a conidium and germinate directly to form a germ tube.
- Zoospores are biflagellate possess fine hairs while the other does not.

Mode of spread and survival:

- The infected tubers and the infected soil may serve as a source of primary infection (Hector, 1926).

- The diseased tubers are mainly responsible for persistence of the disease from crop to crop.
- The air borne infection is caused by the sporangia.
- P.I: Infected potato tubers or oospores.
- Collateral host: Tomato (*Lycopersicon esculentum*), Pepper and egg plant.
- S.I: Conidia dispersed by wind or water.

Favourable conditions:
- Cool moist conditions and
- RH: >90% and with suitable temperature ($12\text{-}24^0$ C) favours the disease.

Dutch rules
- Night temperature below the dew point for 4 hours or more.
- Night temperature not below 10°C.
- Cloudiness on the next day.
- Rainfall at least 0.1mm on the following day (Van Everdingen, 1926).

Management:
- Select healthy tubers for planting.
- Delayed the harvesting.
- High ridging to about 10-15cm height reduces tuber infection.
- Grow resistant varieties such as **Kufri Jyothi, Kufri Badshah, Kufri Jeevan, Kufri Sherpa**, Kufri Naveen, Kufri Alenkar, Kufri Khasi, Kufri Garo and Kufri Moti, etc.
- **Resistant sources:** *Solanum demissum* and *S. Phureja*
  Prophylactic measures:
- Metalaxyl (0.1%) or Mancozeb (0.25%) or chlorothalonil (0.2%) or BM (1%) can be applied at 7 to 10 days intervals in the hills and 10 to 15 days intervals in plains.
- Dip sprouted tubers in 0.2% metalaxyl for 30 min (Shekhawat, 2000).

2. Wart

Causal Organism: *Synchytrium endobioticum*
- Losses seen in temperate regions.
- In India, the disease is restricted to Darjeeling.

Symptoms:
- Host cells at the point of infection are **hypertrophied.**
- White granular swellings form on the eyes of tubers.
- White tumour like outgrowths, called as warts, develop on stems and tubers.
- As the crop matures, warts become black and rot.
- Infected auxillary bud or the leaf is transformed into cock's comb like greenish yellow outgrowth (Hampson, 1996).
- Wart disease is much worse during wet seasons than in dry soil conditions (Singh and Shekhawat, 2000).

Pathogen:

- It is an obligate parasite, which does not produce mycelium but an abundance of dissemination sporangia which are responsible for tumour formation on underground potato organs.
- These sporangia produce zoospores, organs of dissemination and infection.

Disease cycle:

- P.I: Resting sporangia in soil
- S.I: Zoospores dispersed by water

Favourable conditions:

- High soil moisture, optimum temperature of 21^0 C (12 to 28°C), slightly acidic to neutral pH favours disease.

Management:

- Follow strict quarantine measures.
- Grow resistant varieties such as **Kufri Jyoti, Kufri Jeevan** and **Kufri Muthu.**

3. **Early blight**

Causal Organism: *Alternaria solani*

Symptoms:

- It is present in both hills and plains.
- Brown-black necrotic spots with angular, oval shape characterized by concentric rings on leaves.
- Several spot coalesce and spread all over the leaf. Shot holes on tubers.

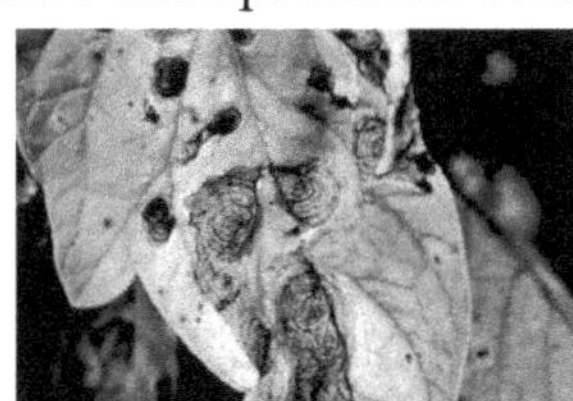 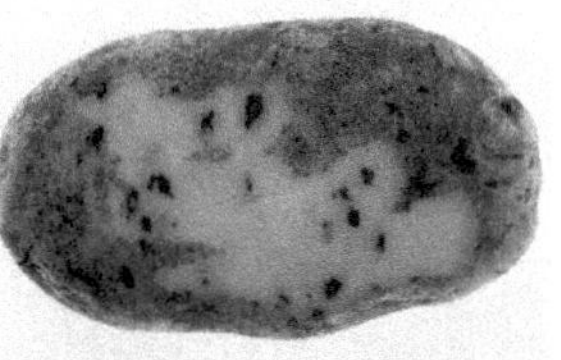

Pathogen:

- Hyphae are light brown or olivaceous which become dark coloured with age.
- The hyphae are branched, septate and inter and intra cellular.
- The coniophores emerge through the stomata or between the epidermal cells.
- The conidia are club shaped with a long beak which is often half the long of the whole conidium.
- The lower part of the conidium is brown while the neck is colourless.
- The body of the conidium is divided by 5-10 transverse septa and there may or may not be a few longitudinal septa.

Favourable condition:

- Dry warm weather with intermittent rain, Poor vigour, Temperature: 25-30°C, Poorly manured crop favours disease.

Mode of spread and survival:

- The conidia and the mycelium in the soil or in the debris of the affected plants can remain viable for more than 17 months.
- These conidia or the new conidia found on the overwintered mycelium bring about the primary infection of the succeeding potato crop.
- Secondary infection is more important in the spread of the disease.
- The conidia formed on the spots developed due to primary infection are disseminated by wind to long distances.
- The conidia from the affected plant may also be disseminated to the adjoining plants by rain and insects.

Management:

- Disease free seed tubers should be used for planting.
- Removal and destruction of infected plant debris should be done because the spores lying in the soil are the primary source of infection.
- Very early spraying with Zineb or captan 0.2% and repeating it for every 15-20 days gives effective control.
- The variety **Kufri Sindhuri** possesses a fair degree of resistance.
- Copper fungicide at least 3–4 weeks after planting to lower down the disease incidence (Reddy, 2010).

4. Black scurf

Causal Organism: *Rhizoctonia Solani*

Economic Importance:

- This fungal disease is prevalent both in the plains and hills and responsible for yield losses up to 25%.
- Actually, infection develops on all parts of the plant, including foliage (Prasad and Agrawal, 1983).
- The fungus attacks young sprout through epidermis and produces dark brown lesions, thereby killing the sprout before emergence, which results in patchy germination (Dutt, 1979).

Symptoms:

- Black speck, black speck scab, russet scab on tubers.
- At the time of sprouting dark brown colour appear on the eyes.
- Affected Xylem tissue causes to wilting of plants.
- Infected tuber contains russeting of the skin.
- Hard dry rot with browning on internal tissue.
- Spongy mass appear on the infected tuber. Seed tubers are source of spread.

- Others symptoms on the tuber include skin cracks, dry-core symptoms where crater like depression is formed on the lenticels (CPRI, 1981), pitting along with shape deformity, hard dry rot with browning of internal tissue (Thirumalachar, 1953) and seed piece decay (Chaudhary, 1983).

Pathogen:
- The mycelium is hyaline when young and brown at maturity.
- Hyphae are septate and branched with a characteristic constriction at their junction with the main hyphae. The branches arise at a right angle to main axis.
- Sclerotia are black.
- A basidium bears four sterimata each with a basidiospore at the end.
- The basidiospores are hyaline, elliptical to obovate and thin walled. They are capable of forming secondary basidiospores.

Mode of spread and survival:
- The fungus is capable of leading a saprophytic life on the organic material and can remain viable in the soil for several years.
- The sclerotia on the seed tubers are the principal source of infection of the subsequent crop raised with these tubers.
- On return of favourable conditions the mycelium present in the soil may develop producing new hypae.

Epidemiology:
- Moderately cool, wet weather and temp 23°C are the favourable for the development of disease.

Management:
- Disease free seed tubers alone should be planted.
- If there is a slight infection of black scurf that can be controlled by treating seed tubers with mercuric chloride solution for 1.5 hr with acidulated mercuric chloride solution for 5 min.
- Treating the soil with pentachloro-nitrobenzene (PCNB) at the rate of 70 kg/ ha lowers the incidence of the disease, but it is too expensive and cumbersome.
- Well sporulated tubers may be planted shallow to control disease.
- The disease severity is reduced in the land is left fallow for 2 years.
- Rapeseed mustard and canola as green manure and crop rotation, effectively reducing *Rhizoctonia solani* (Larkin and Griffin, 2007).

- Treated seed tubers are usually free from black scruff disease. Seed treatment with Boric acid @ 3% for 30 min or seed treatment with bio-agents Trichoderma *harzianum* or *T. viride* @ 4–6 g/kg of seed will lower down the initial inoculum. Field application of *Trichoderma harzianum* and *T. viride@* 100 g/m2 will also be effective to manage the disease.

5. Sclerotium Rot (Stem rot or Southern blight)

Causal Organism: *Sclerotium rolfsii*

Symptoms:
- Affected stems on plants with sclerotium stem rot first show a moist decay at or slightly below the soil surface where infection is initiated.
- Stem lesions expand up and down the stem, and all plant parts can be infected. Stem infection leads to wilting and yellowing of the foliage.
- Tubers are typically infected by way of stolons. The fungus quickly grows over the tuber surface and invades, resulting in a moist cheesy decay.
- Portions of infected plant parts and nearby soil often are covered with the white, radiating mycelium of *S. rolfsii.*
- The mycelium generates small spherical sclerotia (about 1–2 mm in diameter) that are white when young and brown when mature.

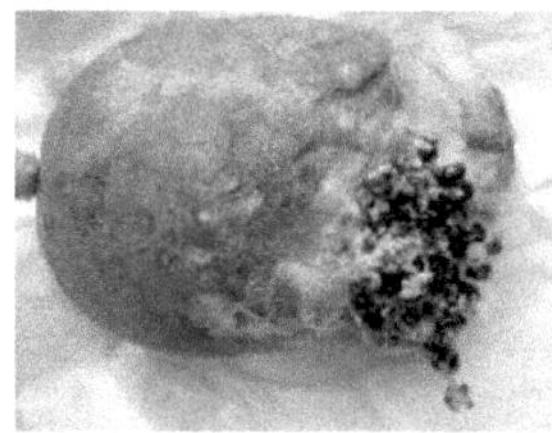

Favourable conditions:
- *S. rolfsii* attacks many field and vegetable crops in warm regions. The fungus persists in soil between crops.
- Germination and infection by the sclerotia are favoured by hot temperatures (80° to 90°F) and moist soil surfaces.
- Sclerotium stem rot is considered to be a problem only in hot climate growing areas. Losses typically occur at the end of the season.
- The fungus can invade dead vines as well as living ones. Extensive tuber losses can be initiated within a few days of harvest if the fungus is present.
- Potato cultivars vary in their degree of susceptibility but current cultivars have not been well classified.

Management:
- Relatively early planting minimizes stem and tuber rot by avoiding the late season high temperatures that favour disease.
- Plant fields infested with *S. rolfsii* before planting fields without infestation.
- Do not store tubers in the ground unnecessarily long before harvest; this allows more time for infection at favourable warm temperatures.

- Rotate to crops that are less susceptible (e.g., non fleshy, root or tuber crops).
- Pre-plant chemigation with metam sodium is recommended for fields known to be infested with *S. rolfsii;* the treatment has afforded good control for at least one season.
- Applications of the soil amendment ammonium bicarbonate made just before harvest will kill mycelium, but not the sclerotia, of the fungus, thus preventing tuber infection for about 3 to 5 days.

6. Dry rot

Causal Organism: *Fusarium acuminatum*

Economic Importance:
- Fusarium dry rot can cause breakdown of potatoes in storage as well as breakdown of seed pieces after planting (Singh, 1986).
- Worldwide, it is one of the most important postharvest diseases of potatoes.
- In the field, symptoms include variable seed emergence and differences in plant size.
- Fusarium dry rot is caused by a number of *Fusarium* species but is generally associated with *Fusarium sambucinum, F. solani, F. culmorum* and *F. avenaceum.*

Symptoms:
- Infections generally begin at wound sites. Once infection occurs, it slowly enlarges in all directions.
- The skin over the infected area sinks and wrinkles, sometimes in concentric rings, due to the fungus drying out the contents of the tuber.
- Internally, infected areas are light brown to black as the fungus kills the cells of the tuber (Rai and Singh, 1981).
- Internal cavities created by dry rot infections generally contain fungal mycelium of various colours.
- The infected areas usually remain dry but at high moisture levels or humidity bacteria invade and cause foul smelling wet infections.
- If infected areas are not removed, the tuber can completely rot and shrivel.
- In the field, symptoms include variable seed emergence and differences in plant size.
- *Fusarium* species can also cause a wilt which includes stunting of growth, chlorosis of leaves and wilting of lower leaves (Khurana, 2000).
- However, infected tubers are more important because in soil, the fungus remains viable only for 9–12 months (Mann and Nagpurkar, 1922).

Mode of Spread and Survival:
- Fusarium dry rot is both seed and soil-borne and is present in most potato growing areas.

- Spread is associated with damage through seed cutting, grading or harvesting.
- Wounds created during these processes allow the *Fusarium* fungi to enter the tuber and spread.

Favourable Conditions:

- Temperatures of 15 to 20°C and high relative humidity aid the growth of fusarium dry rot.
- Lower temperatures and humidity retard the fungus but dry rot development continues even at the lowest storage temperatures (4°C).
- Seed tubers may be infected prior to shipment but not exhibit symptoms until during or after transit. Cultivars differ in their susceptibility to dry rot.
- *Fusarium* species can survive in the soil for a long time as either survival spores or on decaying plant material.
- Untreated wounds or cut seed are susceptible to soil-borne infection.
- Soil attached to tubers at harvest will generally contain spores that can lead to infection during storage.

Management:

- Crop rotation and soil management must be followed to arrest the buildup of the pathogen population. Keep tuber in chamber at 20°C with high humidity.
- Soil amendment by using crop straw and oilcakes helps to reduce the disease. Singh *et al.* (1988) used four crop straws, i.e., gram, soybean, pigeon pea, and cluster bean to reduce the disease incidence.
- Adjustment in planting and harvesting dates is essential to manage the disease. In wilt symptoms of this disease, fungus attacks the plants when they are 40–60 days old. Therefore, the disease is more severe in early planted crop (Singh, 1986).
- By delaying the planting time, disease could be reduced by 36% (Singh *et al.,* 1990c). Seed should be treated with bio-agents *Trichoderma harzianum* and *T. viride* @ 4–6 g/kg of seed.

7. Black leg (Soft rot)

Causal Organism: *Erwinia caratovora subsp. caratovora*

Economic Imporance:

- Introduced into India through seed stocks from Italy.
- Blackleg and soft rot are common diseases during storage and transition. Blackleg disease of potato is not common in India.
- Three soft rot Erwinias, *E. caratovora f. sp atroseptica, Erwinia caratovora f. sp caratovora* and *E. chrysanthemi* are associated with potato causing tuber soft rot and blackleg (Perambelon, 2002).
- It occurs only rarely in the Shimla hills of Himachal Pradesh, Kumaon hills of Uttarakhand, Nilgiri hills, and Bihar plains.

Symptoms:

- Disease occurs in two phases – Blackleg of shoots and soft rot of tubers

Blackleg symptoms:
- Plants are stunted with a stiff, erect growth habit.
- Foliage becomes chlorotic and the leaflets tend to roll upward at the margins.
- Stems of infected plants exhibit an inky black decay.
- The base of the stem is often completely rotted.
- Plants may wilt. In relatively dry soil, only the pith may show blackening.

Soft rot symptoms:
- Soft rot include rotted tissues that are wet, cream to tan in colour, and soft.
- Rot begins on the tuber surface and progresses inward.
- Infected tissues are sharply delineated from healthy tissue by dark brown or black margins.
- Shallow necrotic spots on the tubers result from infections through lenticels.
- Rotting tissue is usually odourless in the early stages of decay, but develops a foul odour as secondary organisms invade infected tissue.
- Soft rot also infects wounded stems and roots.

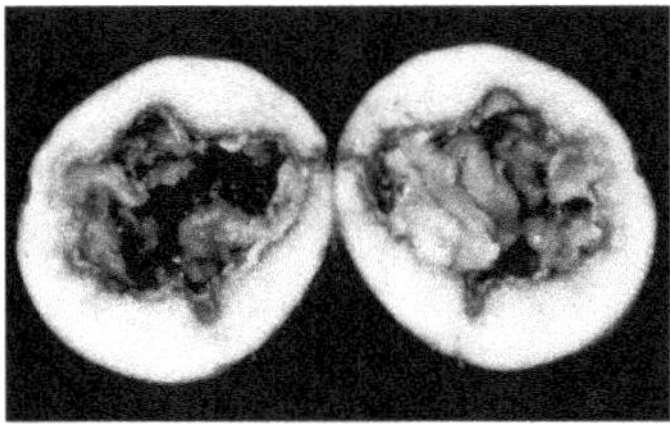

Pathogen:
- It is a gram negative rod shaped bacterium with 1 to 6 peritrichous flagella.

Mode of spread and survival:
- Survive in diseased and contaminated tubers.
- Spread through contaminated soil, tubers and **maggot flies** (*Hymelia* and *Phorlin* sp).

Favourable conditions:
- High humidity (94 – 100%)
- Temperature (21 – 29^{0}C)
- **Late blight and *Fusarium* tuber rot infections predispose soft rot.**

Management:
- Remove all debris from warehouses and disinfect the walls with formaldehyde or copper sulphate.
- Avoid wounding of plants and storage organs.
- Products to be stored should be dry, and the humidity and temperatures of warehouses should be kept low.
- Crop rotation with cereals.
- Crop should be planted in well drained areas and at sufficient distances to allow adequate ventilation.

- Control insects with insecticides.
- Dip cut seed pieces of potato in a solution of Streptocycline 100ppm and CuSo4 40ppm for 30 min.
- The disease can be minimized if tubers treated with 3% Boric acid for 30 min and dry under shade.
- Store the produce either in well-ventilated cool stores and cold stores (Reddy, 2010).

8. Common scab or corkey scab

Causal Organism: *Streptomyces scabies*

Economic Importance:

- It is important disease in Punjab and Himachal Pradesh. In India prior to 1960, it was restricted to hilly regions only.

Symptoms:

- Small brownish and slightly raised spots on tubers.
- Spots enlarge, coalesce and become corky Lesions typically possess a raised margin and slightly depressed center.
- Characteristic symptoms have descriptive names:
- **Russet scab** appears on tubers as superficial tan to brown corky lesions.
- **Pitted scab** is characterized by lesions with depressions beneath the tuber surface.
- **Raised scab** appears as cushion like warty lesions.

 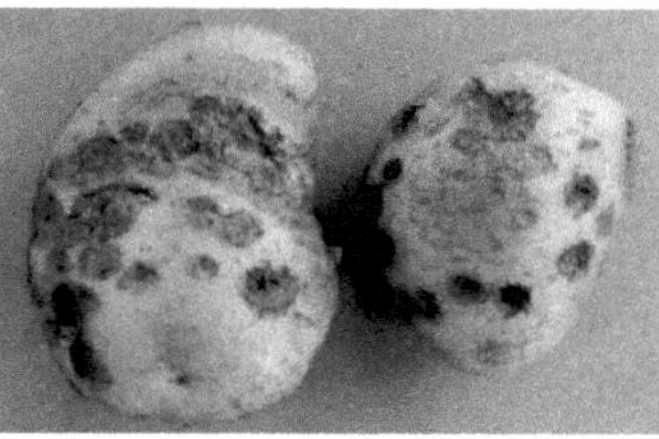

Pathogen:

- Aerial mycelium in pure culture has of prostrate branched threads.
- Sporogenous hyphae are spiral in form.
- Conidia are produced by the formation of septa at intervals along the hyphae, which contract to form narrow isthmuses between the cells.
- Conidia are roughly cylindrical and hyaline.
- The conidia can germinate even at higher temperatures.
- **The growth of the organisam is good in slightly alkaline medium and is checked at pH 5.2.**

Mode of spread and survival:

- P.I: Soil and infected tubers.
- S.I: Soil, water, wind blown soil and infected tubers.
- Pathogen enters through unsuberized lenticels or wounds.

Epidemiology:

- Soil pH (5.2-8.0)
- Soil temperature of 20-22^0 C
- Low soil moisture favours the disease development.

Management:
- Use of disease free tubers.
- Crop rotation with wheat-oat or potato-onion-maize (4yrs).
- Hold the soil pH at about 5.3 by addition of sulphur.
- Green manuring before planting potato (Larkin and Griffin, 2007).
- Dipping of infected tubers in 3% boric acid for 30 min.
- Soil application of PCNB at the time of planting.
- Common scab is severe in alkaline soil and application of alkaline fertilizers like calcium ammonium nitrate should be avoided.
- Infection of the seed tubers can be removed by 1.5hrs dip in mercuric chloride 0.1% solution or by 2h dip in 1 part formaldehyde in 240 parts of water.

9. Brown rot

Causal Organism: *Ralstonia solanacearum*

Economic Importance:
- **First bacterial disease reported in India.**
- First recorded in 1891 from Pune district of Maharashtra by Cappel in 1892.
- **Also referred as bacterial wilt or ring disease or bangle blight.**
- Occurs in Deccan and Central plateau, Assam, West Bengal, Orissa, hills of Uttar Pradesh and Nilgiris.

Symptoms:
- Wilting, stunting and yellowing of foliage followed by collapse of entire plant.
- Browning of xylem in vascular bundles.
- Stems, petioles of the lower leaves and roots become brown and on cutting of infected materials slimy mass of bacteria ooze out.
- Brown ring is formed in the tubers due to discolouration of vascular bundles (ring disease).
- Formation of pockets or cavities around vascular bundles in the pith and cortex.
- When pressed tuber slimy bacterial ooze emerge.
- The tubers may rot at harvest or during storage.

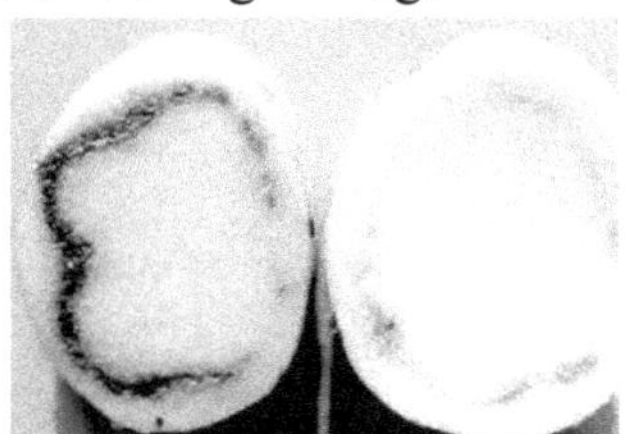

Pathogen:

- G –ve, short rod, 1-4 flagella. Colonies are white to brown in colour.

Mode of spread and survival:

- Infected soil and seed tubers form the main source of the primary infection.
- Brown rot affected plant parts decay and release masses of bacteria in the soil where these may remain viable from season to season.
- The bacteria in the soil are disseminated by wind from one field to the other.
- The infection usually occurs through wounds in the root system.

Favourable conditions:

- Temp 25to 35ºC, RH above 50 % and PH 6.2-6.6 favours for the development of disease. **Acid soil is not favourable.**

Management:

- Crop rotation with maize or soybean for 3 yrs.
- Use disease free tubers for sowing.
- Deep summer ploughing.
- Treat seed tubers with 0.02% streptocycline for 30 min giving 4mm deep sharp cut.
- Disinfestation of cutting knives with sodium hypochlorite (10%) or mercuric chloride.
- Application of stable bleaching powder @ 12 kg/ha has been found to reduce bacterial wilt by 80% when applied in furrows at the time of planting (Shekhawat *et al.,* 1988).
- Certain bacteria like *Pseudomonas fluorescens, Bacillus polymyxa, Bacillus* spp. and Actinomycetes have been found to delay the development of *R. solanacearum* and reduce the incidence of bacterial wilt (Sivamani *et al.,* 1987; Reddy, 2010).

10. Potato witches broom

Causal Organism: *Phytoplasma*

Symptoms:

Early Infection:

- The following symptoms appear on young potato plants propagated from phytoplasma infected tubers.
- They characteristically include formation of many axillary and basal branches with short internodes and narrow leaves.
- Typical witches broom symptoms include plant stunting with proliferated branches carrying small round leaves.
- No flowers develop at plant maturity and infected plants produce hairy sprouts.
- Before harvesting, adventitious aerial tubers are evident on infected potato plants. Tubers collected from infected plants become less dormant and commonly produce hairy sprouts.
- Infected plants produce numerous tiny tubers and sometimes no tubers at all. Severe and typical witches broom symptoms develop on plants grown under greenhouse conditions.

Late Infection:

- These symptoms could be attributed to the insect transmission of PWB phytoplasma from infected to healthy plants.
- Potato seedlings exposed to native leafhoppers started to show symptoms a few weeks later.
- Symptoms on seedlings resembled those of PWB on mature plants and included formation of proliferated branches with narrow leaves on new growth.
- Stems were shortened and tender and, later, affected plants were stunted. Plants produced no flowers but formed small and medium sized tubers.

Management:

- Phytoplasmas are obligate pathogens, similar to plant viruses, which require living hosts to reproduce and survive. So far, there is no appropriate method to control PWB disease.
- Although virus-resistant potato cultivars have been produced, information concerning resistance to phytoplasmas is lacking.
- However, preventive measures may help to reduce the incidence of PWB disease.
- These include controlling and breaking the life cycle of insect vectors. This approach can be implemented before planting potato tubers by destroying weeds that harbour adult leafhoppers or their eggs. Poaceous weeds like wild oats are favourite hosts for *M. quadrilineatus.*
- Spraying with insecticides will eliminate leafhoppers in the weedy edges of the field.
- Avoidance of growing plant species belonging to this family adjacent to potato fields will reduce the vector insect population and eliminate a potential source of inoculum.
- Another recommended cultural practice is to remove symptomatic plants (stunted with narrow leaves) during roguing operations in potato fields.
- Elimination of very small tubers before planting potatoes will reduce phytoplasma infection attributable to tuber transmission.
- Maintenance of appropriate cultural practices and planting potato tubers obtained from certified sources ensures a potato crop with high yield and quality for commercial production.

11. Viral diseases

a) Mild mosaic/Interveinal mosaic

Causal Organism: *(Potato virus X) PV X*

Symptoms:

- Often referred as latent potato mosaic.

- Light yellow mottling with slight crinkling on potato plants.
- Interveinal necrosis of top foliage.
- Stunting of diseases plants.
- Leaves may appear slightly rugose where strains of PV Y combines.

Spread:
- Spreads mechanically through rubbing of leaves, contact of infected plants, seed cutting knives, farm implements.
- Root clubbing of healthy and diseased plants in field.

Management:
- Use disease free seed tubers for planting.
- Rouging of diseased plants.

b) Severe mosaic

Causal Organism: *Potato virus Y (PV Y)*

It is also called **potato leaf drop streak.**

Symptoms:
- Chlorotic streaks on leaves which become necrotic.
- Necrosis of leaf veins and leaf drop streak.
- Interveinal necrosis and stem/petiole necrosis.
- Plant remains stunted in growth.
- Rugosity and twisting of the leaves occurs in combination with PV X and PV A.

Survival and spread:
- **P.I.:** Infected tubers
- **S.I.:** Spread by aphids, *Myzus persicae* and *Aphis gossypii*

Management:
- Use disease free seed tubers for planting.
- Rouging of diseased plants.
- Control aphids with systemic insecticides.

c) Leaf roll

Causal Organism: *Potato leaf roll virus*

Symptoms:

- Upward rolling of leaves, which have a stiff leathery texture.
- Plants stunted and have a stiff upright growth.
- Phloem necrosis of tubers in some varieties.

Spread:

- Infected seed tubers or by **aphids.**

Management:

- Disease free seed tubers for planting.
- Controlling of aphids with systemic insecticides.

11. Potato spindle tuber

Causal Organism: Viroid

Symptoms:

- Plants appear erect, spindly and dwarfed.
- Leaves small, erect and leaflets dark green.
- **Tubers elongated with tapering ends**.
- Tuber eyes are numerous and more conspicuous.

Mode of spread and survival:

- Primary infection by seed tubers.
- Mechanically spread by knives used to cut seed tubers.
- Also transmitted by pollen and seed and contaminated mouth parts of grasshoppers, flea beetles and bugs.

Management:

- Use of PSTVd free potato seed tubers.
- Disinfestation of cutting knives.

Physiological disorders:

1. Hollow heart:

Symptoms:

- This is very common disorder of potato.

- Hollow heart consists of cavities in the tubers, which are lined with brown, necrotic tissues.
- Tubers become over sized and remain empty which leads to the formation of cavity in the centre with the death of the small area of pith cells.
- This condition appears often in varieties which bulk rapidly and produce over sized tubers.

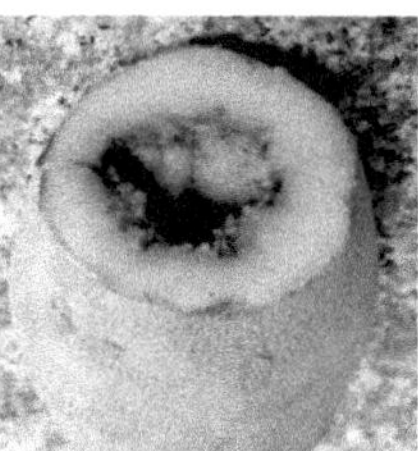

Causes:
- Rapid growth and development of tubers followed by sudden rains or irrigation.
- Excessive use of nitrogen and water application increases the incidence of hollow heart.
- Wide plant spacing promotes bigger tubers and tends to favour hallow heart.
- It may occur in the field when soil temperature rises above 32.2C during growth and maturity of tuber (Bhat, 2016).

Management:
- Follow closer spacing. Avoid excessive application of fertilizers particularly nitrogen.
- Apply irrigation at short interval so that the soil temperature may not exceed 32^0C during tuber development and maturity.
- High potassium levels can reduce hollow heart.
- Select varieties that are less susceptible.

2. Black heart:

Symptoms:
- In this disorders central tissues of the affected tubers show dark grey or black discoloration.
- The discoloration occurs in an irregular pattern, usually with a distinct line between healthy and affected tissues.
- The symptoms are internal only after cutting the potato.
- Seed tubers with black heart should not be used as they are more susceptible to soft rot and have poor emergence problems.
- In advanced stages, the affected tissues may dry out and separate thus forming cavities.
- They are surrounded by disordered tissue and are referred to as **cat's eye** (Hiller and Thornton, 1993).

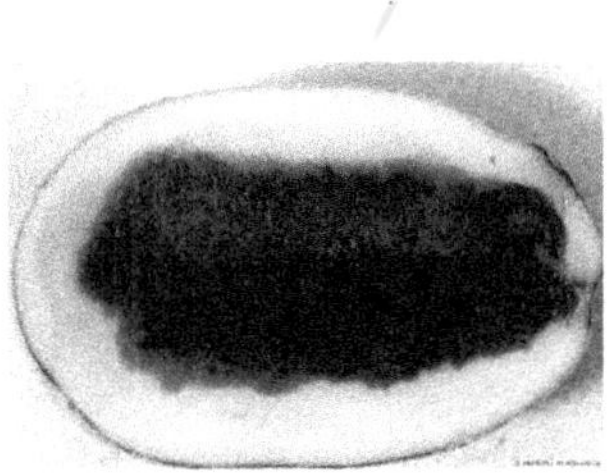

Causes:

- Black heart occurs in conditions of poor oxygen supply, restricted airflow and high respiration, especially when potatoes are stored in piles as air does not get into the centre.
- High soil temperature and water logged soils contribute to black heart development in the field.

Management:

- Provide proper ventilation in storage.
- Avoid raising temperature above 32^0C during transit and storage by avoid piling and stacking too high and keep potato tubers in layers.
- Avoid poorly drained soils and excessive irrigation, to prevent flooding and oxygen reduction (Hooker, 1981).

3. Greening:

Symptoms:

- Exposure of tubers to bright sunlight or longer periods of low light intensity results in greening of potatoes due to the formation of chlorophyll pigment (Bhat, 2016).
- Such tubers glycoalkaloids like solanine and chaconine which are considered poisonous.
- Though consumption of such potatoes is not likely to cause serious health hazard yet such potatoes taste bitter and may cause temporary digestive discomfort.
- Peeling off green skin with layer of the flesh removes most of the solanine content.

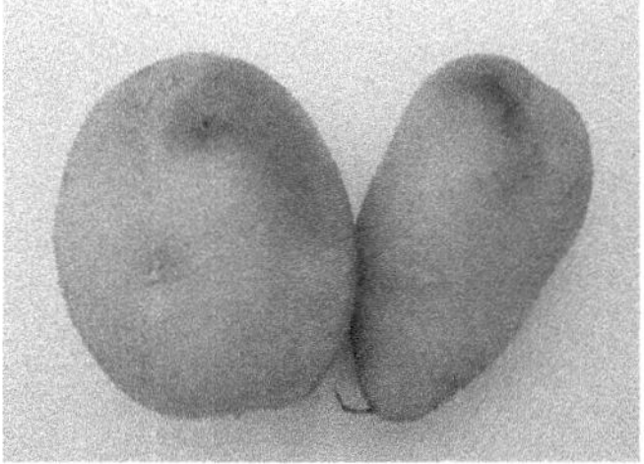

Causes:

- Exposure of tubers to sunlight.
- If harvested potatoes are stored in the home under low levels of light.
- Excessive application of fertilizers may also contribute to this disorder.
- Mechanical injury may also leads to solanine production.

Management:

- Proper earthing up as the tuberization takes place.
- Two earthings are sufficient to keep the potato tubers free from greening.

- Store tubers in darkness after digging up.
- If the home storage area is not completely dark, provide darkness by storing in paper bags to allow air movement.

4. Freezing injury:

Symptoms:

- Freezing injury is characterized by discolouration of the tissue and affects the vascular tissues at the ring called ring necrosis.
- More severe injury leads to blue-black necrotic network in the pith.
- If the tubers are frozen for about 4-5 hr they show no blotch or discolouration but on thawing the whole tuber becomes wet and soft and liquid oozes out of it.
- Tubers show more damage towards proximal end.

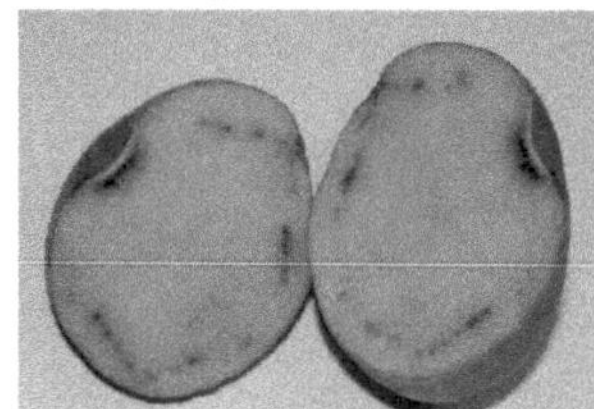

Causes:

- This disorder occurs due to the exposure of tubers to freezing temperature during or after harvest.
- It takes place at -1.5^0C below temperature and results in ice formation in potato tubers.

Management:

- Avoid exposure of tubers to freezing temperature during storage or harvest.
- Adjust the date of sowing so that it does not coincide with low temperature.
- Lift potatoes before there is risk of frost or use frost tolerant varieties if available.
- Avoid storing field-frosted tubers or using them for seed purpose.

5. Growth cracks:

Symptoms:

- Growth cracks are the splitting of the potatoes during growth that leaves deep fissures in the vegetables.
- The splits usually run lengthwise and affecting the overall quality of potato.
- Tubers with external growth cracks are usually unacceptable for fresh market.
- Incidence of growth cracks is greater in case of wider plant spacing or if fewer tubers are set per hill.

Causes:

- Irregular water supply is often responsible for growth cracks.

- A heavy rain or irrigation followed by dry spell causes rapid increase in growth activity and water uptake.
- Chances of cracking increases when potato plants are abruptly provided with optimal growing conditions after a period of poor growth conditions.
- Deficiency of Boron also contributes to cracking.

Management:

- Maintain proper soil moisture during season especially during bulking stage when the plants are large and tubers are rapidly expanding.
- Apply Borax @ 20kg/ha.

6. Internal brown spot:

Symptoms:

- This disorder is characterized by numerous, irregular, dry reddish brown or rust coloured spots beneath the tuber skin, with few or no out ward signs.
- The spots can be anywhere but most commonly found inside the vascular ring and towards apical end.
- Spots consist of group of dead suberised cells that are free of fungi and bacteria.
- There is no external symptom but the tubers lose their value as table potatoes.

Causes:

- Appears particularly in light sandy soils which are not irrigated regularly.
- This disorder has been associated with dry weather, high soil temperature and low soil moisture.
- Storage of immature tubers at high temperature have higher incidence.

Management:

- Application of adequate amount of calcium fertilizer after planting.
- Maintain proper soil moisture and avoid high soil temperature.
- Provide proper storage and growing conditions.

7. Uneven sprouting in the field:

- This problem is practically faced by the farmers.
- Adequate crop stand cannot be maintained.

Causes:

- Planting of tubers just after removal from cold storage.
- Soil moisture deficiency in the field at planting and sprouting.

- Loss of apical dormancy due to cutting of tubers in small pieces.

Management:

- Use tubers for planting after breaking the dormancy.
- Treat the tuber pieces with Dithane M-45 @ 0.25% for 10 min.
- Maintain proper moisture in the field at planting and sprouting.
- Place the tubers for 15 days at room temperature in 30 cm thick layers to induce sprouting and select those tubers having green, thick and multiple sprouts for planting.

References:

Bhat, K. L., (2016). *Physiological Disorders of Vegetable Crops* (p. 258). Daya publishing house, New Delhi.

Bhattacharya, S. K. and Malhotra, V. P., (1979). Control of charcoal rot of potato through crop rotations. *J. Indian Potato Assoc.,* 6, 199–204.

Chatterjee, A. K. and Vidaver, A. K., (1986). Genetics of pathogenicity factors: Application to phytopathogenic bacteria. *Adv. Plant Pathol.,* 4, 1–218.

Chaudhary, R. G., (1983). Cause of potato seed decay in low hills of Arunachal Pradesh. *J. Indian Potato Assoc.,* 10, 111–115.

CPRI, (1958–1960). *Annual Scientific Report, Central Potato Research Institute* (pp. 94– 101). Shimla.

Dutt, B. L., & Pushkarnath, (1960). Resistance of potato varieties to powdery scab. *Indian Potato J.,* 2, 78–82.

Eisenback, J. D., Hirschmann, H., Sasser, J. N. and Triantaphyllou, A. C., (1981). *A Guide to the Four Most Common Species of Root Knot Nematodes (Meloidogyne Species) with a Pictorial Key.* A Coop. Publ. Depts. Plant Pathology and Genetics and U. S. Agency for International development, Raleigh, NC.

Hampson, M. C., (1996). A qualitative assessment of wind dispersal of resting spores of Synchytriumendobioticum, the causal agent of wart of potato. *Plant Dis.,* 80, 779–782.

Harrison, J. G., Searle, R. J. and Williams, N. A., (1997). Powdery scab of potato: A review. *Plant Pathol.,* 46, 1–25.

Hector, G. P., (1926). Appendix II. Annual report of the economic botanist to the govt. of Bengal for the year 1924–1925. *Ann/Dept. of Agric. Bengal,* 1924–1925, 5–9.

Hooker, W. J., (1981). Compendium of potato diseases. *American Phytopathological Soc* (p. 125). St. Paul, MN.

Khurana, S. M. P. and Garg, I. D., (1998). Present status of controlling mechanically and non-persistently aphid transmitted potato viruses. In: Hadidi, A., et al., (eds.), *Plant Virus Disease Control* (pp. 593–609).

Khurana, S. M. P. and Singh, M. N., (1986). Viral and mycoplasmal diseases of potato. *Rev. Trop. Plant Pathol.,* 33, 123–184.

Larkin, R. P. and Griffin, T. S., (2007). Control of soil borne potato diseases using Brassica green manure. *Crop Protec.,* 26(7), 1067–1077.

Mann, H. H. and Nagpurkar, S. D., (1922). Further investigations of the Fusarium blight of potatoes in western India. *Agric. J. India,* 567–576.

Paharia, K. D. and Sahai, D. (1968). Nutritional requirements of potato-isolate of *Macrophomina phaseoli* from potato. *Indian J. Microbiol.,* 10, 107–110.

Patel, D. B., Patel, N. A. and Modi, V. M., (2010). Influence of different dates of potato planting on stem necrosis disease. *International J. Plant Protec.,* 3, 404–405.

Perambelon, M. C. M., (2002). Potato diseases caused by soft rot Erwinia: An overview of pathogenesis. *Plant Pathol.,* 51(1), 1–12.

Phadtare, S. G., (1978). Pink rot of potato- a new report from India. *J. Indian Potato Assoc.,* 5, 174–175.

Pushkarnath, (1976). *Potato in Sub-Tropics* (p. 289). Orient Longman, New Delhi.

Rai, R. P. and Singh, B. P., (1981). A new disease of potato incited by *Fusarium acuminatum* Ell. and Ev. *Current Sci.,* 50, 1037–1038.

Shekhawat, G. S., (2000). Management of potato diseases through host resistance. *J. Mycol. Pl. Pathol.,* 30, 143–150.

Sikka, L. C., Srivastava, S. N. S., Singh, A. K. and Bharadwaj, V. P., (1971). Integrated approach to control *Rhizoctonia solani* on potato. *Indian Phytopath,* 24, 54–57.

Singh, B. P., Nagaich, B. B. and Saxena, S. K., (1988). Studies on the effect of organic amendments on Fusarium wilt of potato. *J. Indian Potato Assoc.,* 15, 60–67.

Sivamani, E., Anuratha, C. S. and Ganamnickam, S. S., (1987). Toxicity of *Pseudomonas fluorescens* towards bacterial plant pathogens of banana (*Pseudomonas solanacearum*) and rice (*Xanthomonas campestris pv. oryzae*). *Current Sci.,* 56, 547–   548.

Srivastava, S. N. S., (1965). The occurrence of silver scurf of potato in India. Sci. and Cult., 31, 537.

Thirumalachar, M. J., (1953). Pycnidial stage of charcoal rot inciting fungus with a discussion on its nomenclature. *Phytopathology,* 43, 608–610.

Van Everdingen, E., (1926). Het. verbandtusschen de weergesteldhieden de aarolppelziekte, *Phytopthora infestans* (the relation between weather conditions and potato blight, *Phytophthora infestans*) Tijdschr. Plantenziekten., 32, 129–140.

Yabuuchi, E., Kosako, Y., Yano, I., Hotta, H. and Nishiuchi, E., (1995). Transfer of two Burkholderia and an Alcoligenes species to Ralstonia gen. nov. Proposal of *Ralstonia pickettii* (Ralston, Palleroni and Doudoroff, 1973) comb. Nov. and *Ralstonia eutrapha* (Davis, 1969) comb. *Nov. Microbiol. Immunol.,* 39, 897–907.

CRUCIFERS

Introduction:

- Cole crops has long been cultivated as an important vegetable crop and a source of vitamins, minerals, and fiber, particularly during cold seasons in temperate climates.
- More recently, cabbage, cauliflower and other cruciferous vegetables (members of the Brassicaceae) have been recognized as important sources of chemoprotective phytochemicals in the diet.
- Cole crops is a productive vegetable based on biomass per area of cultivation.
- However, these crops are affected by many diseases, particularly those caused by fungi and bacteria.

Diseases:

S. No.	Disease Name	Causal Organism
Fungal diseases		
1.	Damping off and wire stem	*Pythium aphanidermatum, Rhizoctonia solani*
2.	Club root	*Plasmodiophora brassicae*
3.	White rust	*Alubugo candida/ Albugo cruciferum*
4.	Powdery mildew	*Erysiphe polygoni*
5.	Anthracnose	*Colletotrichum concentricum*
6.	Downy mildew	*Peronospora parasitica*
7.	Alternaria leaf spot	*Alternaria brassicola*
8.	Black leg	*Phoma lingam*
9.	Cabbage yellows	*Fusarium oxysporum* f.sp. *conglutinans*
Bacterial diseases		
10.	Black rot	*Xanthomonas campestris pv. campestris*
Physiological Disorders of cauliflower and cabbage		
11.	Riceyness	
12.	Fuzziness	
13.	Leafiness	
14.	Browning	
15.	Whiptail	
16.	Buttoning	
17.	Blindness	
18.	Chlorosis	
19.	Hollow Stem	
20.	Frost Injury	
21.	Splitting/ cracking of heads	
22.	Tip Burn	
23.	Bolting	

1. Club root of crucifers or Finger and toe disease

Causal Organism: *Plasmodiophora brassicae*

Economic Importance:

- This is one of the earliest known diseases of crop plants in Europe as early as in 13th century.
- It was extensively studied in Russia by woronin in 1874.
- It occurs worldwide except in china.
- In India it has been reported from many parts.
- It is fairly severe in hilly regions on cabbage, cauliflower and other crucifers.
- Fields once infested with the club root pathogen remain so indefinitely and become unfit for cultivation of crucifers.

Symptoms:
- Infected plants have pale green to yellowish leaves initially.
- Later, infected plants show wilting in the middle of hot, sunny days, recovering during the night.
- Stunting of above ground parts and reduction in size of heads.
- Characteristic symptoms become apparent in advanced stage of root infection as **spindlelike, spherical, knobby, or club-shaped swellings**.
- The swellings may be few, or they coalesce and cover the entire root system.
- **Club root is particularly prevalent on soils with a pH below 7,** whereas it has been observed that the disease is often less serious on heavy soils and on soils containing little organic matter.

Pathogen:
- Primary zoospores are anteriorly by flagellate which is of whiplash type.
- Secondary zoospores are smaller than primary zoospores.

Mode of Spread and Survival:
- Fungus is soil borne and survival in the crop refuses in the form of minute resting spores for at least 10 years.
- Contaminated soil can be caused by wheel of implements, carts, tools and on the feet of human being.

Disease cycle:
- **P.I**: Soil borne resting spores, which survive for longer periods in soil (10yrs.).
- **Collateral hosts:** Broccoli, Brussels sprout, cabbage, cauliflower, Chinese cabbage, mustard, raddish, turnip.
- **S.I**: Resting spores or zoospores carried through irrigation water or by root contact.

Favourable conditions:

- It occurs at a temp range of 12-27^0 C (25^0 C), high soil moisture and neutral to acidic soils 5-7.0 pH.

Management:

- Use of seedlings from disease free fields.
- Plant cabbage and other susceptible cruciferous crops in well drained fields that have a pH slightly above neutral (usually about pH 7.2).
- Crop rotation does not work since pathogen persists long in soil.
- Add hydrated lime to soil to increase pH to 7.2 (6 weeks before planting @ 2.5T/ha).
- Avoid excess irrigation.
- Treat the soil of seed bed areas with chloropicrin, methyl bromide or vapam two weeks before planting.
- **Drenching soil with a solution of Brassicol (Pentachloronitrobenzene).**

2. Downy Mildew

Causal Organism: *Peronospora parasitica*

Economic Importance:

- It is severe in raddish, cabbage, cauliflower, mustard, and knol-khol.

Symptoms:

- Small purplish brown spots on under surface of leaves.
- Small, pale yellow angular spots on upper surface of leaves, with downy growth on the under surface.
- The spots coalesce and the leaves shrivel and dry up prematurely.
- In cabbage, these spots expose the heads to soft rot.
- Cauliflower curds look brownish at the top.
- Stems show dark brown and depressed lesions or streaks which later develop downy growth of fungus.

 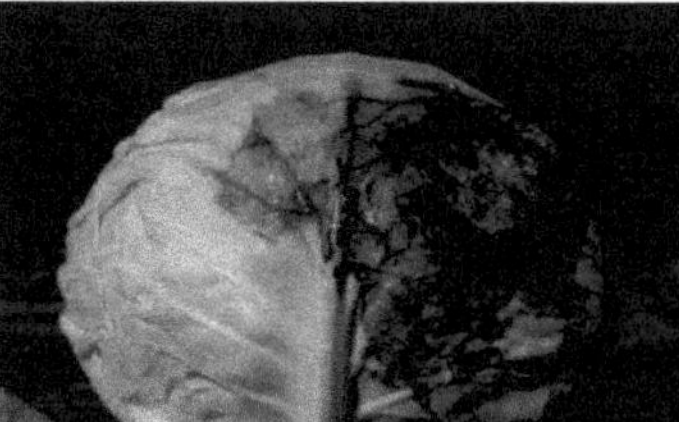 

Pathogen:

- Conidiophores are erect, dichotomously branched; conidia are broadly oval, ellipsoidal and hyaline.

Mode of Spread and Survival:

- The fungus penetrates in the soil through oospores in hosts.
- Secondary spread of the disease is through water and wind borne conidia.

Management:

- Destruction of infected plant debris.
- Avoidance of thick sowing and excessive moist conditions.

- Spray metalaxyl @ 0.25% or COC @ 0.3% or Mancozeb @ 0.2% at 10 days interval.

3. Powdery mildew

Causal Organism: *Erysiphe polygoni*

Economic Importance:

- Seen on cabbage and cauliflower.

Symptoms:

- White powdery spots on the upper surface of leaves, stems, flower parts etc.
- Finally the mildew may cover the entire surface.

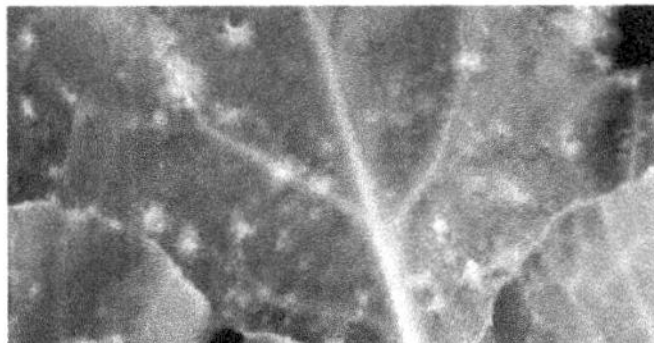

Pathogen:

- Conidiophores are septate.
- The cleistothecia are sharp and globose.

Disease cycle:

- **P.I:** Mycelium in infected plant debris
- **S.I:** Wind borne conidia.

Management:

- Spary inorganic sulphur 0.25% or Dinocap 0.05% (Glawe *et al.,* 2005).

4. Alternaria leaf spot

Causal Organism: *Alternaria brassicola, Alternaria brassicae, Alternaria raphani*

Economic Importance:

- Common on cabbage, cauliflower and mustard.

Symptoms:

- Spots are small, dark coloured.
- They enlarge; soon become circular and 1mm. in diameter.
- Under humid conditions groups of conidiophores will be formed in the spot.
- **Spots develop concentric rings.**
- Finally the spots coalesce leading to blighting of leaves.
- The fungus is seed borne and cause shriveling of seeds and poor germination.
- Linear spots also appear on petioles, stems, pods and seeds.

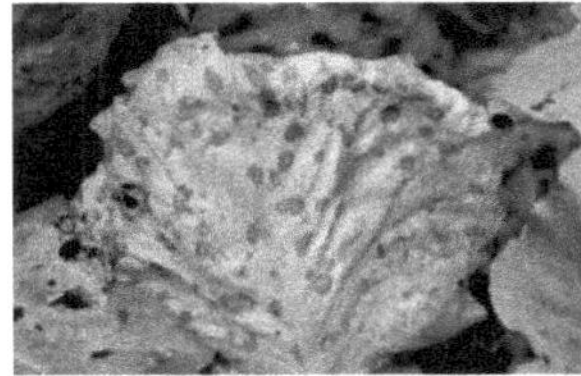

Pathogen:

- The fungal hyphae are branched, septate, inter and intracellular.
- Conidiophores arise singly or in groups of 2 to 12.

- They are simple, erect, cylindrical, slightly swollen at base, septate, pale, smooth and 90 x 5 to 8 mm.
- Conidia are formed in chains of 20 or more.
- They are cylindrical, muriform, tapering slightly towards the apex and the basal cell is rounded (Kashyap *et al.,* 2010).

Mode of Spread and Survival:
- Pathogens are seed borne or the conidia are borne abundantly in moist atmosphere and are disseminated readily by air currents.

Management:
- Hot water treatment at 50^0c for 30min.
- Seed treatment with agrosan.
- Foliar spray with Mancozeb@0.2% or COC@ 0.3% twice.

5. **White rust**

Causal Organism: *Albugo candida (*Synonym: *Cystopus candidus)*

Symptoms:
- White, shiny raised blisters (pustules) on the lower surfaces of leaves, stems and flowers. Pustules coalesce to form irregular patches.
- The epidermis ruptures exposing white spore mass which gives the pustule a powdery appearance.
- Distortion of the floral parts including petals, pistils and anthers due to hypertrophy and hyperplasia.
- Plants malformed beyond recognition.

Pathogen:
- Here, Pathogen is an obligate parasite.
- Mycelium is intercellular producing knob shaped haustoria in the host cells.
- Each sporangium has 4 to 8 zoospores.

Mode of Spread and Survival:
- Over wintering may be through oospores in plant debris in the soil and mixed with seeds and perennial mycelium in weed hosts are primary source of inoculums.
- **P.I:** Oospores in soil and Perennial weeds hosts.
- **S.I:** Sporangia & Oospores carried by wind.

Management:
- Follow sanitary measures, crop rotation and destruction of weeds.
- Spray 0.8% B.M. or any copper fungicide.

6. Wire stem

Causal Organism: *Rhizoctonia solani*

Symptoms:

- Wire stem can be a seed problem where cauliflower or other cruciferous transplants are grown crowded together in unsterilized soil or seedling beds.
- This disease makes the seedlings unsuitable for transplanting since many of the affected plants will die or grow poorly.

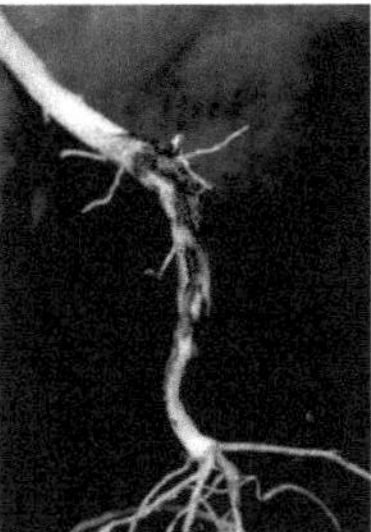

Pathogen:

- The fungus shows branching at right angles near the distal septum in young hyphae.
- Sclerotia are irregular, brown to black and 5mm in dia.
- The fungus produces both terminal and intercalary, barrel shaped chlamydospores.
- In the perfect stage basidia are produced on the host.
- They are barrel shaped, clavate and have four sterigmata.
- Basidiophores are hyaline and ellipsoid.

Management:

- Sterilized soil and seedbed drenches with Copper oxychloride 0.25% will give good disease control.

7. Black leg

Causal Organism: *Phoma lingam*   **P.S:** *Leptosphaeria maculans*

Symptoms:

- It is occurs in most regions, especially in areas with rainfall during the growing period.
- The fungus is carried by the seed and hence it may occur from the early stage.
- Stem of the affected plant when split vertically, shows severe black discoloration of sap stream.
- Whole root system decays from bottom upwards.
- Frequently, the affected plants fall over in the field.

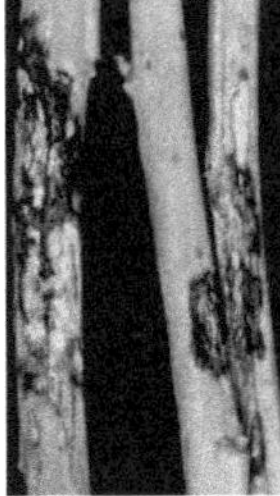
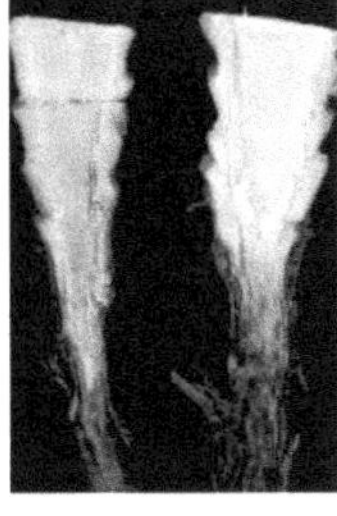

Pathogen:

- Pycnidia are flask shaped, dark coloured and sometimes with papillate ostiole.
- Ascocaeps are globose, and Ascospores are biseptate, ellipsoidal.

Mode of Spread and Survival:

- It can survive for up to four years in seed and three years in infected crop debris.
- The pathogen infects seedlings, forms pycnidia, and produces abundant amounts of spores which exude from the pycnidia in long coils and are splashed to nearby plants to initiate new infections.
- The disease is favored by wet, rainy weather.

Management:

- Seed infection can be prevented by spraying the seed plants with copper oxychloride or with an organo mercuric compound.
- Seed treatment with Captan or Thiram 4g/kg of seed, followed by seed treatment with *Trichoderma viride* 4g/kg.
- **Pusa Drumhead**, a cabbage cultivar has been reported to be tolerant under field conditions.

8. Cabbage Yellows or Fusarium Wilt

Causal Organism: *Fusarium oxysporum* f. sp. *conglutinans*

Symptoms:

- The disease affects the seedlings in nursery stage; however plants exhibit symptoms 2 to 4 weeks after transplanting.
- Disease development is promoted by warm weather conditions.
- Initial symptom appears as the development of yellowish green colour on one side of the plant.
- A lateral warping or curling of the stem and leaves occurs.
- The lower part of the leaf blade adjoining the petiole or midrib wilts and dies.
- The lower leaves turn yellow and later the upper leaves are affected.
- With time, the yellow leaves turn brown and the affected tissue become dry and brittle.
- The speed of progress of disease in the plant depends upon the degree of varietal susceptibility and the soil temperature.

Management:

- The conventional controls such as rotation, seed treatment, fungicide sprays, and destruction of crop refuse are of little value once the fungus has established itself on a farm or in a specific field.
- Therefore, the use of resistant varieties is the only control.

- However, as a preventive measure the vulnerable stage of the young seedlings to the infection can be avoided by very early sowing of cabbage.

9. Sclerotinia rot/ White mould

Causal Organism: *Sclerotinia sclerotiorum*

Symptoms:

- This fungus can cause serious losses in the field, in storage, and under transit and market conditions.
- Generally, damp weather favours the occurrence of the disease.
- Infections may occur on the stem at the ground level, on the leaves at their bases, or where the foliage comes in contact with the soil.
- The infections begin as water-soaked, circular areas, which soon become covered by white, cottony fungal growth.
- The affected tissue becomes soft and watery as the disease progresses.
- The fungus eventually colonizes the entire cabbage head and produces large, black, seedlike structures called sclerotia on the diseased tissue (Ferraz *et al.,* 1999)

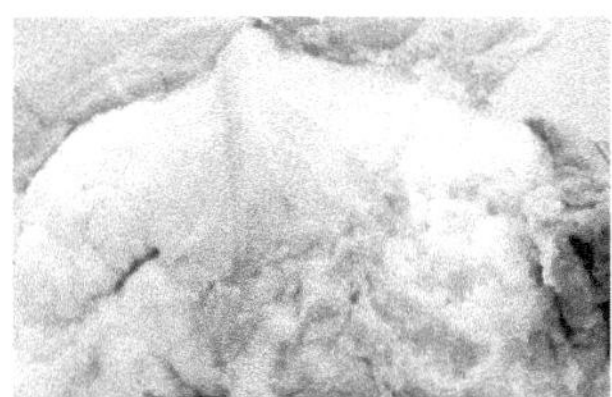
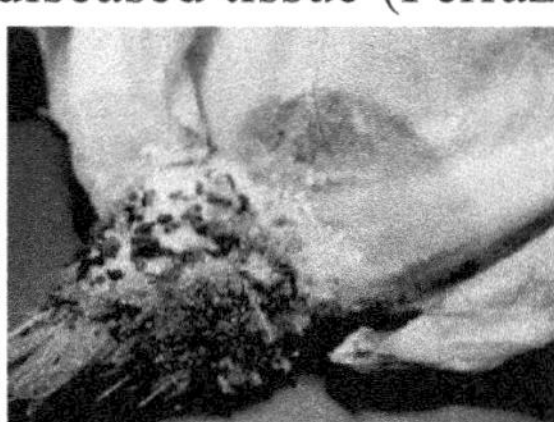

Management:

- The disease can be managed most successfully by combining cultural practices that discourage disease development.
- Planting cabbage in fields that are surrounded by dense woods will restrict air circulation and subsequently delay drying.
- Rows should be planted in the direction of the prevailing winds to promote free flow of air movement within the plants.
- Fields with a history of white mould should be planted with non-susceptible crops such as grains (corn, rye, wheat, etc.).
- Cabbage and other susceptible crops (cauliflower, beans, peas, etc.) should not be planted in fields where white mould has become a problem because continuous cropping of susceptible crops will result in a buildup of the fungus in the soil and increased disease incidence.
- Mechanical injuries to cabbage heads during harvesting operations should be avoided.

10. Black rot

Causal Organism: *Xanthomonas campestris* pv. *campestris*

Economic Importance:

- Serious on cabbage, cauliflower, knol-khol, mustard, raddish.

Symptoms:

- 1st appear near the leaf margins as chlorotic or yellow (angular) areas.

- The yellow area extends to veins and mid rib forming characteristic 'v' shaped chlorotic spots.
- Veins and veinlets turn brown and finally black.
- The vascular blackening extended beyond affected veins to midrib, petiole and stem.
- In advanced stages, infection may reach the roots system and blackening of vascular bundles occurs.
- Bacterial ooze can also be seen on affected parts. If the infection is early, the plants wilt and die.
- If the infection is late plant succumbs to soft rot and die.

Pathogen:
- It is gram negative, short rod with rounded ends and non capsulated.
- It occurs singly, rarely in pairs and motile with single polar flagellum.

Mode of Spread and Survival:
- Bacterium is internally seed and soil borne. It also survives on plant debris.
- **Collateral host:** *Centella asiatica*
- Bacteria enter through stomata of cotyledons.
- Also enters through hydathodes on leaf margin and also through wounds.
- **S.I:** Bacterium through irrigation water or wind splashed rain and also by mechanical means.

Favourable Conditions:
- Black rot is spread rapidly during warm, humid weather, with an optimal temperature range of 27- 30°C at 80-100% humidity.

Management:
- Seed Treatment with HgCl2 solution for 30 min or Agrimycin or Aureomycin 0.01%.
- Hot water treatment at 50^0c for 30 min, for killing seed borne inoculum followed by a 30 min dip in streptocycline 100 ppm.
- Spray Agrimycin-100 or Streptocycline-50ppm at transplanting, curd formation and pod formation.
- Crop rotation for 2-3 yrs with non cruciferous crop. Drenching seed bed with 5% formalin or any antibiotic solution in nursery beds.
- Resistant Varieties: **Cabbage: Cabaret, Defender, Gladiator, Pusa Muktha.**
- **Cauliflower: Pusa ice, Pusa snow ball-K-I-F, Sel-12.**

Physiological Disorders:

- Cauliflower suffers from a number of physiological disorders, which manifest in different type of disease syndromes.
- Some physiological disorders depend mainly on hereditary factor, whereas, other are fluctuation occurring in temperature, air, water, humidity, organic and inorganic nutrition.
- **Important physiological disorders, affecting cauliflower are described below:**

1. Riceyness:

Symptoms:

- It manifests in the elongation on peduncle wearing flower buds, rendering curds, granular, loose and somewhat velvety.
- A premature initiation of floral bud is characterized by riceyness in cauliflower and is considered to be of poor quality for marketing.

Cause:

- At IARI, New Delhi, it has been found that this disorder may result from any temperature higher or lower than the optimum required for particular cultivars.
- Riceyness occurs mainly when harvesting has been delayed.
- If late variety planted early, riceyness develops due to the prevalent of high temperature, however, if can also appear at lower temperature.
- Hereditary factors have also been reported for riceyness.
- Heavy dose of nitrogen and high relative humidity also contributes to riceyness.

Management:

- It can be controlled by cultivation of genetically pure seed and appropriate varieties with recommended cultural practices.

2. Fuzziness:

Symptoms:

- It appears as the flower pedicels of velvety curds elongate.

Cause:

- The anomaly is both hereditary and non-hereditary.
- Cultivation of cauliflower, out of their normal season encourages fuzziness.

Management:

- Sowing good quality seed in right season under proper cultural practices, minimized fuzziness.

3. Leafiness:

Symptoms:

- This disorder is commonly seen by formation of small thin leaves from the curd which reduces quality of curd.

Cause:

- Extremely small green leaves appear in between the curd segment due to inheritable or non-heritable factors.
- Prevalence of high temperatures during curding phase aggravates leafiness.
- Certain varieties are more sensitive to leafiness or bracketing than other.

Management:

- It can be controlled by selection of varieties according to their adaptability.

4. Browning (Brown Rot or Red Rot):

Symptoms:

- It is characterized by sign on the young leaves that become dark green and brittle.
- The old leaves puckered, chlorotic and often drops off.
- Sometimes, the downward curling of older leaves followed by development of blisters when boron deficiency is severe.
- The leaves remain small and the growing point may die.
- However, in later stage, water soaked, light brown to dark brown spots formed on the stem and branches may ultimately lead to the formation of cavities formed on the stem and branches may ultimately lead to the formation of cavities and a hollow stem.
- Curds may also show irregular water soaked spots. Which alter change to a rusty brown colour. The affected curds remain small and acquire a bitter taste.

Cause:

- It is caused by borne deficiency which is influenced by soil pH.
- The availability of boron decreases at neutral soil reaction.

Management:

- This may be controlled by application of borax or sodium borate or sodium tetra borate at the rate of 20 kg/ha a soil application.
- In case of acute deficiency, spray of 0.25 to 0.50 per cent solution of borax at the rate of 1 to 2 kg/ha depending upon growth, soil reaction and extent of deficiency.

5. Whiptail:

Symptoms:

- The young cauliflower plants become chlorotic and may turn white, particularly along the leaf margins. They also become cupped and wither.
- The leaves blades fail to develop properly, and the leaves are ruffled and distorted.
- In older plant, the lamina of the newly formed leaves are irregular in shape, frequently, consisting of only a large bare midribs and hence, the common name "whiptail".

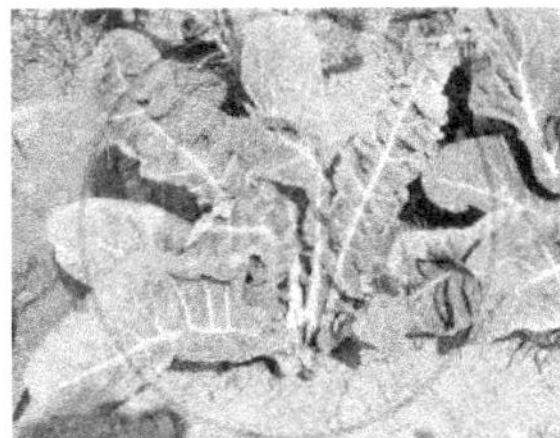

Cause:

- **Deficiency of molybdenum** causes 'whiptail' syndrome, especially, in highly acidic soils.
- Because high manganese concentrations in such soils hinder the uptake of molybdenum which seldom occurs when the soil pH is 5.5 or higher.

Management:

- It can be corrected by application of lime or dolomite limestone to raise the soil pH up to 6.5 or higher.
- Sodium or Ammonium molybdate at the rate of 1-2 kg/ha as soil application can also control "whiptail" of cauliflower.

6. Buttoning:

Symptoms:

- Development of small curds with inadequate foliage in cauliflower is known as buttoning.
- It is also referred to as premature heading.
- The leaves are so small that cannot cover the formed head.

Causative factors:

- Causes of buttoning are transplanting of more than 6 week-old seedlings.
- Planting as early variety in late vice versa leads buttoning.
- Hot and dry weather is unfavourable for vegetative growth of plants, but favourable for inducing curd formation and inhibits further enlargement.

- When soil moisture becomes limiting factor, it checks the growth of the plants, which in turn, causes early formation of curds checks the growth of the plants, which in turn, causes early formation of curds without maintaining their further enlargement.
- Transplanting of seedlings, obtained from poorly managed nursery bed.
- Slow plant growth in the nursery, over crowding, insufficient water, lack of weeding, bad condition of the soil, excessive crowding, insufficient water, lack of weeding, bad condition of the soil, excessive salt concentrations, low lying area or field with shallow and poor top salt may also cause buttoning.
- Vigorously grown nursery plants with thickened stems and sessile foliage being already generative have a tendency of button formation in the field.

Management:
- Nursery should be properly lookafter to avoid any check in the plant growth.
- An adequate amount of nitrogen and water should be applied.
- Do not delay transplanting and Cultural practices should be carried out well in time and water logging and overcrowding should be avoided.

7. Blindness:

Symptoms:
- It means the plant without terminal buds or when the growing point collapse at an early stage and the terminal buds fails to develop and plant becomes blind.
- It occurs in over wintered plants and any practice interfering in growth of the terminal bud may lead to blindness.
- Plant grows without terminal bud and fails to form and curd.
- It is characterized by the leaves that develop are large, dark green, thick and leathery owing to the accumulation of carbohydrates.
- Sometimes, the axillary bud develops but the plant fails to produce a marketable curd.

Cause:
- The main cause of blindness are low temperature when plants are small and when damage occurs to the terminal bud during, handling of the plants or injury by insect-pests.

Management:
- It can be controlled by avoiding young plant from low temperature exposure and care seedlings.
- While planting and handling, seedlings are avoided damage from insect-pests.

8. Chlorosis:

Symptoms:

- Chlorosis shows on interveinal and yellow mottling of lower leaves.
- The affected leaves turn bronze in colour and become stiff.
- In severely deficient plants, abscission of the lower leaves occurs and results into small curd formation.

Cause:
- In cauliflower magnesium deficiency causes chlorosis when grown on highly acidic soils.

Management:
- It can be controlled by applying magnesium oxide @ 300 kg/ha, liming the soil with dolomite limestone to bring the soil pH to 6.5 are an effective control measure.
- Use of a fertilizer containing soluble magnesium, keeps it under control.

9. Hollow Stem:

Symptoms:
- Hollowness caused by boron may be identified by water soaked and discoloured tissue; whereas, hollowness caused by nitrogen, the stem is perfectively clear while with no sign of disintegration.

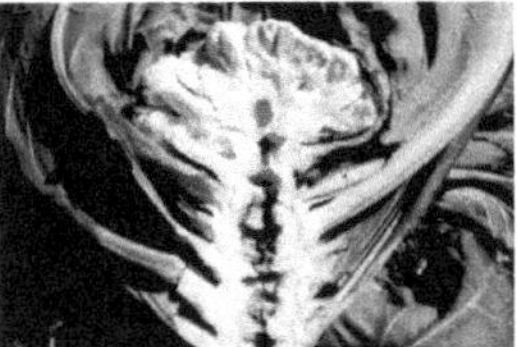

Cause:
- It may be due to boron deficiency and higher supply of nitrogen nutrition.

Management:
- It can be controlled by spraying of borax at 0.1 to 0.3 or soil application of borax @ 15-20 kg/ha.
- If hollow stem is used by boron deficiency. However, for normal type of hollowness, spacing the plants closer together or by reducing the fertilizer doses.

10. Frost Injury:

Symptoms:
- In cauliflower, leaves of young seedling turn yellowish-white on both the surfaces.
- Petioles become flaccid and white, midrib along with adjacent parenchyma and stem may also be injured.

Cause:

- Fully grown curds of cauliflower are more sensitive to frost damage, than the smaller ones.
- However, in cabbage the younger leaves are particularly sensitive to frost, as that the centre of the heads turns brown, while, outwardly the head appears healthy, similar symptoms also occurs in Brussels sprouts.

Management:

- It can be minimized by irrigating the field on anticipating the danger of frost and by raising the field temperature by creating smoke.

11. Pinking:

Symptoms:

- Sometimes curds show pink tinge, this appears due to the exposure of curds to high light intensities.
- Under this condition, anthocyanin form and givesrise pink colour curds. This disorder is not so common.

Physiological disorders of Cabbage:

1. Splitting/ cracking of heads:

Symptoms:

- Splitting of heads may occur due to heavy rains after prolonged drought, excessive fertilizer application and delayed harvesting.
- Early maturing varieties are more prone to head splitting than the late maturing ones.

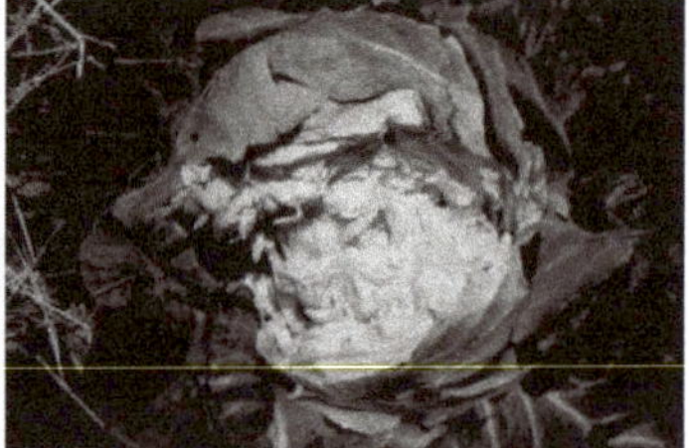

Control measures:

- Do not allow soil dry out. Fertilize properly.

2. **Tip Burn:** Most common disorder.

Symptoms:

- It manifest as brown to black necrotic tissue at leaf tips. Leaves surrounding the growing point are particularly susceptible to this disorder. Tipburn is readily seen when exposed plant structures, such as leaves and curds, are affected. However, damage to the heads of Brussels sprouts, cabbage and Chinese cabbage may go undetected until they are cut open. In severe cases of tipburn, the head is soft and the plant is dwarfed.

Causes:

- Tipburn is related to calcium deficiency in developing tissues.
- Fast growth and high relative humidity favor symptom development.
- Developing leaves, which are already low in calcium, are severely stressed for calcium during times of rapid growth.
- Transpiration and translocation are slowed when relative humidity is high, thus calcium transport is inhibited.

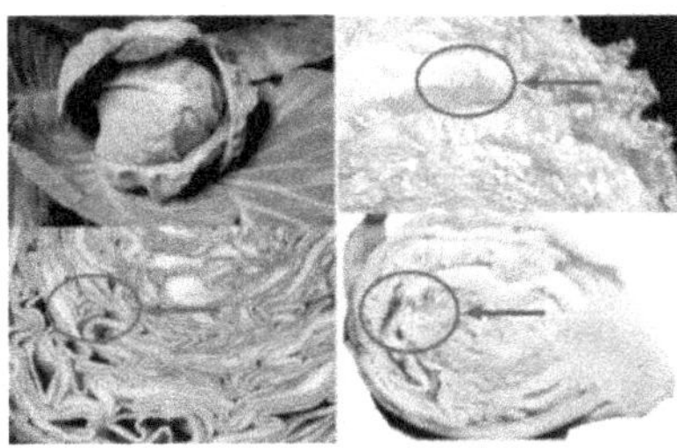

Control measures:

- Two foliar applications of CCC at 1120 or 2240 ppm combined with $CaCl_2$ at 2g/Lor 4 applications of $CaCl_2$ alone reduced the appearance of tip burn.
- Spraying 5 times with 0.7% $CaCl_2$ + 50 ppm NAA.

3. **Bolting**

Symptoms:

- Premature seed stalk development may take place due to sudden rise in temperature.

Control measures:

- Timely planting checks this disorder.

References:

Ferraz, L. C. L., Cafe, F. A. C., Nasser, L. C. B. and Azevedo, J., (1999). Effect of soil moisture, organic matter and grass mulching on the carpogenic germination of sclerotia and infection of bean by *Sclerotinia sclerotiorum. Plant Pathology,* 48, 77–82.

Glawe, D. A., Pelter, G. Q. and Toit, L. J., (2005). First report of powdery mildew of carrot and parsley caused by *Erysiphe heraclei* in Washington State. *Plant Health Progress,* 1–3.

Kashyap, P. L., & Dhiman, S. J., (2010). Eco-friendly strategies to suppress the development of Alternaria blight and black rot of cauliflower. *World Appl. Sci.   J.,* 9, 345–350.

Su, X. J., H. Yu., T. Zhou., X. Z. Li. and Gong, J., (2005). First report of *Alternaria raphani* causing black patches on Chinese radish during post harvest storage in Canada. *Plant Disease,* 89(9), 1015.

Wenham, H. T., (1960). Black root disease of radish caused by *Aphanomyces raphani* Kendr. *New Zealand Journal of Agricultural Research,* 3, 179–184.

CUCURBITS

Introduction:

- Cucurbitaceous crops comprise a large and diverse group of crops.
- Cucurbits are warm-season crops that are cultivated and harvested over spring, summer, and autumn seasons.
- They constitute an important part of a diverse and nutritious diet throughout the world, which are used as salad and pickled (cucumber), cooked (all gourds and squashes), candied, or preserved (ash gourd) vegetables or as dessert fruits (muskmelon and watermelon).
- Also, cucurbits are used as fiber source and for utensil preparations, decorations, and ceremonial and medicinal purposes.
- A wide range of pathogens affect the productivity of cucurbits, which constitute over 200 diseases. The diseases may be caused by fungi, bacteria, viruses, or mycoplasma like organisms.
- The disease may be soilborne, seedborne (carried by seed), spread by wind, or transmitted by insect vectors.
- The diseases caused by pathogen are controlled by fungicides against fungal diseases, bactericide for bacterial diseases, or insecticide in case of viruses transmitted by insect vectors.
- The diseases can be managed by adopting cultural, biological, and chemical methods of disease management.

Diseases of Cucurbits and Their Causal Organisms:

S. No.	Disease Name	Causal Organism
Fungal diseases		

1.	Powdery mildew	*Erysiphe cichoracearum, Sphaerotheca fuligena*
2.	Downy mildew	*Pseudoperonospora cubensis*
3.	Cecospora leaf spot	*Cercospora citrullina, C. melonis, C. lagenarium*
4.	Fruit rot or cottony leak	*Pythium* sp.
5.	Gummy Stem Blight	*Mycosphaerella melonis*
6.	Fusarium wilt	*Fusarium oxysporum f. sp. Melonis, Fusarium oxysporom f. sp. niveum*
7.	Anthracnose	*Colletotrichum orbiculare*
Bacterial diseases		
8.	Bacterial leaf spot	*Erwinia tracheiphila*
9.	Angular leaf spot	*Pseudomonas lachrymans*
Viral diseases		
10.	Mosaic	*Cucumber mosaic virus*
Physiological Disorders		
11.	Pillow	
12.	Leaf silvering	
13.	Blossom End Rot	
14.	Hollow Heart	
15.	Light Belly	
16.	Measles	
17.	Rind Necrosis	
18.	Sunscald	

1. Downy mildew

Causal Organism: *Pseudoperonospora cubensis*

Economic Importance:

- First reported from Cuba in 1868; prevalent in the warm temperate and tropical regions like North America, Europe, and Asia.
- In India, it is present all over the country except in temperate zone in high altitude of the Himalayas.

Host range:

- It occurs on cucumbers, squash, muskmelons, and pumpkins and less frequently on watermelons.

Symptoms:

- **On cucurbits other than watermelons,** small, yellowish areas occur on the upper leaf surface.
- Later a more brilliant yellow colour develops with the center of the lesion turning brown.
- Usually spots are angular because they are restricted by leaf veins.
- When leaves are wet, a downy, white-gray-light blue fungus growth can be seen on the underside of individual lesions.
- The diseased leaves become yellow and fall down.
- Diseased plants get stunted and die.

- Fruits produced may not mature and have a poor taste.
- **On watermelons**, yellow leaf spots may be angular to non-angular and turn brown to black.
- Spores produced on the lower leaf surface are readily spread by the wind.
- Rainy, humid weather favours the development of downy mildew.

Pathogen:
- It is an obligate parasite.
- The mycelium is coenocytic and intercellular with small ovate or finger likes haustoria.
- One to five sporangiosphores arise through the stomata.
- Sporangia are grayish to olivaceous purple, ovoid to ellipsoidal, thin walled with a distal papilla.
- Zoospores are 10 – 13 micron meter. Oospores are not common.

Mode of spread and survival:
- The pathogen survives on the diseased plant debris.
- In warm and humid climates, transmission from old to younger crops takes place all the year round.
- Where warm and dry summers alternate with cooler and wet winters, year round survival is possible on summer irrigated crops.
- They may overwinter as thick walled oospores.
- Sporangia are disseminated by wind.
- **Cucumber beetles are reported to carry the sporangia.**

Favourable conditions:
- The day temperature of 25–30°C, night temperature of 15–21°C and RH> 75% help the disease development.

Fore casting:
- A prediction model based on duration of temperature of 13–30°C and leaf wetness has been developed.

Management:
- Destruction of cucurbitaceous weeds around field.
  Spraying with Metalaxyl 500 g or Metalaxyl + Mancozeb 1 kg/ha or Mancozeb 1kg/ha.
  Spray zineb@0.3% at 10 days interval.

2. **Powdery mildew**

Causal Organism: *Erysiphe* cichoracearum and Sphaerotheca *fuligena*

Economic Importance:

- In India, the disease is prevalent in almost all the states particularly in the warm and dry areas where moisture is present as dew.
- Powdery mildew affects cucumber, muskmelon, bottlegourd, squash, pumpkin, and watermelon.

Host range:

- It attacks pumpkins, muskmelons, squash, bottle gourd, *Coccinia*, cucumber and ridge gourd.
- Bitter gourd is less affected.

Symptoms:

- It is evident as a superficial, powdery, greyish-white growth on upper leaf surfaces, petioles, and even main stems of infected plants.
- Affected areas turn yellow then brown and die.
- In dry seasons, powdery mildew can cause premature leaf drop and premature fruit ripening.
- Some early disease results from spores produced on over wintering cucurbit debris or weeds but the major source of disease inoculum is windblown spores from southern crops.
- Warm, dry weather conditions favour the development of powdery mildew.

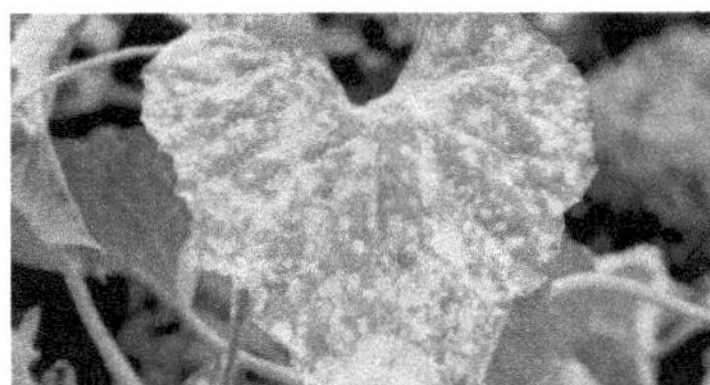 

Pathogen:

- The conidia measure 63.8 x 31.9 micron meter, the cleistothecia are globose which contain 10 – 15 asci.
- In each ascus, ascospores are two and are oval or sub cylindrical.

Mode of spread and survival:

- Perithecia developed on left over cucurbit crop in isolated areas serve as primary inoculum.
- Wild cucurbits harbour the conidial stage of the fungus and release conidia for primary infection to the spring or summer sown cucurbits.
- Conidia are spread by wind, thrips and other insects for secondary infection.

Management:

- Spray Calixin 0.1% or Karathane @0.2%

3. Cercospora leaf spot

Causal Organism: *C. citrullina, C. melonis, C. lagenarium*

Economic Importance:

- Common on watermelon, muskmelon and cucumber.

Symptoms:

- Minute water soaked spots mostly on leaves.
- Spots enlarge rapidly and become circular to irregular with pale brown, tan or white centers and purple to almost black margins.
- Spots coalesce to form large blotches.
- The leaf may dry and die presenting the leaf a scorched appearance.
- Stems and fruits are also attacked.

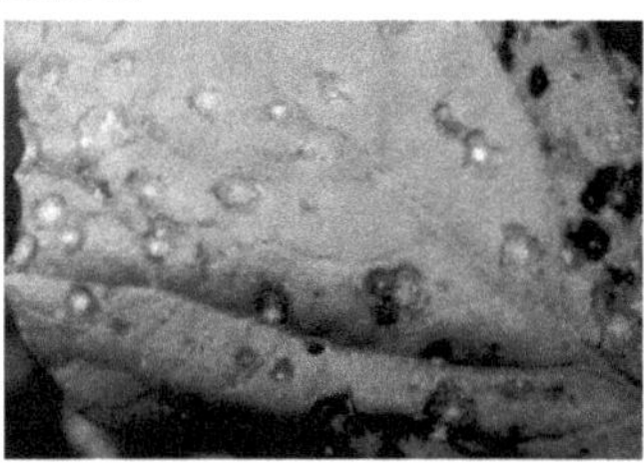

Disease cycle:

- **P.I:** Collateral hosts or plant debris
- **S.I:** Wind borne conidia

Management:

- Maintain good soil drainage and good aeration between vines.
- 2-3 protective sprays with zineb@0.2%.

4. **Cottony leak**

Causal Organism: *Pythium* sp.

Economic Importance:

- Cottony leak, also referred to as Pythium fruit rot, affects most cucurbits; however, it is most common on cucumber and squash.
- Fruit rot is common disease of cucurbits in India.
- It occurs in almost every locality during the rainy season. It is not only field disease but market and transit disease also.

Symptoms:

- This disease generally appears first on portions of fruit in contact with soil.
- Small, water-soaked spots expand rapidly until large portions of the fruit are necrotic and soft.
- Profuse, white fungal growth resembling tufts of cotton can be found on rotted areas when the humidity is high.

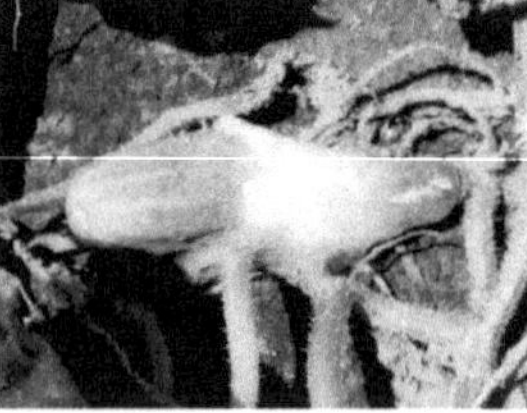

Mode of spread and survival:

- Several species of *Pythium* have been implicated in this disease.
- These soil-borne pathogens can overwinter as dormant spore structures in the residue of many different crops and weeds.
- Infection occurs through wounds or where the fruit touches the wet ground.
- *Pythium* spp. is easily disseminated via water and soil particles.
- Wet conditions promote infection and decay.

Management:

- Manage excess soil moisture by providing good drainage and monitoring irrigation practices.
- Use plastic mulch.
- Fungicides may provide some disease suppression.

5. Gummy Stem Blight

Causal Organism: *Mycosphaerella melonis/ Didymella bryoniae*

Symptoms:

- Infected stems first appear water-soaked and then become dry, coarse and tan. Older stem lesions (dead tissue) reveal small black fruiting bodies (pycnidia) within the affected tissues.
- Large lesions girdle stems and plants wilt in the heat of the day.
- Stem lesions on melons exude a gummy, red-brown substance which may be mistaken for a symptom of Fusarium wilt.
- **Powdery mildew infection, predispose plants to infection.**
- The additional nutrients provided by such injuries enhance gummy stem blight infection.

 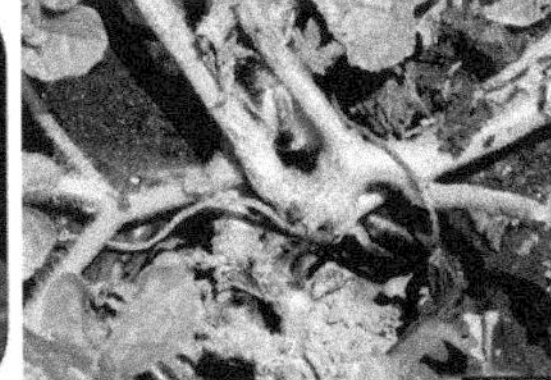 

Mode of spread and survival:

- The pathogen can be seed-borne and, thus, can spread by infected seedlings.
- The inoculum of the pathogen can also come from other cucurbitaceous host plants and weeds and infected plant debris in and around the facility.
- The pathogen produces two types of spores: asexually-produced pycniospores, and sexually-produced ascospores.
- Both types of spores are short-lived once they are released into the environment.
- However, the pathogen can survive up to 2 years as chlamydospores or mycelium on undecomposed, dry plant debris.

Management:

- Use of disease-free seed and transplants is essential to prevent serious crop losses.

- Periodic applications of fungicide like mancozeb @ 0.2% can help limit secondary infections, especially on fruits.
- Fall ploughing and extended rotations with other crops can significantly reduce the amount of inoculum in infested fields.

6. Fusarium Wilt

Causal Organism: *Fusarium oxysporum* f. sp. *melonis* attacks muskmelon and *Fusarium oxysporom* f. sp. *niveum* attacks watermelon.

Economic Importance:
- This disease is known for the last more than 95 years.
- In India, it was reported in 1955 from Maharashtra, it now occurs in many states of the country.
- Yield losses up to 80% have been reported in the worst affected areas.

Symptoms:
- Both fungi contribute to damping-off of seedlings, but most significant losses occur after young plants are infected in the field.
- Plants infected early in the season often produce no marketable fruits.
- Plants that begin to show wilt symptoms at or near maturity produce fewer and lower quality fruits.
- The first symptoms of Fusarium wilt are wilting and chlorosis (yellowing) of older leaves.
- The wilt is most evident during the heat of the day. Plants may appear to recover by morning, only to wilt again in the afternoon.
- Stem cracks and brown streaks often appear near the crown of the plant and are associated with a red-brown exudate.
- Fusarium wilt also causes vascular browning that is visible in stem cross-sections.

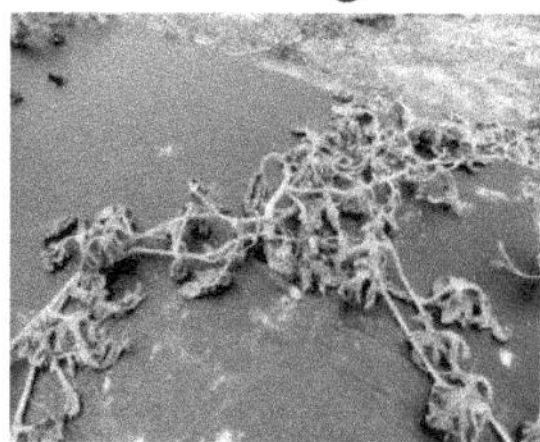

Mode of spread and survival:
- The wilt fungus is introduced to new areas on seed.
- It spreads by wind, equipment and workers.
- It can survive long periods in soil as chlamydospores and in association with melon plant residue.

Management:
- Planting resistant cultivars is the only reliable way to keep infested fields in production.
- Commercially acceptable resistant cultivars exist, but extremely high pathogen populations in the soil can overcome their resistance.

- Therefore, methods to reduce Fusarium populations in the soil also should be employed.
- These methods include extended rotations with crops other than cucurbits and fall ploughing of severely infested fields.

7. Anthracnose

Causal Organism: *Colletotrichum orbiculare* (*Colletotrichum lagenarium*)

Economic Importance:

- The first time reported in 1867 on gourds from Italy; occurs mainly in all humid regions of the world.
- It rarely affects pumpkin. In temperate regions heavy losses occur on fruits of watermelon.

Symptoms:

- The diagnostic features of anthracnose vary with the host.
- Sunken, elongated stem cankers are most prominent on muskmelon, though leaf and fruit lesions also occur. Large lesions girdle the stems and cause the vines to wilt.
- Stem cankers are less obvious on cucumbers, but leaf lesions are very distinct.
- Watermelon foliage affected by anthracnose appears scorched; sunken fruit lesions are easy to recognize.

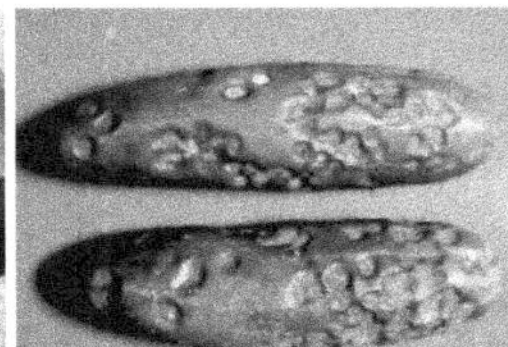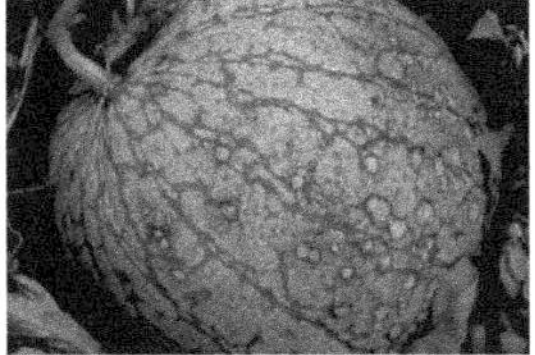

Epidemiology:

- The anthracnose fungus over winters on diseased crop residue.
- There also reported that the pathogen is carried in or on cucurbit seed.
- In wet conditions each spring, the fungus releases airborne spores that begin new infections on vines and foliage.
- Anthracnose usually becomes established in mid-season, after the crop canopy has fully developed.

Mode of spread and survival:

- The fungus can infect muskmelon and watermelon in addition to cucumber.
- The pathogen survives the winter in infected plant residues.
- The fungus can also be associated with seed.
- As with most fungal diseases, long periods of leaf wetness favour disease development.
- Spores are splashed from leaf to leaf, and plant to plant, during irrigation or rain events.
- Several disease cycles can occur in a single growing season, resulting in defoliation of severely infected plants.

Management:

- Seed treatment with Carbendazim 2g/kg of seed.
- Spray Mancozeb 2g or Carbendazim 0.5g/lit.

8. Angular Leaf Spot

Causal Organism: *Pseudomonas lachrymans*

Symptoms:

- Symptoms of the disease firsts appear as small, angular, water-soaked lesions on the leaves.
- When moisture is present, bacteria ooze from the spot in tear like droplets that dry and form a white residue on the leaf surface.
- Water-soaked areas turn gray or tan, die, and may tear away leaving irregular holes.
- Water-soaked spots may also appear on the fruit and are frequently followed by soft rot bacteria.

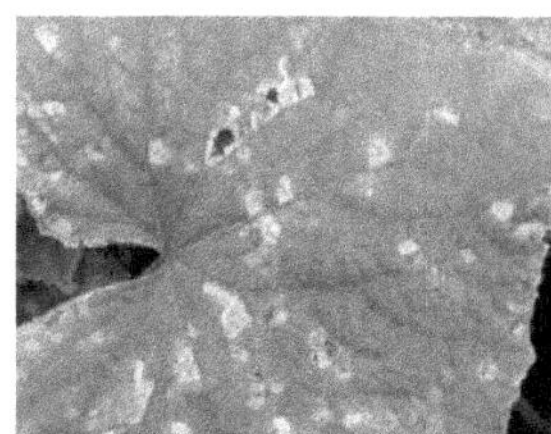

Pathogen:

- The bacterium is a rod with 1-5 polar flagella and forms capsule and a green fluorescent pigment in culture.
- The colonies on beef-peptone agar are circular, smooth, glistening, transparent and white.

Mode of spread and survival:

- Infected seeds may harbour the bacterium.
- They survive in soil or debris from diseased plants for two years.
- They spread by irrigation water.

Management:

- Angular leaf spot may be controlled by planting disease-free seed.
- Rotating with unrelated crops, keeping workers out of fields when foliage is wet and Spray 400ppm Streptomycin sulphate.

9. Bacterial Wilt

Causal Organism: *Erwinia tracheiphila*

Symptoms:

- On cucumber and melon, generally a distinct flagging of lateral and individual leaves occurs. Affected leaves turn a dull green.
- Sometimes wilting occurs on leaves that have been injured by cucumber beetles feeding, but in many cases obvious feeding is not apparent.
- Leaves adjacent to the wilting leaves will also wilt, and eventually the entire lateral is affected.
- The wilt progresses as the bacteria move from the point of entry through the vascular system toward the main stem of the plant. Eventually the entire plant wilts and dies.

- If you cut through the stem of an affected plant and squeeze both cut ends, a white, sticky exudate will often ooze from the water-conducting tissue of the stem. This exudate is composed of bacterial material that plugs the vascular system of the plant.
- Affected stems do not appear significantly discolored. Bacterial wilt is closely associated with either the striped or the spotted cucumber beetle. The bacteria over winter in the bodies of adult cucumber beetles.
- The beetles carry the bacteria when they emerge in the spring. The bacteria are spread either through the faeces of the beetle or from contaminated mouthparts. When the beetles feed on young leaves or cotyledons, they open entry points for the pathogen.
- Once inside the plant, the bacteria travel quickly through the vascular system, causing blockages that in turn result in wilting of the leaves.
- The disease progresses from plant to plant when a carrier beetle moves through the field or when clean beetles pick up the bacteria from a diseased plant and fly to healthy plants. Larvae are not known to carry the wilt organism.

Pathogen:
- It is a motile rod with 4 – 8 peritrichous flagella and capsulated.
- Agar colonies are small, circular, smooth, glistening white and viscid.

Mode of spread and survival:
- The bacteria apparently overwinter in cucumber beetles and they appear to multiply in the beetle.
- The bacterium is not seed borne or soil borne. Bacteria in stems can survive for one month.
- Beetles prefer to feed on plants with bacterial symptoms than on healthy plants.
- Beetle can remain infective for at least three weeks.
- **Striped cucumber beetle and the spotted cucumber beetle help in the spread of the bacterium.**

Management:
- In general, more bacterial wilt is seen on the edges of fields where beetles first encounter plants.
- Larger plantings must be protected by insecticides. Carbaryl (Sevin), Malathion or rotenone insecticides or combination products are registered to treat cucumber beetles. They will provide control of the beetles if applied when beetles first appear in the spring.
- Early control, beginning as soon as the plants emerge, is most important as a single beetle can introduce the bacteria. One to four generations of the beetle may occur on

unprotected plants and applications of these insecticides at weekly intervals may become necessary.

- Apply a light even coating of the insecticide over the entire plant, especially where the stem emerges from the soil (where the beetles often congregate).

10. Cucumber Mosaic

Causal Organism: *Cucumber mosaic virus*

Host range: A virus distributed worldwide, affecting most cucurbits but rarely affecting watermelon.

- Different members of family Cucurbitaceae are attacked by viruses belonging to cucumovirus, poty virus and to bamovirus groups.
- All these viruses produce varied types of mosaic symptoms resulting in considerable losses.

Symptoms:

- New growth is cupped downward, and leaves are severely mottled with alternating light green and dark green patches (Gour *et al.,* 2000).
- Plants are stunted, and fruits are covered with bumpy protrusions.
- Severely affected cucumber fruit may be almost entirely white.

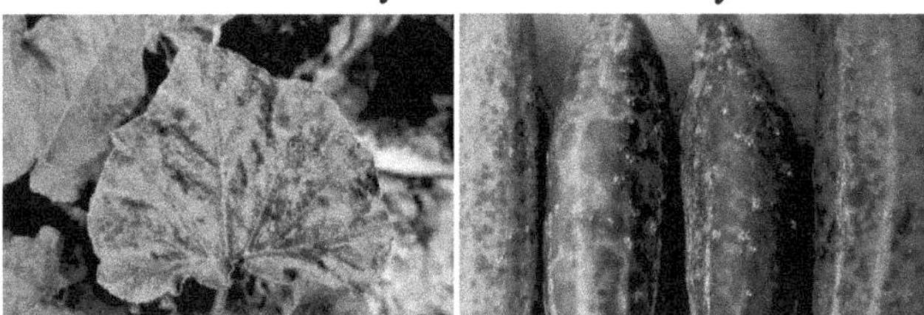

Mode of spread and survival:

- Survive on weeds, ornamentals or other crops.
- Transmitted by mechanical inoculation and by aphids (*Aphis craccivora, Myzus persicae*) and spotted and striped cucumber beetles.
- **Collateral hosts:** Banana, clover, corn, passion fruit, safflower, spinach, sugarbeet, wild cucumber, *Commelina communis, C. diffusa, C. nudiflora, Solanum elaegnifolium, Phytolacca* sp., periwinkle, *Gladiolus* sp., *Impatiens* sp. and *Phlox.*

Management:

- The virus is readily transferred by aphids and survives on a wide variety of plants.
- Varietal resistance is the primary management tool, and eliminating weeds and infected perennial ornamentals that may harbour the virus is critical.
- Spray with any one of the systemic insecticide for vector control like monochrotophos (Storm) or phosphamidon (Famidon), 1.5 ml per liter of water.

Physiological Disorders:

1. **Pillow:**

Symptoms:

- In this disorder, an abnormal white styofoam like porous textured tissue is formed in the mesocarp of the fleshy harvested fruits.

- Vascular tissue with some pillow areas may collapse and become necrotic.

Cause:

- It is a fruit disorder of processing cucumber due to low calcium level in the tissue.

2. Leaf silvering:

Symptoms:

- It is a physiological disorder of summer squash.
- The leaves become silver coloured and contain less chlorophyll; photosynthesis is hampered in the silvered leaves.

Cause:

- This disorder occurs due to moisture scarcity.

3. Unfruitfulness in pointed gourd:

Symptoms:

- Pointed gourd is a dioecious cucurbit. So, male and female plants are separate.
- Female plants produce the fruit whereas male plants act as a pollen donor.
- So required number of male plants should be there in the population of female plants to ensure adequate pollination, fertilization and fruit set.
- A common problem is met with where pistillate flowers in female plants are shed due to lack of pollination and fertilization.
- In some cases, ovary of the unfertilized flower may flow a bit due to parathenocarpic stimulation which also abscises after a few days.

Management:

- Male plants must be grown in the field along with the female plants at the rates of 10-12 male plants per 100 female plants to ensure adequate pollination and fruit set.
- Hand pollination may be done successfully to achieve fruit set.
- Hand pollination to the female flowers should be done in the early morning hours because stigma receptivity decreases with an advancement of the day.

4. Delay in fruit ripening:

Symptoms:

- This problem is particularly important in muskmelon and watermelon.
- Delay in repining is sometime associated with less sweetness and cracking of fruits which occur due to high moisture level and temperature fluctuation at ripening stage.

Management:

- Irrigation should be stopped at the ripening stage to hasten ripening.
- Sowing time should be adjusted in such a way that fruits ripe in hot and rainless condition which hastens ripening and at the same time improve sweetness of the fruits.

5. Blossom End Rot:

Symptoms:

- The blossom end of the fruit develops a dark leathery appearance.
- Symptoms may progress until the entire end of the fruit turns black and rots.

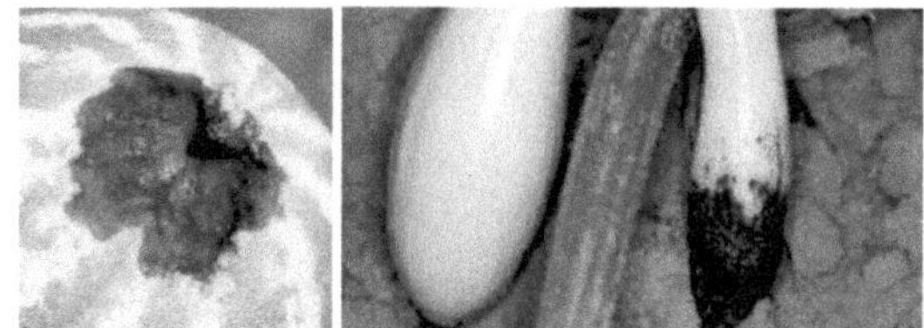

Conditions for Disease Development:

- This disorder is associated with insufficient calcium uptake and alternating periods of wet and dry soil.
- Damage to the root system may also account for decreased calcium uptake and the development of blossom-end rot.

Management:

- Minimized by mulching to maintain constant soil moisture, applying calcium fertilizers and avoiding high levels of nitrogen.
- Drip irrigate crop to control water management.

6. Hollow Heart:

Symptoms:

- Cracks in internal watermelon fruit flesh can occur due to accelerated growth in response to ideal growing conditions.

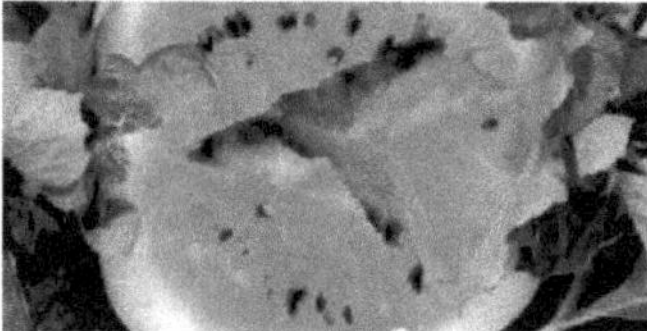

Conditions for Disease Development:

- There is a genetic component to this disorder, but growing conditions can account for much of the variation observed.
- It appears to be associated with conditions that result in poor pollination (enough pollination to set the fruit but not enough to fertilize a high percentage of the ovules) followed by rapid fruit growing conditions (too much fertility, water and high temperatures).

Management:

- Avoid watermelon varieties with a tendency to exhibit hollow heart.
- Implement best practices for irrigation and fertilization programs.

7. Light Belly Colour:

Symptoms:

- This disorder is characterized by the undersurface of cucumber fruit remaining light in color instead of turning dark green.

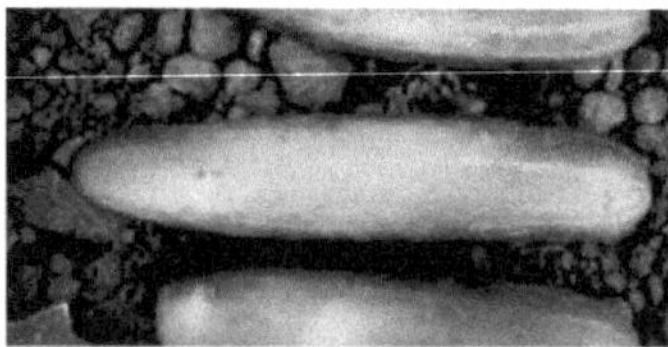

Conditions for Disease Development:

- Commonly occurs on fruit lying on cool, moist soil.

Management:

- It can be partially controlled by avoiding luxuriant vine growth. Avoid excessive nitrogen.

8. Measles:

Symptoms:

- Symptoms are most evident on smooth-skinned melons and cucumbers.
- Small brown spots are scattered over the surface of the fruit.
- The spots are superficial and do not penetrate beyond the outer epidermal layers of the fruit.
- These spots also may occur on leaves and stems (Gautam *et al.,* 2006).

Conditions for Disease Development:

- Associated with environmental conditions favoring guttation.
- The guttation droplets develop high concentrations of salts which burn the epidermis.
- Measles spots occur where a guttation droplet had formed.

Management:

- Control measles by reducing irrigation frequency and duration as fruit approach maturity in fall-harvested crops.
- Irrigation reduction at the later stages of fruit development has not shown any adverse effects on fruit size and soluble solid content.

9. Rind Necrosis:

Symptoms:

- Generally occurs in either cantaloupe or watermelon as dead, hard, dry reddish-brown to brown spots or patches of tissue in the fruit rind.
- Affected areas vary in size from 3mm spots to extensive dead areas throughout the entire rind.
- In watermelon, symptoms are not visible from the outside and are rarely found in the flesh.
- In cantaloupe, dead tissue may extend into the flesh of the fruit.
- Circular, water-soaked depressions also develop on the cantaloupe fruit surface.

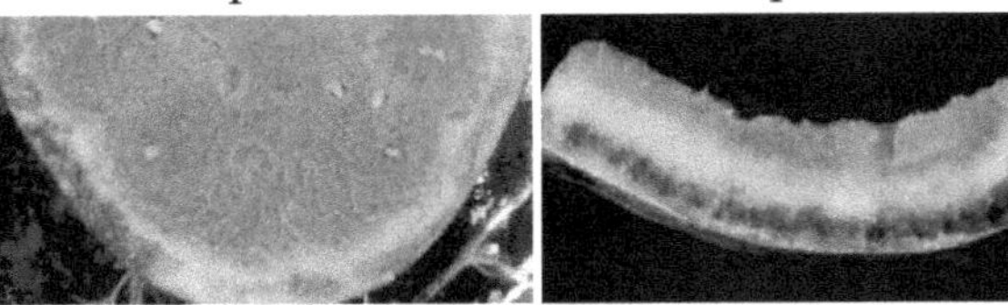

Conditions for Disease Development:
- Not well understood. However, it is thought that environmental conditions which place stress on the plants may trigger the onset of this disorder.
- Susceptibility to rind necrosis varies among varieties.
- The disorder occurs sporadically and is thought to be associated with bacteria that may be present in fruit, but the reasons for symptom development are not understood.
- Drought stress also is reported to predispose melons.

Management:
- Genetic tolerance has been identified in watermelon.
- Avoid drought stress in melon.

10. Sunscald:

Symptoms:
- Papery white areas develop on fruit.

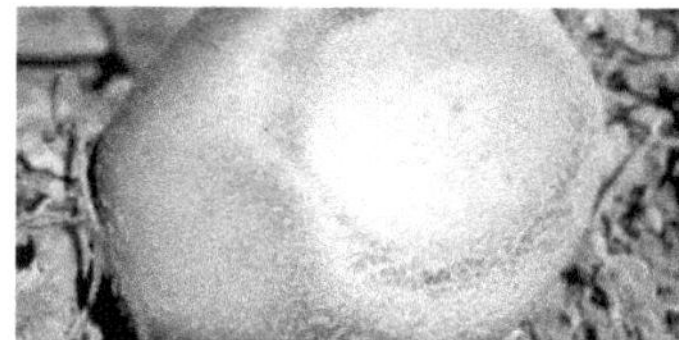
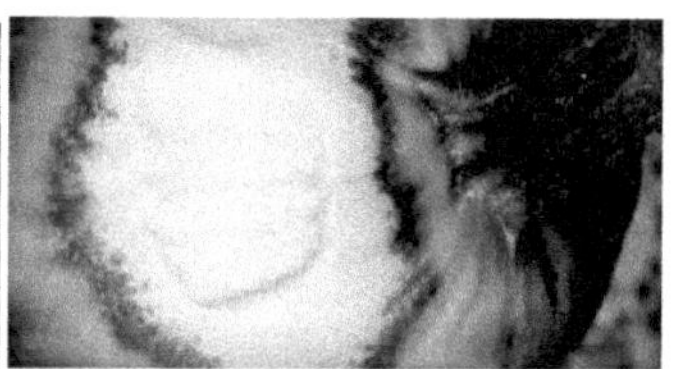

Conditions for Disease Development:
- Develops during hot summer weather when fruit are suddenly exposed to direct sunlight.

Management:
- Minimize by maintaining strong vine growth to ensure the fruit is covered.

References:

Arya, A., (2009). *Diseases of Fruit Trees,* International Book Distributing Co., Lucknow.

Chakrabarti, D. K., Kumar, S., & Chand, G., (2010). *A Guide Book for Diseases of Horticultural Crops (Diseases of Fruits, Ornamentals, Plantation, Spices, Medicinal, Forest and Vegetable Crops)* (pp. 1–152).

Gangwane, L. V., & Khilare, V. C., (2008). *Crop Disease Identification and Management* (p. 244). Daya Publishing House, Delhi.

Gautam, P. L., Ram, H. H., & Singh, H. P., (2006). Cucurbits breeding and production technology. *In: Proceedings of National Seminar on Cucurbits,* Held on 22–23 September, 2005. G.B. Pant University of Agriculture and Technology, Pantnagar, Uttaranchal, India.

Gour, T. B., Babu, T. S. Sriramumlu, M., Reddy, D. D. R., Rao, K. C., Babu, R. R., & Reddy, P. N., (2000). *Pictorial Crop Based Identification Mannuals on Crucifers, Cucurbits, Insect, Pests, Diseases and Nutritional Disorders* (pp. 64–88). Agricultural Information and Communication Center, Acharya, N.G. Rangy Agricultural University, Rajendranagar, Hyderabad.

Gupta, V. K., & Paul, Y. S., (2008). *Diseases of Vegetable Crops* (pp. 100–120). Kalyani Publishers, Ludhiana.

Mehrotra, R. S., & Aggrawal, A., (2008). *Plant Pathology Tata McGraw-Hill Publishing Co. Pvt. Ltd (p. 846).* New Delhi – 110008.

Ram, H. H., (2002). *Vegetable Breeding: Principles and Practices* (pp. 222–274). Kalyani Publishers, Ludhiana, New Delhi, Noida, Hyderabad, Chennai, Kolkata and Cuttack.

ONION & GARLIC

Introduction:

- Onion (*Allium cepa* L.) and garlic (*Allium sativum* L.) is one of the most important commercial vegetable crops grown in India and being used as vegetables, spices or as medicines.

- In India, onion and garlic have been under cultivation for the last 5000 years. India ranks second to China in area and production in both onion and garlic, but ranks 102nd for onion and 74th for garlic in terms of productivity.

- These crops are generally grown throughout the country especially in the states of Maharashtra, Uttar Pradesh, Orissa, Gujarat, Madhya Pradesh, Haryana, Punjab, Rajasthan, Uttaranchal, Jammu and Kashmir, Bihar, Andhra Pradesh and Karnataka.

- The onion and garlic crop is attacked by many diseases and insect pests at different crop growth stages which causes considerable losses in yield.

- Apart from reduction in crop yield, the disease and insect pests also poses harmful effects during harvesting, post harvesting, processing and marketing stages, which lower the quality and export potential of the crops that significantly causes the economic loss.

Diseases:

S. No.	Disease Name	Causal Organism
Fungal diseases		
1.	Purple blotch	*Alternaria porri*
2.	Downy mildew	*Peronospora destructor*
3.	Smut	*Urocystis cepulae*
4.	Smudge	*Colletotrichum circinans*
5.	Blast	*Botrytis* spp.
6.	Stemphylium blight	*Stemphylium vesicarium*
7.	Neck rot and bulb rot	*Botrytis allii, B. squamosa* and *B. Cinerea*
8.	White Rot	*Sclerotium cepivorum*
9.	Black mould	*Aspergillus niger*
10.	Basal Rot	*Fusarium oxysporum* f.sp. *cepae*
Bacterial diseases		
11.	Blue mould	*Penicillium* sp

12.	Sour skin	*Pseudomonas cepacia*
13.	Bacterial Brown Rot	*Pseudomonas aeruginosa*
Viral diseases		
14.	Onion Yellow Dwarf	*onion yellow dwarf virus*
Physiological Disorders		
15.	Tip Burning	
16.	Thick neck	
17.	Premature Bulbing	
18.	Splitting Bulb	
19.	Sunscald	
20.	Bolting	
21.	Watery Scales	
22.	Chemical Injury	
23.	Freezing Injury	

1. Purple blotch

Causal Organism: *Alternaria porri, Alternaria palamdari*

Symptoms:

- This disease occurs mainly at the top of the leaves, the infection starts with whitish minute dots on the leaves with irregular chlorotic areas on tip portion of the leaves.
- Circular to oblong concentric black velvety rings appear in the chlorotic area.
- The lesions develop towards the base of the leaf.
- The spots join together and spread quickly to the entire leaf area.
- The leaves gradually die from the tip downwards.
- Diseased leaves break at point of infection and hang down.
- Infection also seen on outer scales of bulb, seed stalk and neck.
- Severely infected crop dries up.
- Bulbs become dry and papery (Kumar and Palakshapra, 2008).

Pathogen:

- Mycelium is branched, coloured and septate.
- Conidiophores arise singly or in groups.
- They are straight or flexuous, sometimes geniculate.

Mode of spread and survival:

- P.I: Plant debris and seed bulb.
- S.I: Air-borne conidia.

Favourable conditions:
- Warm humid weather with rains or heavy dew.

Management:
- Disease free bulb should be selected for planting.
- Seeds should be treated with Thiram @ 4 g/kg seed. The field should be well drained.
- Three foliar sprayings with Copper oxychloride 0.25 % or Chlorothalonil 0.2 % or Zineb 0.2 % or Mancozeb 0.2 %.

2. Smudge

Causal Organism: *Colletotrichum circinans*

Symptoms:
- Chiefly a disease of **scales** of bulb.
- **Red scaled onions** are usually resistant to the smudge due to the presence of protocatacheuic acid and catechol.
- Damping off in seed bed under wet and warm conditions.
- Disease appears at all stages and also during storage and transportation.
- Sub-cuticular, dark green to almost black smudge appear on the bulb, neck or green leaves that are clinging to bulb after digging.
- Circular lesions with **concentric rings of dark stromata** and mycelium appear on leaves.
- Small, sunken and yellow lesions on inner scales. Pinkish mass of fungal growth on lesions under humid conditions.

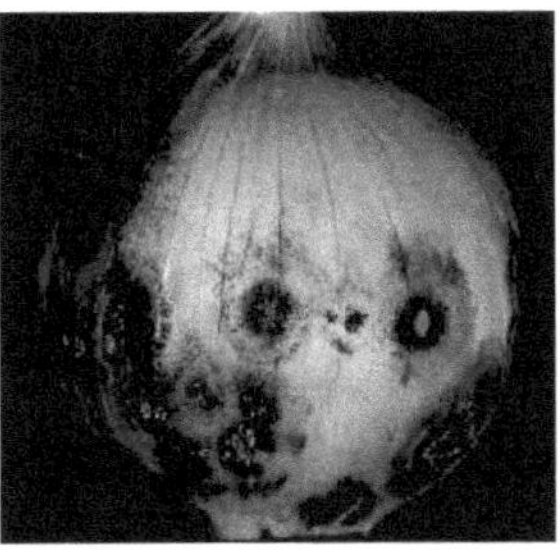

Mode of spread and survival:
- **P.I:** Soil and on infected onions as stromata.
- **S.I:** Wind borne conidia.

Favourable conditions:
- Wet soils with a temperature of 26^0 C.

Management:
- Protection of bulbs from rains after harvest.
- Dry bulbs properly before storage by hot air at 37- 48^0C.
- Spray zineb or captan @0.2% before harvest of crop.
- Resistant varieties are **Nasik red, Pusa Ratna, Pusa Red.**

3. Smut

Causal Organism: *Urocystis cepulae*

Symptoms:

- Fungus attacks cotyledons of young plants soon after their emergence causing dark, elongated eruptive spots.
- On older leaves, the lesions may extend from base to the tip and appear as blisters.
- Lesions develop into thickened areas of several mm in size. Lesions burst open releasing masses of black smut spores.
- Severely affected plants killed within 3-4 weeks of emergence.
- Surviving plants are stunted with stout, brittle, distorted leaves bearing lesions throughout their length.
- Numerous blisters appear on leaves and bulb scales of mature plants which rupture to expose masses of black powdery spores (Sampangi and Mohan, 2017).

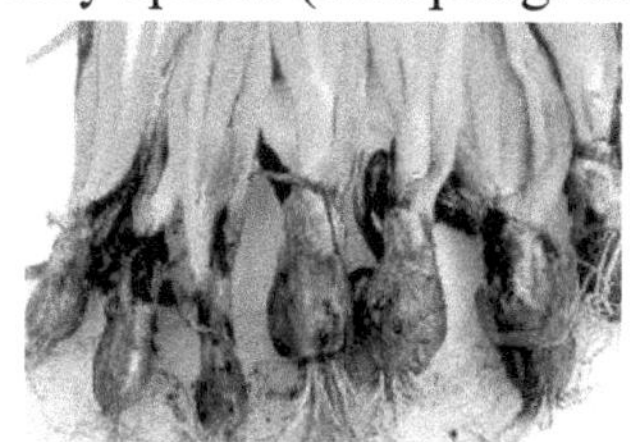

Pathogen:

- The sori of pathogen contain dark coloured and powdery spore masses.
- The spores are found in permentant balls.
- Each ball consists of an enveloping cortex of tined, sterile, bladder like cells with one or two central dark coloured thick walled chlamydospores.
- The spores germinate by means of short promycelium while still in the ball.

Mode of spread and survival:

- The fungus remains viable for 15 years in infected soil by means of spore balls.
- It persists in soil as a saprophyte.
- Onion bulbs and onion transplants are important means of widespread distribution of the fungus.
- Implements also help in the spread.
- Wind borne soil and surface drainage water are important means of local dissemination.
- P.I: Spore balls in infected soil.
- S.I: Windblown soil and surface drianage water, onion bulbs and onion transplants.

Favourable conditions:

- Optimum temperature of 10-20^{0}C.
- Plant is susceptible for 2-3 weeks from the Days after sowing.

Management:

- Seed Treatment with thiram @3 g/Kg seed.
- Crop rotation and use of disease free seedlings.

- Cultivar, **Hardy white bunching** is resistant.
- Spray with captan or ferbam @0.2% along with a sticker.

4. Neck Rot

Causal Organism: *Botrytis allii, Botrytis squamosa* and *Botrytis cinerea*

Symptoms:
- Symptoms are first seen as a softening of the tissues around the neck of the bulb, or more rarely, at a wound. A definite margin separates diseased and healthy tissues.
- Infected tissues become sunken, soft, and appear brownish to grayish in colour, as if they had been cooked.
- These symptoms progress gradually to the base of the bulb. Then the entire bulb may become mummified.
- Hard, irregularly shaped kernel-like bodies, sclerotia, may form between scales, especially at the neck region (Maude and Presly, 1977).

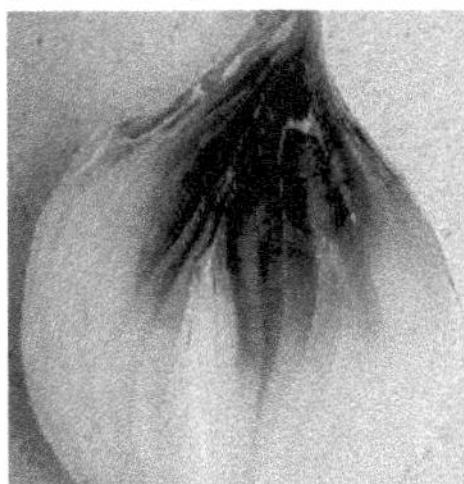

Mode of spread and survival:
- The fungi that cause neck rot survive the winter on previously infected onion debris in the soil, in cull piles and refuse dumps, and in trash in storage sheds.

Epidemiology:
- Symptoms usually appear after harvest, although infections originate in the field.
- Greatest epidemic development occurs when cool (50° to 75°F), moist weather prevails for some days before or during harvest.
- If the weather remains dry during harvest and curing, losses found in storage are usually small.

Management:
- Bulb treatment with Captan /Thiram 0.25%.
- Spraying of Maneb or Mancozeb or Chlorothalonil.
- Fungicides may be applied every 5 - 7 days for disease control.

5. Downy mildew

Causal Organism: *Peronospora destructor*

Symptoms:
- White downy growth appears on the surface of the leaves.
- Finally the infected leaves are dried up.

Pathogen:

- The sporangiophores are non septate, long and swollen at the base.
- Sporangia are pyriform to fusiform, attached to the sterigmata by their pointed end.
- These sporangia germinate by one or two germ tubes.
- The coenocytic mycelium is intercellular with filamentous haustoria.
- Oogonia are formed in the intercellular spaces.

Mode of spread and survival:

- The fungus attacks the seed stalks in a seed crop and has been found on and in the seed as mycelium but true seeds do not help in carryover of the fungus from one season to the next.
- The main sources of perennation are the diseased bulbs used for propagating the crop in many areas and oospores present in diseased crop residues.
- If infected bulbs are planted, the fungus grows up with the foliage produces sporangia and these spread the disease to other plants.

Management:

- Three spraying with Mancozeb 0.2 % is effective.
- Spraying should be started 20 days after transplanting and repeated at 10-12 days interval.

6. Leaf Blight (Blast)

Causal Organism: *Botrytis* spp.

Symptoms:

- It is the major disease of onions in cool climate areas.
- Light infections do not affect yields but heavy infections causing major yield reductions can occur.
- Hundreds of white specks are seen on the foliage.
- The disease then spreads very rapidly and tops of the entire crop may be killed (Nainwal, 2013).

Pathogen:

- It is characterized by its conidiophores which present an appearance of grape bunch.
- The conidiophores are tall, erect and branches irregularly or dichotomously.
- They are dark and septate. The terminal cells swell to produce sporogenous ampullae.

- On each ampulla numerous conidia arise simultaneously on short denticles.
- The conidia are hyaline or tinted, aseptate and globose to ovoid.

Management:
- Bulb treatment with Captan /Thiram 0.25%. Spraying of Maneb or Mancozeb or Chlorothalonil.
- Fungicides may be applied every 5 - 7 days for disease control.

7. White Rot

Causal Organism: *Sclerotium cepivorum*

Symptoms:
- The leaves become yellow and die-back and when the plants are pulled up, roots are found to be rotten and the base of the bulb covered with a white or grey fungal growth.
- Later, numerous small black spherical sclerotia are produced.
- The bulb of the onion completely rots.

Mode of spread and survival:
- The disease is worst in warm summers or in the case of winter onions during warm spell in autumn or spring.
- Sclerotia persist in soil for eight years.
- The primary inoculum consists of spherical small black sclerotia produced in infested fissure of *Allium* spp. during previous years.
- Scelerotia are transported from field to field by flood water.

Management:
- Crop rotation and clean seed are the only effective control.
- Heavy manuring with organic manures reduces the disease in the crop.
- Seed dressing with Benomyl, Carbendazim or Thiophanate-methyl (100 to 150 g/kg seed) gives effective control.

8. Black mould

Causal Organism: *Aspergillus niger*

Symptoms:
- Infection usually is through neck tissues as foliage dies down at maturity.
- Infected bulbs are discoloured black around the neck, and affected scales shrivel.
- Masses of powdery black spores generally are arranged as streaks along veins on and between outer dry scales.
- Infection may advance from the neck into the central fleshy scales.
- In advanced disease stages, the entire bulb surface turns black, and secondary bacterial soft rot may make the bulb soft and mushy.

- No external symptoms may be found with some bulbs.

Management:

- Seeds should be treated with Thiram @ 4 g/kg seed.
- The field should be well drained.
- Growers must follow crop rotation and harvested bulbs must be thoroughly cured to reduce potential storage losses.
- Soil drenching with Copper oxychloride 0.25 %.
- Three foliar sprayings with Copper oxychloride 0.25 % or Chlorothalonil 0.2 % or Zineb 0.2 % or Mancozeb 0.2 %.

9. Basal Rot

Causal Organism: *Fusarium oxysporum* f. sp. *cepae*

Symptoms:

- The leaves turn yellow and then dry up slowly.
- The affected plant shows drying of leaf tip downwards.
- The entire plant shows complete drying of the foliage.
- The bulb of the affected plant shows soft rotting and the roots get rotted.
- There will be a whitish mouldy growth on the scale.
- This disease can begin in the field and continue on in storage.

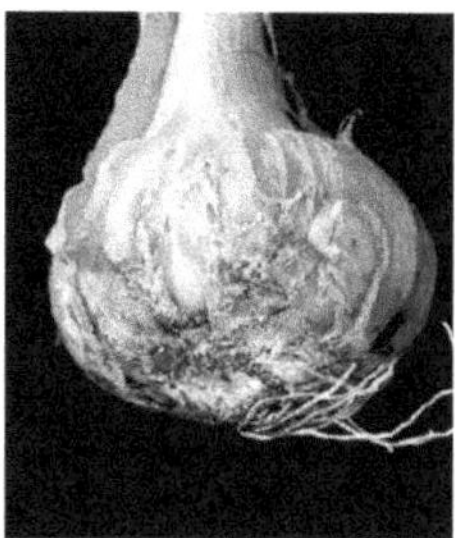

Pathogen:

- The fungus produces many chlamydospores which are thick walled resting spores and microconidia which are one celled and thin walled (Sumner, 1995).

Mode of spread and survival:

- The pathogen is soil borne and the optimum temperatures for development are 28-32°C.
- Infection occurs through the root either directly or through wounds.

Management:

- Growers must follow crop rotation and harvested bulbs must be thoroughly cured to reduce potential storage losses.
- Onions are very sensitive to low soil copper levels.

- In order to optimize crop production and disease susceptibility, additional soil copper fertility may be needed especially on mucky and sandy soils.
- Soil drenching with Copper oxychloride 0.25 %.

10. Stemphylium Blight

Causal Organism: *Stemphylium vesicarium*

Symptoms:

- It is a serious problem in Northern parts of the country especially in the seed crop.
- This disease is very common on onion leaves and flower stalks.
- Infection occurs on radial leaves of transplanted seedlings at 3- 4 leaf stage during late March and early April.
- The symptoms appear as small yellowish to orange flecks or streaks in the middle of the leaves, which soon develop into elongated spindle shaped spots surrounded by pinkish margin.
- The disease appearing on the inflorescence stalk causes severe damage to the seed crop.

Management:

- Field sanitation and collecting and burning of crop residues minimize the spread of infection.
- Spraying Mancozeb (0.25%) along with Monocrotophos (0.05%) with sticker triton on appearance of disease at fortnightly interval controls the disease.

11. Blue mould rot

Causal Organism: *Penicillium* sp

Symptoms:

- Blue mould generally appears during harvesting and storage. Symptoms develop slowly on the bulbs.
- Initial symptoms include water soaked areas on the outer surface of scales.
- Later, a green to blue green, powdery mould may develop on the surface of the lesions.
- Infected areas of fleshy scales are tan or gray when cut. In advanced stages, infected bulbs may disintegrate into a watery rot.
- Many species of Penicillium can cause blue mould.
- These fungi are common saprophytes on plant debris and senescent plant tissue.

Pathogen:

- It produces an enormous number of spores on a broom like conidiophore.
- Some of these spores are in the air at all times.
- They can be carried to long distances by wind. In moist air they germinate readily.

Mode of spread and survival:

- Invasion of onion bulbs and garlic is usually through wounds, bruises, or uncured neck tissue.
- Once inside the bulb, the mycelium grows through the fleshy scales, eventually sporulating profusely on the surface of lesions and wounds.
- Optimum conditions include moderate temperatures 70° to 77°F (21° to 25°C) and high relative humidity.

Management:

- To reduce the risk of blue mold, promptly cure the bulbs so the necks are dry.
- Additionally, use the following other cultural practices.
- Minimize bruising or wounding bulbs during harvest and handling, as well as from insect damage.
- Store bulbs at a maximum temperature of 41°F and at low relative humidity.

12. Bacterial brown rot

Causal Organism: *Pseudomonas aeruginosa*

Symptoms:

- It is very serious disease of onions in storage.
- The infection occurs through the wounds.
- The rot begins at the neck of the bulbs which later gives foul smell through the neck when squeezed.

Management:

- Proper curing and rapid drying of the bulbs after harvesting is essential for controlling the disease.
- Affected bulbs should be discarded before storage.

- If rains occur during maturity, spraying of Streptocycline (0.02%) is recommended.

13. Sour skin

Causal Organsim: *Pseudomonas cepacia*

Economic Importance:

- It is first described in 1950, has been reported from onion-growing areas all over the world.
- Losses often appear in stored onions, but infection usually begins in the field.
- The disease can be serious in individual fields, with yield losses of 5–50%.
- Sour skin is primarily a disease of onions, but other *Allium* species are reported to be hosts.

Symptoms:

- Primary symptoms on onions include a slimy (but initially firm), pale yellow to light brown decay and breakdown of one or a few inner bulb scales.
- Adjacent outer scales and the center of the bulb may remain firm.
- Externally, bulbs appear sound, but the neck region may often after leaves have collapsed.
- In advanced stages, healthy scales can slip off during handling. Young leaves some times die back, starting at the tips.

Pathogen:

- Bacterial cells are rods that measure $1.6\text{-}3.2 \times 0.8\text{-}1.0$ µm; they occur singly or in pairs; and they are motile by means of tufts of polar flagella.
- Most strains produce non-fluorescent, yellowish or greenish pigments, but the pigments may be of a variety of colours.
- It is an obligate aerobic bacterium. The optimum growth temperature is 30–35°C. No growth occurs at 4°C, and most strains grow at 41°C.
- Denitrification is negative while nitrate is reduced to nitrite.
- It is oxidase positive and arginine dihydrolase negative and can liquefy gelatin.

Management:

- Control measures include proper maturing of the crop and quick drying after topping and harvest.
- Since contaminated irrigation water has been implicated in the spread of the pathogen, the use of recycled or irrigation runoff water should be avoided.
- Season long overhead irrigation provides a favourable environment for infection by pathogen, whereas furrow irrigation results in almost complete absence of the disease.

- In experimental plots, the final four or five sprinkler irrigations were accompanied by increases in sour skin of 150– 300%.
- Where sour skin is a potential problem, changing from sprinkler to furrow irrigation, at least from bulbing to the end of the season, is advisable where feasible.

14. Onion Yellow Dwarf

Causal Organism: *onion yellow dwarf virus*

Symptoms:

- This is a viral disease caused by onion yellow dwarf virus. It is transmitted mechanically as well as by insect vectors.
- The symptoms of the disease are severe stunting of the plants, dwarfing and twisting of the flower stalk.
- The affected leaves and stems change their normal green colour to various shades of yellow and leaves tend to flatten and crinkle and as a result bend over.

Management:

- Removal and destruction of the diseased plants checks the spread of the disease.
- Healthy bulbs should be used for seed production.
- Spraying of Malathion (0.1%) or Oxydemeton Methyl (Metasystox) (0.1%) to control the vectors checks further spread of the disease.

PHYSIOLOGICAL DISORDERS:

1. Tip Burning:

Symptoms:

- Tip burn is a kind of necrosis at the margins of young developing leaves.

Causes:

- The susceptibility to tip burn is genetically governed, but influenced by environmental components.
- Tip burn may be promoted both by factors causing luxuriant vegetative growth.
- The principal cause of tip burns in the onion is the deficiency of potassium in the tips of onion leaves.
- The other factors responsible are increased light intensity coupled with high temperature, high soil pH and repeated use of brackish water.

Management:

- Foliar application of K_2SO_4 @1% twice at weekly interval.

2. Thick Neck:

Symptoms:

- Any factor that keeps the plants into vegetative phase without forming bulbs or delays bulbing causes thickening of neck.
- Sometimes the onion plants fail to start bulbing and keep on their growth continued under certain conditions.
- Excessive growth without forming bulbs leads to thick-necked bulbs.
- Onion forms bulb more quickly at higher temperature. The plants can be kept in vegetative phase without forming bulbs at low temperature coupled with short days.
- For bulbing, plants need long days and high-temperature. The prolonged low temperature at bulbing stage increases thickening of neck.

Causes:

- Excessive use of nitrogenous fertilizer will produce bulbs with thick neck.
- Late maturity due to cool summer results in bulbs with a thick neck.
- This problem is always found associated with high yielding varieties in order to make sufficient leaf area for higher yield. Therefore, these varieties have to keep their growth continued.

Management:

- Avoid excessive use of nitrogenous fertilizers.

3. Premature Bulbing:

Symptoms:

- Premature bulbing is the start of bulb initiation very rapidly, soon after transplanting of seedlings in the field.
- This occurs when the seedlings are transplanted too late in the season; at this stage photoperiod and temperature both are favourable for bulbing but not for vegetative growth.
- High temperature and long day conditions are favourable for bulbing but not for vegetative growth.
- Seedlings when transplanted under such conditions will start bulbing without attaining sufficient growth.

Causes:

- Late planting of over wintered seedlings leads to premature bulbing.

- Dense planting or too high plant population per unit area also causes premature bulbing in onion.

4. Splitting Bulb:

Symptoms:

- Splitting occurs due to the presence of multiple growing points in a single bulb and also said to be associated with the genetic makeup of a cultivar.

Causes:

- Splitting or doubling of bulbs also takes place under some adverse conditions and imbalanced nutrition.
- High temperature and short day conditions encourage the development of lateral shoots.
- Any kind of injury to the plants during cultural operations may lead to splitting of bulbs.
- A long water stress period at initial growth stage or a long drought spell followed by irrigation or rain is responsible for doubling of bulbs.
- The use of un-rotten animal dung and urine in the field also leads to splitting of onion bulbs.

Management:

- Deep planting of onion seedlings reduces bulb splitting.

5. Sun scald:

Symptoms:

- Sunscald generally occurs when the onion bulbs are left in the field for curing after harvest.
- However, sometimes it may occur even before harvest in the standing crop, when onion bulbs are out of the soil either due to their large size or due to shallow planting of seedlings.

Causes:

- This disorder usually develops when the temperature is very high, and humidity or soil moisture is excessively low. Under such conditions, the tissues directly exposed to sun become soft and slippery.

Management:

- In standing crop to avoid this injury the sun exposed bulbs may be covered with soil by earthing up operation.
- The field should be provided with irrigation at short interval to keep the soil and bulb temperature low, and seedlings should be planted little bit deeper into the soil to avoid exposure of bulbs to direct sun during development phase.

- After harvest, the bulb should never be left in the field.

6. Bolting:

Symptoms:

- It is the most a serious disorder of onion crop. It refers to the emergence of seed stalk previous time of their formation and adversely affects the formation and development of bulbs.
- The bolting is an undesirable character, which could be due to directly, affects the bulb yield of onion.
- Genetic factors, poor quality seed, photoperiod, change in temperature and cultural practices affecting the growth govern this process.
- Due to bolting weight of the bulb is reduced and the woody stalk of the inflorescence remains at the core of the bulb which reduces the quality of the bulb and dehydrated products.

Causes:

- Very high nitrogen doses suppress bolting in the onion bulb crop. Bolting increases with an increase in size of the sets used as planting material.
- Onion seeds if sown too early in the season and seedlings complete their basic vegetative phase (juvenile phase) before the fall in temperature will receive sufficient cold stimulus from atmosphere to synthesize flowering hormone and promote bolting.
- A week exposure to chilling temperature optimum for flowering, followed by long photoperiod will favour the development of seed stalks rather than rapid bulbing.

Management:

- Always sow the seeds at the proper time.
- Use of over fertilizer should be avoided.
- Adjustment time for transplanting in such a way that the crop may be exposed to moderate temperature at bulbing.
- The Rabi crop is mature for coincides with high temperature compared to kharif crop.
- Growing non-bolting varieties like Early Grano, Texas Early Grano, etc.
- Transplant healthy seedling for 6 to 7 weeks old.
- Supply of the recommended dose of nitrogen and cuts the seed stalk at early stage.

7. Watery Scales:

Symptoms:

- The symptoms are the development of thick and leathery outer most skin.

- Fungi or bacteria may infect these scales; however, the attack of these bacteria and fungi is not the sole cause of this disorder.
- Onion is sensitive to high levels of carbon dioxide, either that is present in internal scales or in the external atmosphere when the onions are stored in controlled atmosphere storage.

Cause:

- If the carbon dioxide concentration exceeds 13%, it results in development of watery scales.

Management:

- In controlled atmosphere storage, carbon dioxide about 10% causes an internal breakdown.
- The higher concentration of carbon dioxide in the storage is more harmful to onions than low oxygen atmosphere.
- Proper storage facilities should be maintained for storing the onions.

8. Chemical Injury:

Symptoms:

- Chemical injury, known as alkali scorch, generally occurs when onions are stored in storage.
- This develops due to alkali impregnated/printed jute bags used to pack the onion bulbs.
- Higher concentration of ammonia gas in storage sometimes may cause serious injury to the onion bulbs.
- Ammonia injury is also same as that of injury caused by printed alkali material.
- The symptoms of ammonia injury are the development of dark brown to black spots.

9. Freezing Injury:

Symptoms:

- The sensitivity of onion bulbs to freezing injury depends on the genetic makeup of a cultivar.
- The cultivars having very high total soluble solids are not found sensitive to freezing injury because the bulbs of such cultivars have a very low freezing point.
- The sensitivity of onion bulbs to freezing injury depends also on water content.
- The bulbs with less water content have more resistance against freezing injury.

Cause:

- Many varieties could be stored successfully without any freezing injury, even at $-2°C$ temperature, although below this temperature, the freezing injury is developed.

Management:

- It is usually done by cultivating the fields, if such an occasion is anticipated.
- Cultivating field outcome layer of moist soil at the surface that acts as insulation.
- This holds the day's warm the soil around the bulb and root crop.

- The downside to refining the possible increase of the disease caused by throwing up contaminated soil on tender onion tissue.

References:

Alberto, R. T. 2014. Pathological response and biochemical changes in *Allium cepa* L. infected with anthracnose twitter disease. *Plant Pathology Quarantine.* 4(1), 23-31. 3.

Amani A. Sayed , Abd-El- razik, A. A., Abd-ElRahman, T. M. and Eraky, A.M.I. 2014. Influence of certain carbon and nitrogen sources on antagonistic potentiality of *Trichoderma harzianum* and *Bacillus subtilis* against *Botrytis allii* the incitant of onion neck rot. *Journal of phytopathology and Pest Management,* 1(2), 9-16.

Vincelli, P.C. and Lorbeer, J.W. 1989. Blight-alert: A weather-based predictive system for timing fungicide applications on onion before infection periods of *Botrytis squamosa. Phytopathology,* 79, 493-498.

Walker, J.C. 1925. Two undescribed species of Botrytis associated with the neck rot disease of onion bulbs. *Phytopathology,* 15,708-713.

Wilhite, S.E., Lumsden, R.D. and Straney, D.C. 1994. Mutational analysis of gliotoxin production by the biocontrol fungus *Gliocladium virens* in relation to suppression of Pythium damping-off. *Phytopathology,* 84, 816-821. 53.

Yadav, P.M., Rakholiya, K.B. and Pawar, D.M. 2013. Evaluation of bioagents for management of the onion purple blotch and bulb yield loss assessment under field conditions, *The Bioscan,* 8(4), 1295-1298

BEANS

Introduction:

- Common bean (*Phaseolus vulgaris* L.) is one of the most widely cultivated food legume species in the world for local consumption and exportation purposes.
- It is a worldwide food-secure and nutritious worldwide crop to people of all income categories.
- Bean is attacked by certain pathogenic fungi causing wilt, root-rot and leaf spot diseases which seriously affected both plant stand and yield production. (Fininsa, 2001; Abiy *et al.,* 2006; Tadesse *et al.,* 2009).
- These organisms can occur individually throughout the growing season.

Diseases:

S. No.	Disease Name	Causal Organism
Fungal diseases		
1.	Cercospora leaf spot	*Cercospora* sp.
2.	Rust	*Uromyces phaseoli typical*
3.	Powdery mildew	*Erysiphe polygonii*
4.	Anthracnose	*Colletotrichum lindemuthianum*
5.	Angular leaf spot	*Pseudocercospora griseola*

6.	Drt root rot	*Rhizoctonia solani, Macrophomina phaseolina*
Bacterial diseases		
7.	Bacterial wilt	*Curtobacterium flaccumfaciens* pv. *flaccumfaciens*
8.	Halo blight	*Pseudomonas savastonai pathovar phaseolicola*
9.	Bacterial blight	*Xanthomonas campestris pv phaseoli*
Viral diseases		
10.	Bean common mosaic	*Bean common mosaic virus*
11.	Yellow mosaic	*Bean Yellow Mosaic Virus*

1. Anthracnose

Causal Organism: *Colletotrichum lindemuthianum*

Symptoms:

- All the above ground parts are affected at any stage of crop growth.
- However, the characteristic symptoms appear on pods.
- On cotyledons spots are sunken dark brown or black with pink spore mass.
- Seedling infection results in collapse of seedling.
- Spots on leaves appear on lower side and are black. Later these may also appear on upper surface.
- When the infection is severe, the affected plants wither off.
- Black, sunken, circular spots of varying sizes appear on pods with bright red, yellow or orange margins.
- The centre of these spots later turns grey or pink due to sporulation of the pathogen.
- The border of these spots appears raised.
- On lima beans, symptoms are sooty appearing spots on leaves and pods.
- Anthracnose develops primarily during the spring and fall when the weather is cool and wet, and not during our hot, dry summers.
- Lima beans are particularly susceptible.

Pathogen:

- Mycelium is branched, septate, hyaline at first and dark colored with age.
- Acervuli develop beneath the cuticle.
- Conidia are borne on short conidiophores.
- Setae are few, brown and septate.
- Conidia are one celled, hyaline and cylindrical with rounded ends or with one end slightly pointed.

Mode of spread and survival:

- The fungus is seed borne and can survive from one season to another in debris from infected plant as well as in diseased seed.
- The fungus can remain alive in seeds even after the seeds are dead.
- **P.I:** Through **seed** and collateral hosts
- **S. I:** Conidia by splashing rain water or air borne conidia
- **Host range:** All vegetable beans and cowpea, mungbean, blackgram etc.

Epidemiology:

- Anthracnose is favored by cool temperature (16°) and wet conditions. The heavy and frequent rains with moderate temperature (19 to 25°C) and high RH (more than 70%) favor the progress of the disease in terms of vertical and horizontal spread (Kumar *et al.,* 1999).
- Wet periods for about 12 hours or more favors the occurrence of infection.

Management:

- Prevent this disease by using certified disease-free seed for planting and removing all plant debris after harvest.
- Anthracnose can survive in the soil for two years on plant debris or be brought to the garden on infected seeds.
- Do not plant bean seeds in an area that had disease for two to three years.
- Avoid overhead watering and avoid splashing soil onto the plants when watering.
- Fungicide sprays of fixed copper are the only recommended chemical that can be used on lima beans for anthracnose control.
- Seed treatment with Carbendazim@2g/kg seed.
- Protect the crop by spraying 0.2 % Benlate or Bavistin or Zineb or Maneb @ 2Kg/ha at 7-10 days interval (Reddy, 2010b).

2. Rust

Causal Organism:

On Beans: *Uromyces phaseoli typica*

On cowpea and others: *Uromyces phaseoli vignae*

On dry bean: *Uromyces appendiculatus*

- It is **autoecious** macrocyclic rust, *i.e.,* produces all the stages on bean plant.

Symptoms:

- The symptoms mostly appear on leaves, though often they are found on petiole and stem of some hosts.
- The rust pustules appear on either sides but more common on lower surface.
- The Uredosori are minute, roundish, slightly raised and reddish brown coloured (Hagedorn and Inglis, 1986).
- These contain rust spores and appear in groups.
- Later in the season with the formation of teliospores, the sori turn dark brown or black.
- Diseased leaves may wither or fall off under severe infection.

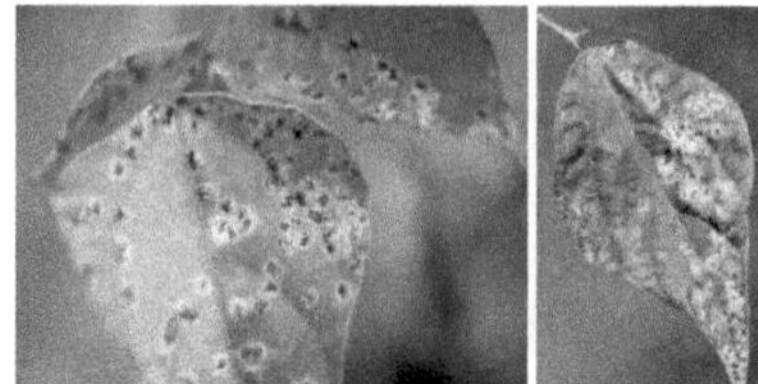

Pathogen:

- Uredospores are echinulate, oval and yellowish brown in colour.
- Teliospores are dark brown coloured, elliptical and ovate, pedicillate, and smooth walled, single celled with warty papillae at the top.

Mode of spread and survival:

- **P.I:** Survives through teliospores in cooler regions and on collateral hosts.
- **S.I:** Wind borne Uredospores.
- **Host range:** French beans, green gram, black gram and cowpea.

Management:

- The fungus survives the winter in the soil, on plant debris and even on poles used the previous year.
- In gardens where rust has been severe, crop rotation is important.
- Adjust sowing dates to avoid severe infection of plants in the field.
- Protect the crop with mancozeb or zineb @ 2 kg/ha or wettable sulphur @ 0.3% (Reddy, 2010b).
- As plants begin to bloom, sulfur or chlorothalonil can be sprayed weekly on snap and green beans only.
- Do not apply chlorothalonil to lima (butter) beans. Wait seven days between spraying and harvest when using chlorothalonil on beans, and 14 days on Southern peas.
- Three sprays of fungicides Tridimefon @ 0.1% or Tridemorph at 45, 60, and 75 days after sowing are reported to give the best control of disease and the highest bean yields (Singh, 2003).

3. Powdery Mildew

Causal Organism: *Erysiphe polygonii*

Symptoms:

- Leaves are covered with patches of a whitish to grayish powdery growth.
- New growth appears contorted, curled or dwarfed and may turn yellow and drop.
- Pods are dwarfed and distorted.
- This is mostly a problem on fall beans.
- Powdery mildew is spread by wind and rain.
- It is seed-borne in nature. Infection and disease development is easily favored by moderate temperature (21°C) and low humidities (65% RH) (Hogedorn and Inglis, 1986).

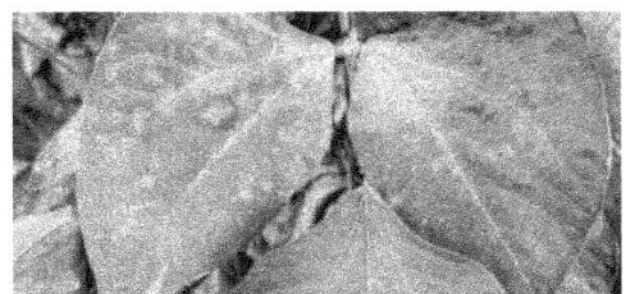

Pathogen:
- The mildew pathogen develops mycelial threads between a few cells near the epidermis and grows root like structures, haustoria that slowly withdraw food from the living plant tissue.
- After the fungus covers the upper and sometimes the lower leaf surface with fungus threads, the threads can produce many short multicellular fungus stalks, each of which bears a few spores resembling beads in a chain.

Mode of spread and survival:
- The fungus is capable of attacking different leguminous hosts and survives in conidial or perithecial form.
- The conidia are easily carried by wind, rain and insects.
- The spores are short lived and usually die in about 2 days if they do not reach a suitable host.
- When humidity is high and the leaf surface is dry, the spores germinate readily in few hours and the germ tubes enter the plant.
- Some strains produce sexual perithecia with asci which can remain alive from one season to the next.

Management:
- Avoid crowding plants by allowing adequate space between rows.
- On Southern peas, sulfur can be used.
- When the disease is first noticed, sprays or dusts of sulfur are recommended for use on snap and green beans only.
- Do not use sulfur on young plants.

4. Cercospora leaf spot

Causal Organism: *Cercospora* sp.

Symptoms:
- This fungal disease, caused by *Cercospora* species, occurs primarily on the lower leaves of plants as irregular, tan spots.
- Severe infection causes excessive leaf drop and stunting of the plant.

Epidemiology:
- Infection is worse during periods of extended rainfall, high humidity and temperatures between 75 to 85° F.

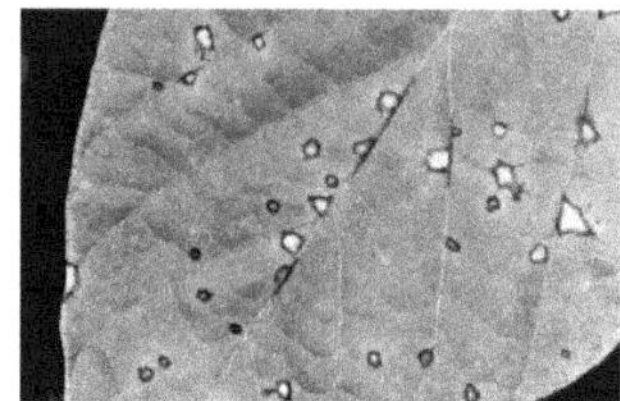

Management:

- Use disease free seed for planting.
- Remove all debris in the garden after harvest.
- Do not plant beans in the same area for two to three years.
- There are no resistant varieties or recommended chemicals for this disease in the home garden.

5. Bean Root Rots

Causal Organism: *Rhizoctonia solani, Pythium* and *Fusarium solani*

- Root rots are widespread diseases in the world and are often considered as a major constraint to bean production, reducing both yield and quality (Abawi and Widmer, 2000).
- Depending on the pathogen(s) involved in the development of the disease, general root rot symptoms might include any combination of various traits such as poor seedling establishment, dampingoff, uneven growth, leaf chlorosis, premature defoliation, death of severely infected plants, and lower yield (Abawi *et al.,* 2006; Schwartz *et al.,* 2007).
- Fusarium root rot, Pythium root rot, Rhizoctonia root rot, and Sclerotinia root rot are important root rot diseases which reduce significantly the bean yield worldwide. Root rot problem is caused by soil-borne fungus.

Symptoms:

- Many fungi, including *Rhizoctonia solani, Pythium* species and *Fusarium solani*, form species phaseoli, live in the soil and will infect young seedlings or the seeds of bean plants.
- Seedlings fail to emerge after planting when the seeds rot in the soil or young seedlings may be stunted.
- Plants are usually affected slightly above or below the soil line with a watery soft rot.
- Roots of the plant usually die and leaves are turning yellow.
- The disease is favored by 22 to 32°C temperatures, high soil moisture and by acidic soils (Hogedorn and Inglis, 1986).

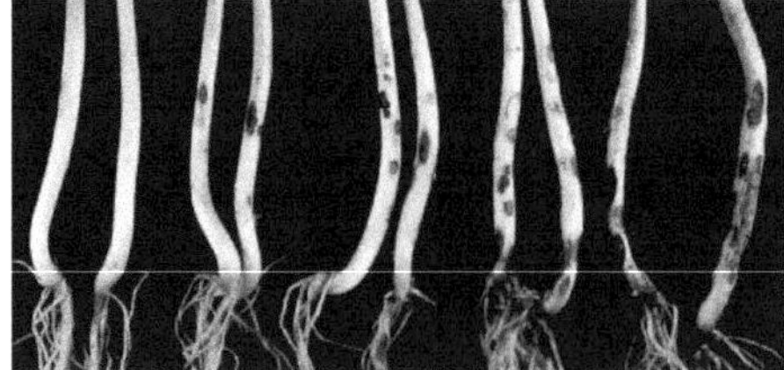

Management:

- Do not plant beans in low, poorly drained areas.

- Plant on raised beds.
- Plant after the soil has warmed to 69° F at a 4 inch depth.
- Reduce disease buildup in the soil by rotating locations in the garden where you plant bean or pea with other vegetables.
- Try to avoid injury to the root system, which often occurs during planting, through cultivation or due to a large population of nematodes in the soil.
- Remove crop debris immediately after harvest.
- Plant seeds previously treated with captan.

6. Charcoal Rot or Dry Root Rot

Causal Organism: *Macrophomina phaseolina*

Economic Importance:

- The disease is also known as **ashy stem blight, root rot, ashy grey stem** and ***Macrophomina* rot.**

Symptoms:

- The initial symptom is yellowing of leaves, which soon dry up.
- The plant may wilt within a week after the appearance of symptoms.
- When the stem is examined closely, dark lesions may be seen on the bark at the ground level.
- On uprooting infected plants, dry rot symptoms may be seen on the basal stem and the main roots.
- The tissues are weakened and break off easily.
- Black sclerotial bodies are formed on the diseased tissue a few days after infection.

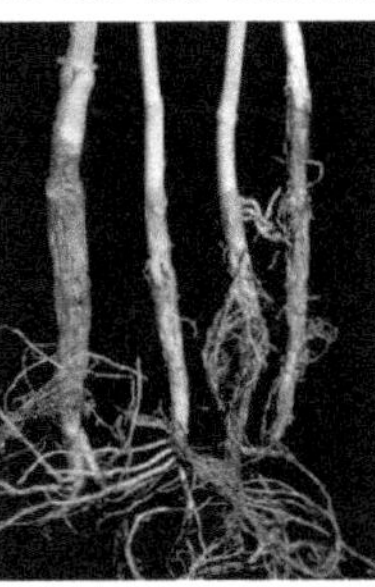

Pathogen:

- The sclerotial stage of the fungus is known as *Rhizoctonia bataticola* (Taub.) Butler.
- The mycelium is superficial or immersed, hyaline to brown, branched, septate and often tree-like in form.
- The pycnidia are at first buried beneath the lead-grey epidermis in which many sclerotial bodies are generally mixed.
- The conidiophores are more or less straight, sometimes crooked with a truncate tip.
- The conidia are one celled, more or less fusiform, straight or slightly curved.
- One end of the conidium is often pointed and the other is blunt.
- Sclerotia are readily produced, both on the plants in the field and in cultures.
- These are jet black, smooth, hard round to oblong or irregular in shape.

Disease cycle:
- The pathogen perpetuates as sclerotia in the soil and in infected seed.
- Survival is longer in dead host tissues than in free conditions in the soil.
- The fungus is a poor competitor in soil but readily colonizes plant debris.
- Population of the fungus increases when susceptible hosts are continuously grown in the field.
- When infected seed is sown in the field, it also introduces the fungus in the field.
- The sclerotia germinate and the mycelium cause primary infections.

Epidemiology:
- Environmental factors contributing to soil moisture stress/ water deficit predispose the plant to infection.
- Soil temperature of 28°C or more favours disease development.

Management:
- Collect and destroy the infected plant debris.
- Follow long crop rotations with non-leguminous crops.
- Solarization of infected soils during summer months can also help in reduction of soil borne inoculum.
- Use disease free seed and treat them with carbendazim or benomyl (0.2%).
- Application of biocontrol agents like *Trichoderma viride* and *Aspergillus niger* have also been found promising but need further confirmation.

7. **Angular bean leaf spot**

Causal Organism: *Pseudocercospora griseola or Phaeoisariopsis or Isariopsis griseola.*
- Hosts are *Phaseolus vulgaris* (common bean, field bean, French bean, kidney bean, string bean), cowpea, soybean. Other hosts include *Desmodium* species and *Dolichos lablab.*

Symptoms:
- Spots are usually seen first at flowering.
- Two types of symptoms occur depending on the leaf type.
- On the trifoliate (3 leaflets) leaves, angular spots up to 3mm wide, grey and then light brown, sometimes surrounded by a yellow halo, but limited by the veins.
- On the primary (single) leaves, the spots are up to 15mm diameter and are often with rings, like a target.
- Fungal mould grows on the undersides of both types of spot, and produces the spores.
- On the pods and stems, dark, sunken, oval to circular spots of varying size occur.
- The spots may join together. Seed becomes infected beneath the spots on the pods. They become discoloured.

Mode of survival and spread:

- Spread is by airborne spores released from the spots on the leaves.
- Spread over long distances occurs on seed.
- The fungus is splashed in rain from the infected seed to the leaves.
- The fungus survives between plantings in the remains of the crop, on "volunteer" plants, and on seed, where it can survive for at least 12 months.

Epidemiology:

- The disease is favoured by moderate temperatures (16-28°C), rain or high humidity, alternating with dry times (Strausbaugh and Forster, 2003).
- The wet periods allow spore germination, infection and production on the spots; dry periods allow spread of the spores in the wind.

Management:

- Make sure that the seed is certified free of the fungus.
- Collect and burn or bury as much of the crop as possible after harvest.
- Do not plant one crop of bean after another in the same land; use a rotation of at least 2-years.
- Treat seed with carbendazim (Reddy, 2010a).
- If fungicides are needed for control of leaf or pod spots, use a copper fungicides or mancozeb.

8. Bacterial wilt or tan spot

Causal Organism: *Curtobacterium flaccumfaciens* pv. *flaccumfaciens*

Symptoms:

- It includes a series of chlorotic and necrotic areas on leaves accompanied by overall plant wilt, often permanent, leading to plant.
- The symptoms first appear as foliar wilting and chlorotic areas leading to necrosis on leaves surrounded by a yellow halo.
- Subsequent symptoms are leaf wilting during periods of warm and dry weather or periods of moisture stress due to the pathogen presence within the vascular system, which interferes with normal water movement from roots into the foliage.
- Hence, the infected plants may recover when the temperature is lower at night or during cloudy or wet weather.
- Tearing or shredding of the necrotic leaf tissues is common under wind-driven rain and hailstorms, giving a ragged appearance to leaves with symptoms.

- Disease severity and plant mortality are often higher on seedlings and young plants, particularly if they originate from infected seeds.
- Symptoms on seedlings emerged from infected seeds are commonly seen at the cotyledon and/or the second trifoliate leaf stage.
- In such a situation the seedling rarely survives and will die within a few days post-emergence.

Mode of spread and survival:
- There are two types of field infection.
- Primary infection involves the invasion of bean seedlings as they emerge from the soil.
- This occurs when the seed is infected or when an emerging seedling comes into contact with infected plant material.
- Secondary infection is due to spread from primary source to other growing plants often involving only one or two isolated plants or it may cover an entire field or area.
- In severely diseased fields, nearly all infection is secondary (Reddy, 2010a).

Management:
- This bacterial pathogen can be managed, but not eliminated, through crop rotation, sanitation, sowing only treated certified seeds, varietal selection, and avoiding stress and excessive moisture on foliage (Popovic *et al.,* 2012).
- Plant resistant varieties. **Heirlooms and other older bean varieties, like pinto or red kidney, are susceptible to the disease** (Belachew *et al.,* 2015).

9. Bacterial Blight

Causal Organism: *Xanthomonas campestris* pv. *phaseoli*

Symptoms:
- There are two widespread bacterial blights that affect most types of beans, common blight (*Xanthomonas campestris pv phaseoli*) and halo blight (*Pseudomonas syringae pathovar phaseolicola)* (Fininsa, 2001; Fourie, 2002).
- The stems, leaves and fruits of bean plants can be infected by either disease.
- Rain and damp weather favour disease development.
- Halo blight occurs primarily when temperatures are cool.
- Light greenish-yellow circles that look like halos form around a brown spot or lesion on the plant.
- With age, the lesions may join together as the leaf turns yellow and slowly dies. Stem lesions appear as long, reddish spots.
- Leaves infected with common blight turn brown and drop quickly from the plant.

- Common blight infected pods do not have the greenish-yellow halo around the infected spot or lesion.
- Common blight occurs mostly during warm weather.

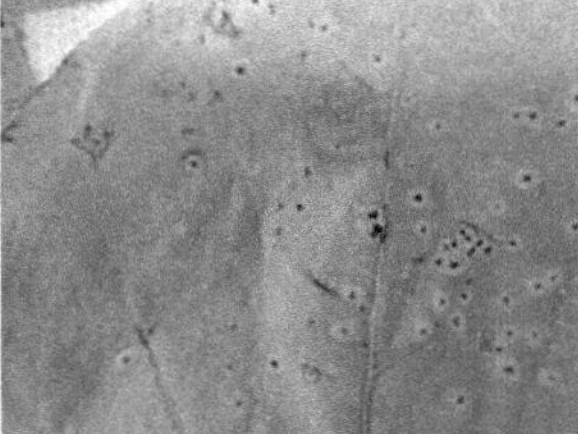

Pathogen:
- The bacterium is gram negative rod, non capsulated and motile with single polar flagellum.

Mode of spread and survival:
- The pathogen is seed borne and the disease spread through wind splashed rains from diseased to healthy plants.
- In new area disease spreads through infected seeds.

Management:
- Both of these diseases come from infected seeds. The diseases spread readily when moisture is present.
- Avoid overhead watering and do not touch plants when the foliage is wet.
- The bacteria can live in the soil for two years on plant debris. Do not plant beans in the same location more frequently than every third year.
- Buy new seeds each year.
- Fixed copper can be applied at ten day intervals. Wait one day between spraying and harvest.

10. Yellow mosaic

Causal Organism: Bean Yellow Mosaic Virus, Mungbean yellow virus or Phaseolus virus-2 *(ss DNA virus)*

Symptoms:
- Bright yellow patches appear on leaves.
- Yellow areas alternate with dark green areas of the leaf blade.
- Younger leaves show more severe mottling and chlorosis.
- Leaves completely turn yellow and gradually become necrotic.
- Plants are stunted and flower and pod set is reduced.
- Pod formation is reduced and if produced, they are deformed having shrivelled and undersized seeds.
- The causal agents of these symptoms may be nutrient imbalance or herbicide injury or result from infection by one of several viruses.

Mode of spread and survival:

- **P.I:** Collateral hosts
- **S.I:** Whitefly, *Bemisia tabaci*
- Not transmitted by sap, seed and pollen.
- **Host range:** French bean, Soybean, Red gram, *Xanthium strumarum, Eclipta alba*, etc.

Management:

- Remove collateral hosts and destroy.
- Spray metasystox@0.1% for vector control.

11. Common bean mosaic virus/ Green mosaic: *Bean common mosaic virus (ss RNA)*

Symptoms:

- Affects only beans (*Phaeolus vulgaris* and other *Phaseolus* species).
- Symptoms vary according to the variety of bean affected, time of infection and environmental conditions.
- Leaves show mosaic pattern, *i.e.*, light green areas alternate with dark green areas.
- Diseased leaves become rough, and show **blisters** on the leaf lamina.
- Leaf size, petiole length and plant height reduced.
- Leaves curl downward.
- Diseased plants produce fewer pods which are smaller in size.
- Seeds become smaller, malformed and aborted.

Survival and spread:

- Seed, sap, graft and aphid transmissible.
- **Infected seeds** are primary means of spread.
- *Aphis craccivora, Macrosiphum pisi, Aphis gossypi, A. medicaginis, Myzus persicae* and *Brevicoryne brassicae* transmit the virus in a non-persistent manner.

Management:

- There are no recommended chemical controls for these problems.
- Many of these viruses are transmitted by aphids and are also transmitted through seed.
- For this reason it is unwise to save seeds from year to year.
- Use of disease free seed.

- Vector control with systemic insecticides.

12. Golden Mosaic: Golden Mosaic Virus)

Symptoms:

- Golden mosaic is a serious disease of beans. This disease is first reported by Capoor and Verma (1948) from India.
- Disease is characterized as systemic, bright yellow or golden mosaic pattern in leaves. The chlorophyll of the leaves is partially or completely destroyed.
- Infected plant remains dwarf. Infected pods may be malformed, stunted, and show mosaic pattern.
- Seeds remain discolored and small in size. Pod production is generally reduced.
- Disease is transmitted by white fly *Bemisia tabaci*. The virus is readily transmitted by bud grafting.
- Successful transmission of this virus requires unusually warm temperature, i.e., 25° to 30°C.
- Likewise whitefly transmission is optimum at warm temperature i.e., 26.5°C (Hagedorn and Inglis, 1986).

Management:

- Follow crop rotation in the field. Destruction of infected plants from field is very important.
- It is essential to isolate field from virus reservoir plants and from insect vector sources plants, i.e., soybean, tobacco, tomato, cotton.
- Soil application of insecticide Carbafuron or Fensulfothion or Disulfoton or Disyston or Phorate @ 1.5 kg ai/ha at the time of sowing followed by 3–4 sprays of Dimethoate or Monocrotophos both @ 0.05% at 10 days interval significantly controlled the white fly population and disease spread.
- Spraying of 2% mineral oil has proved very effective in checking the spread of the disease (Singh, 1981).

Physiological Disorders:

- Disturbance in normal functioning of the plant due to external, physical, chemical or mechanical agents lead to physiological disorders.
- Bald head and sneak head, sunscald, and ozone injury are considered as important physiological disorders of bean crop.

1. Bald Head And Sneak Head:

Symptoms:

- Bald head is wide spread and common in occurrence. Severely stunted and malformed bean seedlings are the typical symptoms. This is the result of mechanical injury to bean and lima bean.
- Seed during threshing, seed with severely mutilated coats are removed in the milling and cleaning processes while those which have been injured only internally are ones which produce bald head and sneak head plant.

- Normally because of the lack of the normal growing tip, such plants are designated as baldhead plants.
- Sneak head, a malady brought about by chewing of the germinating seedlings by seed corn maggot has symptoms which develop those of bald head (Bhat, 2016).
- Seed with low moisture content are more prone to mechanical injury resulting in bald head.

Management:
- Take extreme care in all of the mechanical aspects of seed harvesting, cleaning, handling, and planting.
- The moisture content of seed should not be less than 14–15%.

2. Sunscald:

Symptoms:
- It probably occurs almost everywhere beans are grown but rarely cause significant yield loss.
- Initially very tiny brown or reddish spots upon the upper or outer valve away from the center of the plant.
- These spots gradually increase in size until they appear as short streaks running backwards and downward from the vertical towards the dorsal suture.
- Sun scalding is caused by the concentration of the sun's heat on leaf tissue.
- Intense sunlight primarily causes sunscald but high temperature may also be responsible for this problem (Bhat, 2016).

Management:
- Optimum use of fertilizers and irrigation management are important to lower this problem.

References:

Ayele, H., (1991). *Importance of haricot bean export to the Ethiopian economy.* In: Research on Haricot Bean in Ethiopia, an Assessment of Status, Progress, Priorities and Strategies (pp. 31–34).

Addis Ababa, Ethiopia. Baudoin, J. P., Camarena, F., Lobo, M. and Mergeai, G., (2001). *Breeding Phaseolus for intercrop combinations in Andean highlands.* In: Cooper *et al.,* (eds.), Broadening the Genetic Bases of Crop (pp. 373–384). Oxford, UK, CABI Publishing.

Belachew, K. M., Gebremariam, M. and Alemu, K., (2015). Integrated management of common bacterial blight (*Xanthomonas axonopodis pv. phaseoli*) of common bean (*Phaseolus vulgaris*) in Kaffa, Southwest Ethiopia. Malays. *J. Med. Biol. Res.,* 2(2), 147–152.

Bhat, K. L., (2016). *Physiological disorders of other vegetable crops.* In: Physiological Disorders of Vegetable Crops (p. 92). Daya Publishing House. New Delhi.

Bhosale, S. B., Jadav, D. S., Patil, B. Y. and Chavan, A. M., (2014). Fungal disease of *Alternaria alternata* associated with soybean (*Glycine max* (L.) Merr.) and its biological control by efficient plant extract. *Indian Journal of Applied Research,* 11(4), 79–81.

Capoor, S. P. and Verma, P. M., (1948). Yellow mosaic of *Phaseolus lunatus* L. *Current Science,* 17, 152–153.

Popovic, T., Starovic, M., Aleksic, G., Zivkovic, S., Josic, D., Ignjatov, M. and Milovanovic, P., (2012). Response of different beans against common bacterial blight disease caused by *Xanthomonas axonopodis pv. phaseoli. Bulg. J. Agric. Sci.,* 18, 701–707. Ramappa, H. K., (1988). *Studies on Nematode Parasites of French Bean and Their Control.* M.Sc. (Agri), Thesis, University of Agricultural Science, Bangalore.

Reddy, P. P., (2010a). *Bacterial and viral diseases and their management.* In: Plant Protection in Horticulture (Vol. 3, p. 288). Scientific Publishers, Jodhpur, India.

Reddy, P. P., (2010b). *Plant Protection in Horticulture: Fungal Diseases and Their Management* (Vol. 2, p. 359). Scientific Publishers, Jodhpur, India.

Reddy, P. P., Singh, D. B. and Ram, K., (1979). Effect of root-knot nematodes on the susceptibility of pusa purple cluster brinjal to bacterial wilt. *Current Science,* 48, 915–916.

Schwartz, H. F., Gent, D. H., Gary, D. F. and Harveson, R. M., (2007). *Dry bean, Pythium wilt and root rots.* High Plains IPM Guide, a Cooperative Effort of the University of Wyoming. University of Nebraska, Colorado State University and Montana State University.

Vadhera, I., Sheila, B. N. and Bhat, J., (1995). Interaction between reniform nematode and Fusarium solani causing root rot of french bean. *Indian J. of Agriculture Science,* 65, 774–777.

Vincente, N. E., Sanchez, L. A. and Acosta, N., (1991). Effect of granular nematicides and the fungus *Paecilomyces lilacinus* in nematode control in watermelon. J. *Agric. Univ. P.R.,* 75(3), 307–309.

PEAS

Introduction:

- Pea (*Pisum sativum* L.), the famous plant in which G.H. Mendel worked out Mendel Laws and Genetic Principles, is a noble and aristocratic vegetable.
- The crop is cultivated for its tender and immature pods for use as vegetable and mature dry pods for use as a pulse. In both cases, seeds are separated and used as vegetable or pulse.
- Peas are highly nutritive and contain high content of digestible protein (7.2 g / 100g), Carbohydrate (15.8 g), Vitamin-C (9 mg), phosphorus (139 mg) and minerals.
- Tender seeds are also used in soups. Canned, frozen and dehydrated peas are very common for use during off-season.

- Like any legume crop, pea is an integral component of sustainable agriculture due to its soil enriching and conditioning properties.
- Garden pea is grown mainly as a Rabi crop which normally sown in October and November and harvested in the month of February and March.
- Being a leguminous crop has capacity of fixing atmospheric nitrogen in the soil.
- In spite of high yielding varieties and improved agronomic practices the productivity of pea is low.
- Diseases are one of the most limiting factors responsible for low yield per hectare.
- Among the diseases, powdery mildew (*Erysiphe polygoni*), Downy mildew (*Peronospora pisi*), wilt (*Fusarium oxysporum f.sp. pisi*), Rust (Uromycesfabae) and Ascochyta blight (*Ascochyta* spp.) are the most important diseases of pea in India (Sharma, 1998).

Diseases:

S. No.	Disease Name	Causal Organism
Fungal diseases		
1.	Pythium seed and root rot	*Pythium ultimum*
2.	Downy mildew	*Peronospora pisi*
3.	Powdery mildew	*Erysiphe polygoni*
4.	Rust	*Uromyces fabae*
5.	Anthracnose	*Colletotrichum pisi*
6.	Ascochyta blight	*Ascochyta pisi*
7.	Fusarium wilt	*Fusarium oxysporum* f.sp. *pisi*
8.	Cercospora leaf spot	*Cercospora canescens*
Bacterial diseases		
9.	Bacterial blight	*Pseudomonas syringae pv. pisi*
Viral diseases		
10.	Pea mosaic	*Pea seedborne mosaic virus*
11.	Enation	*Pea enation mosaic virus*
Physiological Disorders		
12.	Marsh spot	

1. Downy mildew

Causal Organism: *Peronospora pisi*

Economic Importance:
- Downy mildew of pea was first discovered by Berkeley in England in 1846 (Chupp and Sherf, 1960), and since then, it has been found in all parts of the world.
- Dixon (1981) has also reported that downy mildew of peas is widely distributed all over the world.
- Olofsson (1966) and Biddle *et al.* (1988) reported yield losses of 30% in Sweden and 45% in the UK, respectively.

- In India, the disease is prevalent throughout the Indo-i plain and causes considerable yield loss.

Symptoms:
- A grayish white, moldy growth appears on the lower leaf surface, and a yellowish area appears on the opposite side of the leaf.
- Infected leaves can turn yellow and die if weather is cool and damp.
- Stems may be distorted and stunted.
- Brown blotches appear on pods, and mold may grow inside pods.

- Following infection, the mycelium develops in the intercellular spaces penetrating the stem, the leaf stalks, and even the pods through the veins (Kosevskii and Kirik, 1979).
- Pod infection develops from conidia deposited on young pods rather than by mycelial growth through the peduncle and pedicel (Mence and Pegg, 1971).
- Later in the season, oospore develops in the senescent tissues and can survive in the soil for up to 15 years (Van der Gaag and Frinking, 1997).

Pathogen:
- The vegetative stage is probably diploid like in other species of Peronospora (Tommerup, 1981).
- The fungus is an obligate parasite which can only grow on living plant tissue.
- Forma specialis pisi can only infect Pisum species and not species of the genus Vicia within the tribe Vicieae (Campbell, 1935).

Favourable conditions:
- High humidity and low temperatures (5- 15°C) for few days are ideal for infection and development of disease.

Mode of spread and survival:
- The oospores can survive for a long time in the soil. Oospores survive for 10–15 years in the soil (Olofsson, 1966).
- Primary infection by oospores in soil, seed and water Secondary infection by sporangia through rain splash or wind (Shaw, 1981).

Management:
- Metalaxyl is effective when applied as a foliar spray@ 100g in 300 liter of water/ha (Brokenshire, 1980).
- The cultivar 'Dark Skin Perfection', PWR-3 is more resistant to downy mildew than some other cultivars used for the production of peas for canning and freezing (Stegmark, 1988).

2. Powdery mildew

Causal Organism: *Erysiphe polygoni*

Economic Importance:

- The disease is widespread and often economically important in semi-arid regions of the world. The disease was first reported in India from Dehradun by Butler in 1918.
- In dry and warm condition the disease becomes more destructive, while downy mildew flourishes in humid weather condition.

Symptoms:

- It attacks leaves first producing faint, slightly discolored specks from which grayish white powdery growth of mycelium develop.
- Powdery growth spread over leaf, stem and pod.
- The leaves turn yellow and die.
- The fruits do not either set or remain very small. It causes defoliation.
- Later stages, powdery growth also covers the pods (Yarwood *et al.,* 1954).

Mode of spread and survival:

- Powdery mildew spores are carried by air and once active, will continue to spread in dry conditions.

Favourable conditions:

- Warm (temperature 15-25°C), humid (over 70% relative humidity) conditions for 4-5 days late in the growing season, during flowering and pod filling, favours disease development.

Management:

- Spraying with wettable sulphur 0.1% or Dinocap 0.2% is effective (Surwase *et al.,* 2009).
- Resistant varieties are **Gloris-de-quimpes, P-431, P-456, P-185, P-38, T-10** and **T-56** (Azmat *et al.,* 2010).
- *Trichoderma harzianum* (0.5%) was found effective and economical for controlling the disease and giving better seed yield (Surwase *et al.,* 2009).

3. Pea rust

Causal Organism: *Uromyces fabae*

Economic Importance:

- The rust fungus was first identified by Jordi in 1904 (Buchheim, 1922). In India, pea rust pathogen *U. viciae fabae* by Sydow and Butler on *Vicia faba* from Pusa, Bihar in 1906.

Symptoms:

- Leaves of infected plants exhibit many small, orange-brown pustules usually at the lower surface.

- Severely infected leaves wither and may drop from the plant.
- Larger pustules occur on the stems and isolated pustules may be found on the pods.
- Severe infection may result in reduced seed size and may cause yield losses of up to 30%.

Mode of spread and survival:
- Euphorbia and infected vegetation residues are sources of the infection.
- The agent is not transferred by seeds.

Favourable conditions:
- Frequent precipitations, plentiful dews and air temperature of 20-25°C promote disease development (Kushwaha *et al.,* 2006).
- Dry and hot weather restrains the disease development.

Management:
- Singh and Tripathi (2004) reported that KFP 106, DMR 11, HUP 8603, Type 163, and KPMR 22 showed a good level of resistance, which being conditioned by a number of genes.
- Fungicidal application using Tridemorph 0.1% or Mancozeb 0.25% effectively controls the disease (Sugha *et al.,* 1998).

4. Ascochyta blight
Causal Organism: *Ascochyta pisi*

Economic Importance:
- **Ascochyta blights** occur throughout the world and can be of significant economic importance.
- Three fungi contribute to the ascochyta blight disease complex of pea.
- *Ascochyta pinodes* (sexual stage: *Mycosphaerella pinodes*) causes *Mycosphaerella* blight. *Ascochyta pinodella* (synonym: *Phoma medicaginis* var. *pinodella*) causes *Ascochyta* foot rot, and *Ascochyta pisi* causes Ascochyta blight and pod spot.
- Of the three fungi, *Ascochyta pinodes* is of the most importance.
- These diseases are conducive under wet and humid conditions and can cause a yield loss of up to fifty percent if left uncontrolled (Bretag *et al.,* 1995; Tivoli *et al.,* 1996).
- Srivastava and Gupta (1990) reported pea blight (*Ascochyta pisi*) from Sikkim, where it caused heavy losses from December to March.

Symptoms:
- Early symptoms are most commonly observed under the plant canopy, on lower leaves, stems, and tendrils, where conditions are more humid.
- Symptoms first appear as small, purplish-brown and irregular flecks.

- Under continued humid conditions, the flecks enlarge and coalesce, resulting the lower leaves becoming completely blighted.
- Severe infections may lead to girdling of the stem near the soil line, which is known as foot rot.
- Foot rot lesions are purplish-black in colour and may extend above and below the soil line.
- Foot and stem lesions girdle and weaken the stem, leading to crop lodging and yield loss.
- Disease lesions develop on pods under prolonged moist conditions or if the crop has lodged.
- Pod lesions are initially small and dark, but may become extensive and lead to early pod senescence.
- Severe pod infection may result in small, shrunken or discoloured seed; or alternatively, seed may show no symptoms.

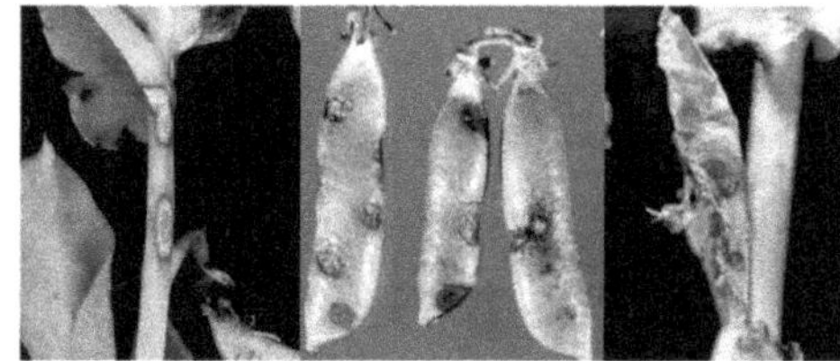

Mode of spread and survival:
- Ascospores carried long distances by wind.
- The asexual conidia travel short distances to new hosts via water splashes from rain.
- Infection originates from diseased seed or from spores growing on debris in the soil near pea plants.

Favourable conditions:
- Favorable conditions are warm humid conditions with a temperature is about 15° C to 25° C (Susuri, 1976).

Management:
- Sow disease-free seed.
- Follow rotation crop.
- Seed treatment with Carbendazim @ 1g/kg of seed or Hot water seed treatment (52 C for 10 min) to lower the infestation.
- Spray the crop with Mancozeb @ 2.5g/lit if noticed during the growth period or Spray Wettable sulphur at the rate of 2.3g/lit of water (Warkentin *et al.,* 1996).
- The disease can be reduced by reduction of the crop refuse by burning either in the field or after threshing (Bedlan, 1985).

5. White rot

Causal Organism: *Sclerotinia sclerotiorum*

Disease symptoms:

- The infection may occur at any part of the foliage, mainly the stem or branches.
- The maximum infection develops at the flowering stage of the crop, when petals fall on ground and these catch infection immediately and mycelial growth of fungus invades the stem and branches.
- At the point of infection, a dry discolored spot develops.
- It gradually girdles the entire stem and also progresses up and down.
- As a result of tissue necrosis, the portion of the plant beyond the point of infection wilts.
- If the infection is at the base of the main stem, the entire plant wilts.
- If it occurs on branches, partial wilting occurs.
- The diseased tissues become whitish and may be shredded.

Mode of spread and survival:

- The infection caused by hard sclerotia left in soil or in plant debris.

Favourable conditions:

- When adequate moisture is available and temperature ranges between 4 and 20°C.
- However, light is essential for stimulation of apothecial production.

Management:

- Plants become susceptible after or around flowering and earlier sowing suffer severe damage, hence late sowing (November) is recommended.
- Need based sprays of Carbendazim @ 0.1 % at fortnightly intervals starting from disease appearance.

6. Root rot

Causal Organism: *Pythium ultimum*

Symptoms:

- Reddish brown to black streaks appear on primary and secondary roots.
- These streaks coalesce at later stages, leading to girdling of lower stem.
- Red discoloration of the vascular system can be seen, especially near cotyledon attachment.
- Stunted growth, yellowing and necrosis appear on the basal foliage.

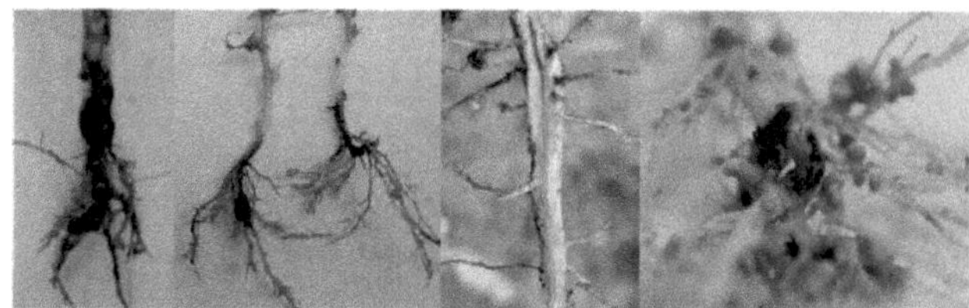

Mode of spread and survival:
- Primary infection by soil, seed and water.
- Secondary infection by conidia through rain splash or wind.

Favourable conditions:
- Cool, wet weather conditions.
- Favourable conditions are higher soil temperatures 25° to 30°C and moderate soil moisture.

Management:
- Avoid soil compaction, choose well-drained fields.
- Avoid overcrowding and deep planting.
- No commercial cultivars of peas have root-rot resistance.
- Planting cultivars that are adapted for growing region may reduce stresses.
- Ensure application of *Rhizobium* inoculant good for pea growth, and can boost disease resistance.
- Using high quality seed and treating the seed is the best way to manage early root rots.
- Crop rotation reduces the inoculum build-up of root rots.

7. Wilt/ St. John's wilt

Causal Organism: *Fusarium oxysporum* f.sp. *pisi*

Economic Importance:
- It was first reported in Minnesota by Bisby in 1918 (Chupps and Sherf, 1960).
- Only symptoms were identified.
- Fungus was identified in 1928 in Wisconsia.
- In India, the occurrence of Pea wilt report was made available by Patel *et al.* (1949) from Bombay.
- Losses up to 60% were reported in the crop during the years of epiphytotics in Himachal Pradesh (Kumar, 1983).

Symptoms:
- Symptom of the disease is more pronounced in 3 to 5 week old plants.
- In young seedlings, cotyledons droop and wither.
- Yellowing of lower leaves and stunting of plants.
- The xylem vessels develop brown discoloration and get distorted.
- Leaflet margins curl downward and inward.
- The stem may be slightly swollen and brittle near the soil.
- Internal woody stem tissue often is discolored, turning lemon brown to orange brown.

- Externally, the root system appears healthy; however, secondary root rots are likely to occur on plants wilted for long periods. Eventually, wilted plants may die (Schroeder and Walker, 1942).

Pathogen:
- The fungus hyphe is septate, delicated, white to peach colored, usually with a purple tinge.
- Microconidia are borne on simple phialades arising laterally on hyphae or from short, less branched conidiophores.
- These are oval ellipsoid to cylindrical or curved and measures 5–12 x 2.2–3.5 micrometer.
- Macroconidia are borne on elaborately branched conidiophores or on the surface of sporodochia.
- These are thin-walled, 3–5 septate, fusoid-subulates pointed at both ends and measure 27–46 x 3–4.5 micrometer.
- Chlamydospores are both terminal and intercalary.

Mode of spread and survival:
- Primary infection by Soil, Seed, Water.
- Secondary infection by Conidia through rain splash.

Favourable conditions:
- A soil temperature of 23° to 27°C is most favourable for Fusarium wilt.
- Hot weather and warm soils.

Management:
- Treating the seeds with Carbendazim (2g/kg of seed) protects the seedlings during the initial stages of growth.
- Soil drenching with Copper oxychloride 0.25% (Neweigy *et al.,* 1985).
- Seed treatment with antagonists like *Trichoderma viride* and *Trichoderma harzianum* was found effective in the management of pea wilt both under glasshouse and field conditions (Verma and Dohroo, 2005c).

8. Bacterial blight

Causal Organism: *Pseudomonas syringae* pv. *pisi*

Economic Importance:
- It was first described in Colorado in 1915 by Sackett.
- The disease has since been found in many parts of the world and on every continent.

- Under wet spring conditions or in overhead-irrigated systems, the disease can be severe and significantly reduce yields.
- Losses are generally proportional to disease severity or incidence.

Symptoms:
- Initially water soaked lesions on all aboveground tissue; lesions eventually turn brown and necrotic.
- Lesions on leaves may take on an angular shape; stem infections appear around nodes, stipules and leaflets.
- Infected flowers shrivel and decay and lead to pod and seed infection.

Mode of spread and survival:
- The pathogen is seedborne and is very prevalent in seed stocks.
- It resides in seed both externally and internally, and can survive for three years in infected or infested seed.
- The seedborne nature provides the pathogen with a primary means of long distance dispersal.
- The bacterium can be spread from infested/infected seeds to healthy seeds at harvesting by machinery or during the milling process.
- The bacterial blight pathogen can survive in infected pea debris for over a year, but does not survive well in soil, especially in organic soil.

Management:
- Cultivars resistant to specific races are available and offer a very effective means of controlling bacterial blight.
- However, the race of the pathogen prevalent in a location should be determined before a resistant cultivar is selected for planting.
- A 2-year rotation in combination with pathogen-free seed or seed disinfested with 1% sodium hypochlorite is appropriate.

9. Pea enation mosaic

Causal Organism: Peppper enation mosaic virus (PEMV)

Economic Importance:
- This is one of only a few viruses with unique properties and hence has been assigned to a separate virus group.
- The virus mainly infects legumes in the temperate regions of the world.

- In addition to pea, PEMV also infects broadbean (from which the virus was first described in New York in 1935), sweet pea, and alfalfa and probably overwinters in many common perennial legumes.

Symptoms:
- Infected pea plants develop mosaic and chlorotic vein flecking (appears as translucent windows) and veinal enations (blister like outgrowths), which are very characteristic for PEMV.
- Plants are stunted, and proliferation of basal branches is common.
- Pods are distorted, split open, and may show prominent enations.

Mode of spread and survival:
- The virus is spread in nature most efficiently by the pea aphid *(Acyrthosiphon pisum)* and to a lesser extent by the green peach aphid *(Myzus persicae).*
- The virus is transmitted in a persistent (circulative) manner.

Management:
- Many American cultivars are resistant to PEMV.
- The method of virus transmission and the behavior of the pea aphid are two factors aiding in the control of PEMV.
- Spraying plants with insecticides reduces the incidence of the virus because of the persistent nature of spread and because the pea aphid readily colonizes peas and broadbean.
- The aphids can be controlled before much secondary spread occurs. Removal of perennial legumes bordering the planting area also reduces the primary virus reservoir.

10. Pea mosaic
Causal Organism: *Pea seedborne mosaic virus* (PSBMV)
Economic Importance:
- It is not a problem for commercial fields in New York at this time.
- The virus is readily seed borne in pea, with up to 90% infected seed reported in some commercial seed lots.
- Seed coats may split as the seed approaches maturity, but the likelihood of this occurring varies among varieties.
- This characteristic is not unique to virus infection.
- The virus has been found in the "plant introduction" collection, its distribution being increased by exchange of infected seed lots.

Symptoms:

- The virus has previously been known as pea leafroll mosaic virus or pea fizzletop virus.
- In pea, the symptoms consist of leaf narrowing and downward leaf rolling, accompanied by a mild mosaic. Plants are somewhat reduced in size.

Mode of spread and survival:
- The virus is predominantly spread by seed, although it is also spread in nature by aphids (*Myzus persiccae, Aphis craccivora*) in a non persistent manner.

Management:
- Most Perfection-type pea varieties are very susceptible, and no resistant varieties are presently available.
- Resistance is conditioned by a recessive factor. Spray water to knock aphids off plants.

PHYSIOLOGICAL DISORDERS:
1. Marsh spot:
Symptoms:
- The deficiency causes the formation of a brown spot in the centre of many of the peas produced, and the produce is spoilt for human consumption and for use as seed.

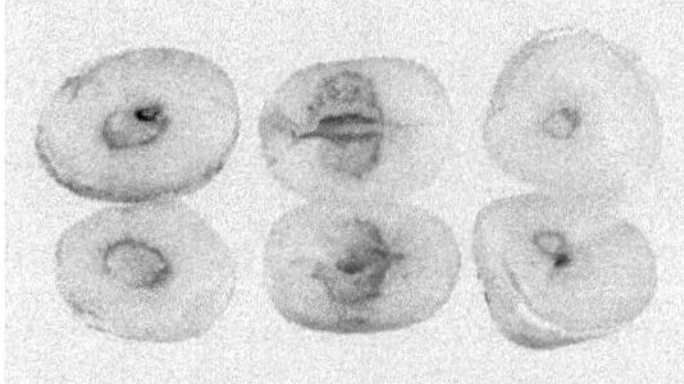

Causes:
- Marsh spot is a disorder of peas, which is due to deficiency or unavailability of manganese.
- It is particularly associated with organic and alkaline soils.

Management:
- When symptoms appear in a crop, 5 kg/ha of manganese sulphate with a wetter, or an equivalent application of a manganese spray, should be applied at once in a high volume of water.
- Similar treatment must also be carried out when an affected crop is at first pod stage, and repeated 10 - 14 days later, in order to prevent the formation of marsh spot.
- In some seasons flowering is prolonged and a third manganese application will be necessary.

- The amount of manganese in some formulations (e.g. chelated manganese) may be too low to be effective at the rate recommended.

References:

Anwar, S. A., Bhutta, A. R., Raut, C. A., & Khan, M. S. A., (1994). Seed borne fungi of pea and their role in poor germination of pea seed. *Pakistan J. Phytopathology,* 6, 135–139.

Ayub, A., Rahaman, M. Z., Ali, S. and Khatun, A., (1996). Fungicidal spray to control leaf rust of lentil. *Bangladesh J. Plant Pathol.,* 12, 61–62.

Azmat, M. A., Nawab, N. N., Shahid, N., Abdul, R., Khalid, M., Khan, A. A. and Khan, S. H., (2010). Single gene recessive controls powdery mildew resistance in pea. *Inter. J. Veg. Sci.,* 16, 17–24.

Bains, S. S., Dhiman, J. S. and Singh, H., (1993). Occurrence of *Peronospora pisi* with *Uromyces viciae fabae* on leaves on pea genotypes. *Indian Phytopathol.,* 48, 365–366.

Barilli, E., Sillero, J. C., Aparicio, M. F. and Rubiales, D., (2009). Identification of resistance to *uromyces pisi* (Pers.) Wint. In: Pisum spp. germplasm. *Field Crop Research,* 117(2), 198–203.

Batra, L. R. and Stavely, R., (1994). Attraction of two spotted spider mites to bean rust uredinia. *Plant Dis.,* 78, 282–284.

Bedlan, G., (1985). *Pea leaf and pod spot.* Pflanzenschutz, 147, 14–15.

Biddle, A. J., Knott, C. M. and Gent, G. P., (1988). *Pea Growing Handbook* (p. 264). Processors and Growers Research Organization, Peterborough, UK.

Buchheim, A., (1922). *On the biology of Uromyces pisi* (Pers.) Winter. Preliminary note. Centralbl. fur Bakt. Ab., 2, 507–508.

Butler, E. J., (1918). *Fungi and Diseases in Plants.* Thacker Spink and Co., Calcutta, India.

Campbell, L., (1935). *Downy Mildew of Peas Caused by Peronospora Pisi* (De Bary) Syd (Vol. 318, p. 42). Washington Agric. Exp. Sta. Bull.

Peshne, N. L., (1966). A comparative study of morphology, physiology and pathogenicity of Nagpur and Poona isolates of *Fusarium oxysporum f. sp. pisi.* Ann. Agril. Res. Abst. Grad. Res., W. K. 1960–1965, *Agric. Coll. Mg. Space Res.,* 12, 174–175.

Prasad, P. and Dewedi, S. N., (2007). Fungicidal management of field pea (*Pisum sativum* L) powdery mildew caused by *Erysiphe polygoni* DC. *Prog. Res.,* 2, 116–118.

Shaw, C. G., (1981). *Taxonomy and evolution.* In: Spencer, D. M., (ed.), The Downy Mildews (pp. 17–29, 636). Academic Press, New York, USA. Shroff, S., & Chand, R., (2010). Pre-infection Biology of aeciospores of *Uromyces fabae. Inter J. Curr. Trends Sci. Tech.,* 1(2), 1–10.

Sitara, U., Niaz, I., Naseem, J. and Sultana, N., (2008). Antifungal effect of essential oils on in vitro growth of pathogenic fungi. *Pak. J. Bot.,* 40, 409–414.

Verma, S. and Dohroo, N. P., (2005a). Effect of sowing dates on development of Fusarium wilt of autumn pea caused by *Fusarium oxysporum f. sp. pisi, Plant Dis.* Res., 20, 177–179.

BEETROOT

Introduction:

- Beet root (*Beta vulgaris* L.) is a popular herbaceous biennial root vegetable in the family Chenopodiaceae grown for its edible root.
- Beet root grown for its fleshy roots which are used as cooked vegetable, salad and for pickling and canning.
- Young plants along with tender leaves are also used as pot herbs.
- Beet root is a rich source of protein (1.7 g/100 g), carbohydrates (88 mg), calcium (200 mg), phosphorus (55 mg) and vitamin C (88 mg).
- Leaves are rich in iron (3.1 mg), vitamin A (2100 I.U.), thiamine (110 μ g) and ascorbic acid (50 mg/ 100 g).
- Under Indian conditions, about 10–15% of the crop is destroyed by the diseases.
- Out of 25 diseases known in the country, about 15 are economically important. Among the diseases caused by fungi, seed/seedling disorders, foliar diseases, root rots of adult plants and nematodes both in root and seed crop are more destructive.

S. No.	Disease Name	Causal Organism
Fungal diseases		
1.	Seedling disease of beet	*Phoma betae* *Pythium ultimum* *Aphanomyces cochlioides*
2.	Cercospora leaf spot	*Cercospora beticola*
3.	Phoma blight and heart rot of beet	*Phoma betae*
4.	Downy mildew	*Perenospora schachtti*
5.	Powdery mildew	*Erysiphe betae*
6.	Fusarium yellows and root rot	*Fusarium oxysporum* f. sp. *betae*
7.	Rhizoctonia root rot and blight	*Rhizoctonia solani*
Viral diseases		
8.	Beet yellows	*Beet yellow virus*
9.	Beet mosaic	*Beet mosaic virus*
10.	Beet Curly-top	*Beet curly top virus*
11.	Purple Leaf of Beet	*Tobacco mosaic virus*
Physiological Disorders		
12.	Heart rot or Crown rot	
13.	Zoning	

1. Cercospora leaf Spot

Causal Organism: *Cercospora beticola*

Economic Importance:

- It was first described in 1876.
- In India, it was reported in Punjab.

Symptoms:

- This is a commonly occurring disease on foliage of beet roots.
- High humidity usually favours the spread of this disease.
- Numerous small circular spots appear on the leaf surface.
- The spots increase in size, becoming brownish or purplish in colour.
- Individual spots are usually circular but several may coalesce into larger areas of dead tissue.
- The spots dry up giving a shot-hole appearance to the leaves.
- In case of severe infection spots cover the entire leaf surface resulting in pre-mature death and dropping of the leaves.
- As leaves die, the crown becomes cone-shaped with a rosette of dead leaves at the base.
- Defoliation occurs throughout the growing season resulting in reduction in root size and yield. Older leaves are mostly affected.

Pathogen:

- Conidia are borne singly at the tip of conidiophores.
- They are hyaline, elongate, filiform and multiseptate. Perfect stage is not known.

Mode of spread and survival:

- The pathogen is carried with the seed.
- The chief overwintering inoculum is in infected plant debris, in which mycelium remain viable.
- The fungus can overwinter in debris from diseased plants, in weed hosts and in beet seeds.
- The fungus can survive 12 – 18 months. The conidia are disseminated chiefly by air.
- Insects, splashing water, cultivation tools, workers and irrigation water also spread of the disease. Moist weather is essential for sporulation.

Management:

- Removal and destruction of affected plants and practicing crop rotation are beneficial in controlling the disease.
- Spraying with Copper oxychloride (0.3 %) thrice at an interval of 15 days controls the disease effectively.

2. Powdery mildew

Causal Organism: Erysiphe betae

Economic Importance:

- The disease has been widespread in several Western States since 1974.
- Fungal spores may blow in from overwintering sources.
- Overwintered infected seed beets may also be sources of infections.
- The fungus tolerates a wide range of environmental conditions.

Symptoms:

- Small, discrete, white patches on both leaf surfaces.
- Patches coalesce until white mycelium and spores cover the entire leaf.
- Leaves later become yellow, then purplish brown, and finally necrotic.

Management:

- Foliar sprays of tridimefon (Bayleton) are also used for powdery mildew control.

3. Downy Mildew

Causal Organism: Perenospora schachtti

Symptoms:

- The disease is mostly prevalent during the cooler months.
- Symptoms appear as irregular greasy greyish areas on the leaves.
- Under moist conditions, these areas expand rapidly and a white powdery growth appears on the lower surface of the affected leaves.
- Affected leaf dries and shrivels quickly.
- Flower shoots on infected plants become stunted and distorted.
- The entire inflorescence has a compact appearance and excessive leaf development may give an appearance witches broom.
- The fungus survives on the crop residues in the soil and is also carried by the seed.

Pathogen:

- *Peronospora* produces sporangia abundantly on the cotyledons and is splashed from there to other plants.
- The sporangia germinate by means of a germ tube and not by zoospores.

Management:

- Preventive measures such as good field sanitation, crop rotation and use of resistant cultivars are recommended.
- Seed treatment with Thiram (2.5-3 g/kg of seed) protects the emerging seedlings from the disease attack.
- Spraying with Dithane Z-78 (0.3 %) thrice at an interval of 15 days is also recommended as an effective control measure.

4. Phoma leaf spot and root rot:

Causal Organism: *Phoma betae*

Pleospora boslingii (P.S.)

Economic Importance:
- Phoma blight/ heart rot was observed in 1876 in France.
- It is wide spread in Kashmir valley of India.

Symptoms:
- It attacks all plant parts. Pre-emergence damping-off occurs with heavily infested seed.
- Some emerged seedlings may show brown discoloration in the hypocotyl after infection has occurred.
- Spots on leaves are up to 2 cm in diameter, brown, round to oval, with dark concentric rings near the perimeter.
- Small dark pycnidia are found throughout the spots in concentric rings.
- Older, lower leaves are generally more susceptible than younger leaves, and the leaf spot phase of the disease is generally less destructive than the root rot phase.
- Pycnidia are also found on seed stalks in dark necrotic streaks with grayish centers.
- Symptoms on roots begin near the crown as small, dark, sunken spots that become soft and water-soaked and finally turn dark brown to black with prominent black lines separating the diseased and healthy tissues.
- Older infected tissues become black, dry, shrunken and somewhat spongy.
- Cavities lined with grayish-white mycelium may occur within these spongy tissues.
- Pycnidia are uncommon in root tissue.

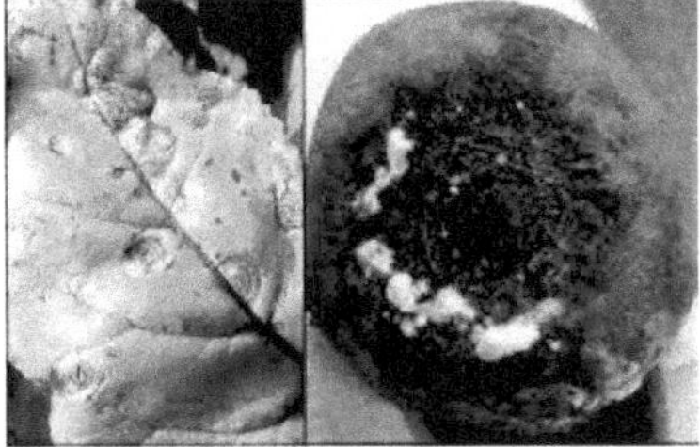

Pathogen:
- It produces elliptic, aseptate, hyaline conidia, usually containing two large guttules.
- The conidia escape as spore tendrils from dark brown, ostiolate, subglobose pycnidia immersed in infected plant tissues.
- It forms pseudothecia containing asci with yellow-green, muriform ascospores.

Disease Cycle:

- It is commonly introduced into fields through seed.
- The pathogen can be spread within a field through water-splashed conidia, surviving in the soil on infested plant debris, and on alternative weed hosts.
- The pathogen can be spread farther distances between fields through windblown ascospores.

Management:
- The use of clean seed will reduce the incidence of the disease.
- Other measures include planting after the soil is warmth, and promoting vigorous plant growth by supplying sufficient boron and other nutrients.
- Also, a four-year crop rotation is important.
- Close topping and harvest wounds should be avoided in roots that are to be stored.
- Creating an environment conducive to wound healing during storage is recommended.
- Corky tissue, which serves as a barrier to microbial invasion, develops in 10 to 14 days at 10°C and a relative humidity of 95% or greater, provided there is adequate air movement.
- Seed treatment fungicides may reduce levels of seed-borne inoculums.
- **Use fungal antagonist *Lactesaria arvalis* as a soil amendment, as seed ball treatment.**

5. Sclerotium root rot

Causal Organism: *Sclerotium rolfsii*

Economic Importance:
- It is also known as Southern blight. It occurs in latter part of the Feb-April.

Symptoms:
- Affected plants show yellowing and wilting of leaves.
- Such plants can be easily pulled out.
- Fleshy roots are partially or completely decayed.
- Numerous, mustard seed sized brown sclerotia are found on the decaying plant parts.

Disease cycle:
- **P.I:** Soilborne.
- **S.I:** Sclerotia.

Management:
- Crop rotation. Hot water treatment at 52°C for 10 min.
- Deep summer ploughing buries sclerotia.

- Infected crop debris should be collected and burnt.
- Soil can be drenched with fungicides.

6. Mosaic

Causal Organism: *Beet mosaic virus*

Symptoms:

- Symptoms appear as conspicuous mottling with chlorotic, zonate ring spots on the leaf surface.
- When these ring spots develop their center are usually green.
- Virus infected plants remain stunted and may lose some leaves.

Mode of spread and survival:

- The disease is normally transmitted and spread by aphids.

Management:

- Destruction of infected plants and controlling the aphid population by spraying
- Malathion (2ml/litre of water) prevents the spread of the disease.

7. Curly-top

Causal Organism: Beet curly top virus (BCTV), Beet severe curly top virus (BSCTV) & Beet mild curly top virus (BMCTV)

Symptoms:

- External symptoms of curly top virus infection may appear in leaves, stems, flowers, fruits, or roots of infected plants.
- Generally, mottling is absent, but infected plant parts may become distorted through curling, twisting, rolling, stunting, etc.
- Leaves become thickened and leathery.
- Curly top virus may impair both yield and quality of the root of an infected plant.
- Some of the most pronounced symptoms resulting from curly top virus attacks are internal and non-observable with the unaided eye.
- Such internal symptoms consist of death of the food conducting vessels, as well as of extreme variations from the normal in numbers and sizes of cells composing the plant tissues.

Pathogen:

- Beet curly top virus particals are 18 – 22 nm in dia.
- The thermal death point of the virus is 80°C and longevity in vitro is 8 days.

Mode of spread and survival:

- The beet **leaf hopper** *(Circulifer tenellus)* is the vector of BCTV.
- The first generation leafhoppers migrate out of the range lands to sugar beet fields, carrying the virus with them.
- Leafhoppers produce several generations each year, which migrate through susceptible crops spreading the virus.
- As the crops mature and dry, the leafhoppers move back into the over wintering areas in search of the winter host.
- Leafhoppers acquire BCTV by feeding on infected host, either the winter host or crop plants.
- Leafhoppers are able to acquire the virus during very short feeding times.
- The leafhopper retains the ability to transmit BCTV for a month or more after acquisition. The vector may maintain the virus during its over-wintering period.

Management:

- Losses can be reduced by the use of resistant varieties; adopting sanitary measures including the eradication of susceptible weeds and susceptible volunteer crop plants from a previous planting; regulating the time of planting in order to avoid the main flights of the beet leafhopper; use of barriers of trap crops and early removal and destruction of infected plants.
- Spraying Malathion (2ml/litre of water) controls the population of beet leaf hoppers.

8. Beet Yellows

Causal Organism: *Beet yellow virus (BYV) and beet mild yellowing virus (BMYV)*

Economic Importance:

- It was first observed in 1934 in Holland.
- **There are two fungi causing yellows together or alone.**
- **BMYV makes the plants more susceptible to Powdery mildew fungal attack.**

Symptoms:

- This disease is transmitted mainly through aphids.

- The important symptoms of the disease include yellow spots on the young leaves in the initial stages of infection.
- As the disease progresses, the leaves exhibit irregular yellow patches alternating with normal green colour of the leaves.
- The older leaves of infected plants become chlorotic, noticeably thickened, leathery and brittle.
- The foliage becomes abnormally red or yellow and often dies.

Pathogen:
- Beet yellow virus (BYV) and beet mild yellowing virus (BMYV) both can occur alone or together to result in yellows.
- Beet mild yellowing virus makes the plants more susceptible to fungal attack i.e. Powdery mildew.

Mode of spread and survival:
- The viruses are spread to healthy plants by aphids.
- Beet yellow virus persists in aphids for few hours, but once infected with beet mild yellowing virus and aphids remains infective for most of its life cycle.
- **The main field vector is *Myzus persicae* but other aphids may spread the viruses, eg. The black bean aphid (*Aphid fabae*) can also spread BYV but not BMYV.**

Management:
- Control measures include removal of infected plants and weeds from the field.
- The disease incidence can be minimised by controlling the population of aphids by spraying Oxydemeton Methyl (Metasystox) 25 EC (2ml/litre of water).

9. Purple Leaf of Beet

Causal Organism: *Tobacco mosaic virus*

Symptoms:
- This viral disease is caused by a strain of tobacco mosaic virus (TMV).
- The infected plants are stunted and leaves have a tendency to stand erect and come closer, unlike the healthy plants where the leaves are broad, long and profuse.
- Leaves of infected plants show an unusual intense purple colour, white the young emerging leaves show it prominently.
- Few leaves develop minute necrotic lesions all over the lamina.

Mode of spread and survival:
- The virus is readily transmissible through sap.

Management:
- Removal and destruction of virus-infected plants and weed hosts helps in minimising disease.

Physiological Disorders:

1. Heart rot or Crown rot:

Symptoms:
- The leaves die in the crown which is covered with small deformed leaves.
- The older leaves wilt and become necrotic.
- The entire crown becomes necrotic and starts to decay.
- In the fleshy root, internal and external black spots of necrotic tissue develop.

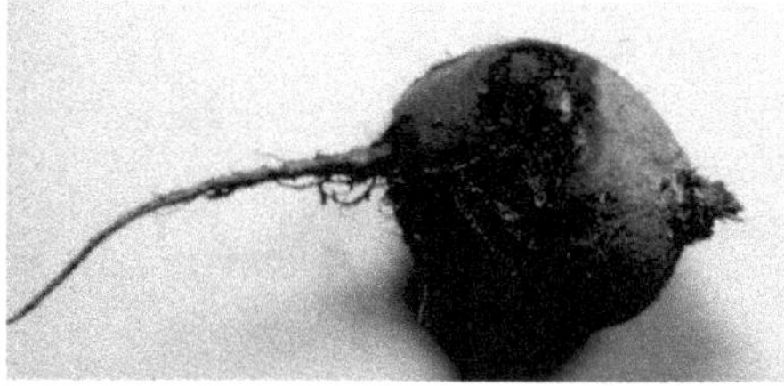

Cause:
- The disorder is caused by boron deficiency.

Management:
- Soil application of borax (10-15 kg/ha) or foliar spray of boric acid (0.2%), 2-3 times at vegetative stage can check it.
- Avoid the sowing of beet in acidic soils. Avoid drought conditions by supplying reduced irrigation.

2. Zoning:

Symptoms:
- In zoning, alternate dark and light coloured rings are formed on the beetroot.

Cause:
- It occurs due to high temperature above 30°C, wide range fluctuations in day and night temperature and irregular supply of moisture during root growth and development.

CARROT

Introduction:

- Carrot (*Daucus carota* L) is one of the principal root vegetables of India.
- It is grown in different parts of the country throughout the year for its roots which are consumed as salad and cooked vegetable and is processed in many forms.
- Originating in central Asia carrots are broadly classified into two groups – Asiatic or tropical type and European or temperate type.
- Asiatic or tropical types are mostly purple or black coloured and set seed in Indian plains.
- European or temperate types are mostly orange coloured due to high carotene content, a precursor of vitamin A and possess light tops, small core and are mostly self coloured having wide range for a carotene, TSS and total sugars (Simon, 1990; Rubatzsky *et al.,* 1999).
- The symptoms and the pathogens associated with diseases will be studied under the present lecture.

Diseases:

S. No.	Disease Name	Causal Organism
Fungal diseases		
1.	Cercospora leaf spot	*Cercospora carotae*
2.	Alternaria leaf blight	*Alternaria dauci*
3.	Powdery mildew	*Erysiphe polygoni*
4.	Downy mildew	*Peronospora trifoliarum*
5.	Watery soft rot	*Sclerotinia sclerotiorum*
6.	Black rot	*Alternaria radicina*
Bacterial diseases		
7.	Bacterial soft rot	*Erwinia carotovora p.v. carotovora* & *Erwinia carotovora p.v.atroseptica*
8.	Bacterial blight	*Xanthomonas campestris pv.carotae*
9.	Yellows	*Phytoplasma*
Physiological Disorders		
10.	Cavity spot	
11.	Carrot splitting	
12.	Forking	

1. Cercospora Leaf Blight

Causal Organsim: *Cercospora carotae*

Symptoms:

- The disease produce severe blighting on carrot leaves and petioles if wet weather is prolonged during the growing season.

- Entire leaves and petioles may die on severely infected plants.
- The symptoms first appear along the margins of the leaves, often causing the leaves to curl.
- Spots inside the leaf edges are small, roughly circular, and tan or gray to brown with a dead center.
- As the lesions increase in number and size, the entire leaflet withers and dies.
- The fungus attacks younger leaves and plants in preference to older ones.
- In heavily infested fields, however, both older and younger leaves are subject to attack.
- The pathogen also produces lesions on the petioles and stems. The lesions may merge and girdle the stems, causing the leaves to die.

Pathogen:
- Conidiophores are in terminating in growth and show scars where conidia attached.
- The conidia are slightly obclavate, hyaline and many celled.

Mode of Spread and Survival:
- The fungus subsists on seed and diseased crop residues.
- Stromatic masses in diseased tissues are the main source of survival from season to season.
- They produce conidia which are transmitted by wind or water.
- The fungus pathogen can grow in the culture at 45°F to 98°F temperatures with the optimum between 66° and 82°F (Chupp and Sherf, 1960).

Management:
- The leaf blight pathogens can survive from one year to the next in infected plant debris.
- Therefore, a two-to three-year rotation is recommended to allow for natural decline in the pathogen population.
- The use of disease-free seed is strongly recommended because the fungus can survive on or in the seed.
- Early applications of Captafol (Foltaf) (0.2%), Copper oxychloride (0.3%), starting at the first sign of infection, effectively control leaf blights on carrots.
- Best control is achieved when fungicides are applied at high pressure and in sufficient water to reach the lower leaves in a dense canopy.

2. Alternaria Blight

Causal Organism: *Alternaria porri* f. sp. *dauci*

Symptoms:

- Alternaria leaf spots first appear at the margin of the leaflets and are dark brown to black and irregular in shape.
- Lesions produced on the petioles and stems are dark brown and often coalesce and girdle the stems.
- As the disease progresses entire leaflets may shrivel and die, appearing scorched.
- Alternaria leaf lesions are generally more prevalent on older foliage and plants than on young foliage.
- The disease spreads rapidly on the older leaves of a maturing crop after the rows have closed.
- This is due in part to poor air circulation among the older lower leaves in the canopy and to the moisture-holding capacity of the dense foliage.

Epidemiology:
- The pathogen requires the presence of moisture for infection. Heavy dews are almost as favorable for infection as are the rains.
- The optimum temperature for growth and infection by Alternaria is 82F (Chupp and Sherf, 1960).

Management:
- The disease can be kept under check if a well-drained soil is selected and suitable crop rotation is adopted.
- Since the fungus can survive in the seed, hot water treatment at 50°C for 15 minutes is recommended.
- Seed treatment with Thiram (3g/kg of seed) before sowing is effective to control the disease.
- Crop rotation and destruction of infected plant material in the field will minimize the disease infection, Fungicidal applications with Foltaf (0.2%), Copper oxychloride (0.3%) satisfactorily controls the disease (Reddy, 2010).

3. Powdery Mildew

Causal Organism: *Erysiphe polygoni*

Symptoms:
- The symptoms appear as white powdery growth on the leaves and petioles causing the leaves to turn brown and wilt.

Management:

- Spraying Bavistin (0.1%) or Benlate (0.1%) at an interval of 8-10 days effectively controls the disease.
- IL76-326 is resistant.

4. Watery soft Rot: *Sclerotinia sclerotiorum*

Economic Importance:

- Sclerotinia rot of carrot, also referred to as watery soft rot or cottony rot was first reported on field carrots in Belgium by M. E. Coemans in 1860, while on stored carrots it was first described by E. Rostrup in 1871 (Mukala, 1957).

Symptoms:

- Carrots are susceptible to this disease, especially late in the season and during storage.
- The disease is present in soil or storage areas and often shows up after the crop has been harvested.
- Symptoms can be identified in the field as characteristic white mould with black sclerotia present on the crown of infected carrots (Kora *et al.,* 2008).
- In storage, a soft, watery rot with white mould and black sclerotia characterizes the disease.

Management:

- Crop rotation, weed control (to improve air circulation), planting on raised beds, winter flooding, rapid cooling prior to storage and meticulous sanitation of all storage components are all necessary to reduce losses from this disease (Weber, 2003).

5. Black Rot

Causal Organism: *Alternaria radicina*

Symptoms:

- This disease can be seed and soil-borne and is characterized by a shiny black decay at the crown area and a greenish-black mould on the taproot.
- The infected tissue is greenish black to jet black due presence of masses of black spores.
- This disease affects the roots in the field well as in storage.

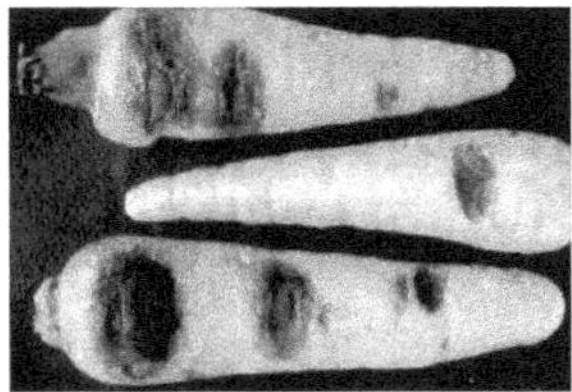

Management:
- Proper field sanitation and practicing rotation helps to keep the disease under control.
- The root surface should kept dry and stored at 0°C with 95 % relative humidity.

6. Bacterial soft Rot

Causal Organism: *Erwinia carotovora p.v. carotovora* and *Erwinia carotovora p.v. atroseptica*

Symptoms:
- Bacterial soft rots of carrots occur only when soil conditions are wet or storage conditions are poor.
- Soft water-soaked, irregular lesions appear on the roots.
- Initially these lesions are superficial but soon spread to cover the inner tissues.
- The foliage may remain green until the disease on the tuber advances considerably.
- The entire plant wilts when complete rotting of the tuber takes place.
- A foul odour is given out from the decayed roots.
- Abundant moisture on the root surface favours disease incidence.

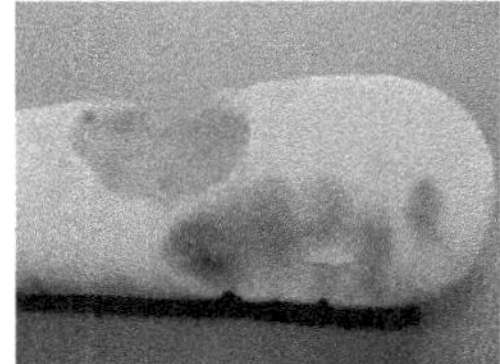

Pathogen:
- It is large, gram negative and motile with large peritrichous flagella.

Mode of Spread and Survival:
- Soil is the principal source of primary inoculum for stored carrots.
- Soil that contains debris from plants that were diseased the previous year is the most important inoculum source.
- The pathogen lives and multiplies within the soil.
- If soft rot occurs on carrot roots in fields, the inoculum source can be traced back to carrot foliage from which it moves directly down to the roots.
- Harvest bruises, freezing injury, fungus invasion and insect wounds offer penetration sites.

Management:
- Planting on raised beds in poorly drained areas may also reduce bacterial infections.
- Careful harvest handling, grading and sanitation are the only ways to reduce the problem.

- The diseased roots should not be stored along with the healthy tubers.
- The root surface should kept dry and stored at 0 C with 95 % relative humidity.
- Dipping in a solution of 1:500 of sodium hypochlorite before storage or transits reduce the disease.
- Spraying fungicide Carbendazim @ 2 g/l of water at an interval of 8–10 days is effective for the management of the disease (Reddy, 2010).

7. Bacterial leaf blight

Causal Organism: *Xanthomonas hortorum* pv. *carotae*

Symptoms:

- The bacterium causes irregular brown spot on leaves, dark brown streaks on petioles and a blighting of floral parts.
- Lesions on foliage begin as small yellow spots.
- Soon the centre of the spots they become dry and brittle with an irregular halo.

Pathogen:

- The bacterium is rod shaped and polar flagellum.

Mode of Spread and Survival:

- The bacterium is borne in and on seed from diseased seed plants.
- They also live in soil.
- Rain or irrigation water splashes bacteria from cotyledons or soil to young seedlings.
- Insects also carry the bacterium mechanically.
- Under rainy warm conditions, epidermis occurs rapidly.

Disease Cycle & Epidemiology:

- The carrot leaf blight pathogens survive on or in the seed and on diseased crop debris in the soil.
- The fungal pathogens produce spores that become airborne and are spread predominantly by wind.
- The bacterial pathogen is spread primarily by wind-driven rain or by irrigation water.
- Moisture is essential for infection by all blight organisms because bacterial cells and fungal spores require surface moisture and warm temperatures to germinate.
- The higher the temperature, the shorter the wet period required for infection.
- When temperatures are warm or when moisture in the form of rain, dew, or irrigation water is persistent, the threat of infection and rapid spread of leaf blight organisms is high.

Management:

- Spraying early with Copper oxychloride 0.25 %.

8. Carrot Yellows

Causal Organism: *Phytoplasma*

Symptoms:

- The affected leaves become yellow accompanied by vein clearing.
- Dormant buds in the crown grow out into chlorotic shoots, which give a withers broom appearance on the top.
- Size and quality of roots are reduced and malformed.
- The internal texture of roots show marked changes causing reduction in value carrots for fresh market as well as for processing.
- Roots of infected plants have a bitter taste with astringent flavour.

Mode of spread and survival:

- The disease is mainly transmitted by the **six-spotted leaf hopper (*Macrosteles divisus*)** although other species may also be involved.

Management:

- Weed control especially of those acting as alternate host eliminates the disease.
- Effective control of aster leaf hopper by spraying with Carbofuran, Acephate (Lancer) and Dimethoate.
- Carbaryl and Parathion (Metacid) reduced leaf hopper number.

Physiological disorders:

1. Cavity spot:

Symptoms:

- This disorder appears as a cavity in the cortex, in most cases the subtending epidermis collapses to from a pitted lesion.

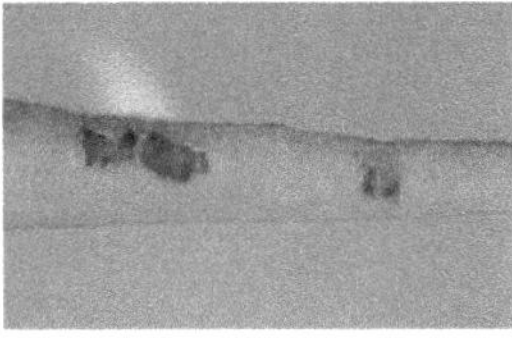

Causes:

- The cavity spot disorder is induced by deficiency of Ca (Maynard *et al.*, 1963).
- This is associated with an increased accumulation of K which leads to a decreased accumulation of Ca.

Management:

- Increase in Ca level in the growing medium leads to significant reduction in the incidence of cavity spot (Bhat, 2016).

2. Carrot splitting:

Symptoms:

- Splitting or cracking of carrot roots is a major problem in many carrot growing areas (Bhat, 2016).
- As clear by its name, roots get splitted making it unfit for market.

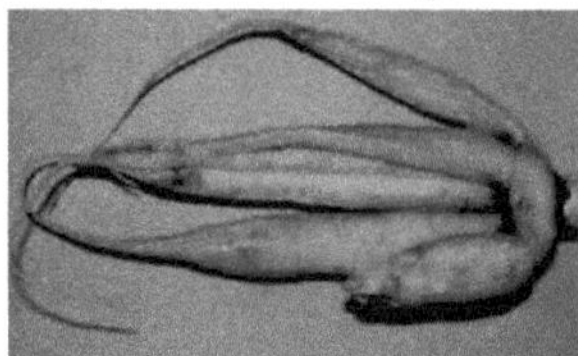

Causes:

- It is reported that this tendency towards is controlled by genetic factors but a number of other factors are also involved.
- Long drought followed by heavy rainfall is major reason for root splitting in carrot.
- In soils with high content of N and chloride, splitting of roots is increased (Boss and Some, 1986).
- High soil concentrations of ammonium compounds caused more serious splitting than by other forms of nitrogen.
- If roots are large, there are chances of splitting as compared to small ones.

Management:

- Follow proper management practices like proper irrigation, right spacing and optimum amount of N application.
- Prefer other forms of N fertilizer source than ammonium compounds.

3. Forking:

Symptoms:

- There is secondary elongating growth in the roots that gives a look of fork like structure to the root.

Causes:

- It occurs in heavy soil due to the soil compactness.
- Un-decomposed organic manure favours elongated root in carrot.

Management:

- It can be corrected by reducing the moisture from the field, by balanced irrigation and also by sowing the carrot in sandy loam or light soil having soils of loose and friable in nature.

References:

Adams, P. B. and Ayres, W. A., (1979). Ecology of *Sclerotinia* species. *Phytopathology,* 69, 896–899.

Ahlawat, Y. S. and Chenulu, V. V., (1984). Radish mosaic-A new disease caused by turnip mosaic in India. *Trop. Agric. (Trinidad).* 61, 188–192.

Ahuja, S., (1983). *Studies on the Variability in Infection of Root Knot Nematode Meloidogyne incognita on Potato* (p. 4). Third Nematology Symposium, Himachal Pradesh Agricultural University, Solan.

Bhat, K. L., (2016). *Physiological disorders of other vegetable crops.* In: Physiological Disorders of Vegetable Crops (p. 92). Daya Publishing House. New Delhi.

Bora, L. C. And Bhattacharyya, A. K., (2000). Integrated management of black rot of cabbage caused by *Xanthomonas campestris* (Pammel) Dowson. *J. Agric. Sci. Soc. NE India,* 13, 229–233.

Boss, T. K. And Some, M. G., (1986). *Vegetable Crops in India.* Naya Prokash, Calcutta, India.

Chupp, C. and Sherf, A. F., (1960). *Vegetables Diseases and Their Control* (p. 693). The Ronald Press Company, New York.

Cook, G. E., Steadman, J. R. and Boosalis, M. G., (1975). Survival of Whetzelinia sclerotiorum and initial infection of dry edible beans in Western Nebraska. *Phytopathology,* 65, 250–255.

Couper, G., (2001). *The Biology, Epidemiology and Control of Sclerotinias clerotiorum on Carrots in North East Scotland.* PhD thesis, University of Aberdeen, Aberdeen, Scotland, UK

Kora, C., McDonald, M. R. and Boland, G. J., (2003). Sclerotinia rot of carrot, an example of phenological adaptation and bicyclic development by *Sclerotinia sclerotiorum. Plant Disease,* 87(5), 456–470.

SWEET POTATO

Introduction:

- Sweet potato (*Ipomoea batatas*) is an herbaceous perennial in the family Convolvulaceae grown for its edible storage roots.
- The sweet potato plant is a branching, creeeping vine with spirally arranged lobed, heart shaped leaves and white or lavender flowers.
- The plant has enlarged roots called tubers which act as an energy store for the plant.
- The tubers can be variable in shape and can be red, yellow, brown, white or purple in color.
- Sweet potato vines can reach 4 m (13 ft) in length and the plant is usually grown as an annual, harvested after one growing season.
- Sweet potatoes may also be referred to as yams or Spanish potatoes and originate from Central America.

- Sweet potato tubers are eaten cooked as a vegetable or may be processed into flour or starch.
- The leaves can be eaten fresh or after cooking.
- The symptoms and the pathogens associated with diseases will be studied under the present lecture.

Diseases:

S. No.	Disease Name	Causal Organism
Fungal diseases		
1.	White rust	*Albugo ipomoe- panduratae*
2.	Fusarium root and stem rot	*Fusarium solani*
3.	Alternaria leaf spot and stem blight	Alternaria spp.
4.	Black rot	*Ceratocystis fimbriata*
5.	Leaf and stem scab	*Sphaceloma batatas*
Bacterial diseases		
6.	Bacterial soft rot	*Erwinia chrysanthemi*
7.	Bacterial wilt	*Ralstonia solanacearum*
8.	Soft rot or pox	*Streptomyces ipomoea*
Viral diseases		
9.	Sweet potato virus disease	*Sweet potato feathery mottle virus (SPFMV)* and *Sweet potato chlorotic stunt virus (SPCSV)*
Physiological Disorders		
10.	Chilling Injury	

1. Alternaria leaf spot & Leaf and stem blight

Causal Organism: *Alternaria bataticola*

Economic importance:

- Leaf spot and stem blight of sweet potato caused by *Alternaria bataticola* is foliage and stem disease that is very important in Eastern and Central Africa and Brazil.
- Although no literature has been found on the losses caused by this disease, it has been known to cause important damage due to plant death.

Symptoms:

- Brown lesions on leaves with concentric rings resembling a target.
- Lesions are usually restricted to the older leaves and may be surrounded by a yellow halo.
- Small gray-black oval lesions with lighter centers may occur on stems and leaf petioles and occasionally on leaves.
- Stem and petiole lesions enlarge and often coalesce resulting in girdling of the stem.
- Defoliation may occur (Walker, 1952).

Pathogen:

- The mycelium of pathogen is fuscous brown to almost hyaline, septate, and branched.
- Colonies on agar are gray- green. Conidiophores are single or in bundles, unbranched, erect or slightly curved, 2-7 septate, pale brown to fuscous-brown, 47-80x7mm.
- Conidia are solitary, elongate, obclavate muriform, transversely 5-12 septate, longitudinally 0-8 septate, pale to fuscous-brown, smooth walled, conidium body.
- The conidial beak is long, filiform, colourless to pale brown, septate, often branched once and occasionally up to three times and measures 16-128 x 3-6mm.

Mode of spread and survival:

- The fungus survives in soil and plant debris.
- The air-borne conidia are spread through infected planting material by wind, splashing rain, and water.
- High relative humidity or free water is necessary for infection and sporulation, conditions common in tropical regions due to continuous rain.

Management:

- Destroy all sweet potato crop residue immediately following harvest.
- Plant resistant or tolerant sweet potato varieties where available.
- Plant only disease-free seed material.
- It has been suggested that red-skinned are more resistant than white-skinned varieties.
- Use mancozeb to control *Alternaria* spp. in other crops and can probably be effective against pathogen.

2. Black rot

Causal Organism: *Ceratocystis fimbriata*

Symptoms:

- Stunted plants; wilting plants; yellowing plants; dropping leaves; plant death; circular brown-black patches of rot on tubers.

Management:

- Only disease-free seed material should be planted.
- Sweet potato should not be planted in sites where sweet potato has been grown during the previous 3-4 years.
- Transplant material should be collected from plant by making cuts above-ground.
- Seed material should be treated with an appropriate fungicide prior to planting.

3. Fusarium root and stem rot

Causal Organism: *Fusarium solani*

Symptoms:

- Swollen and distorted base of stems; deep, dark rot extending deep into tuber and forming elliptical cavities; growth of white mould.

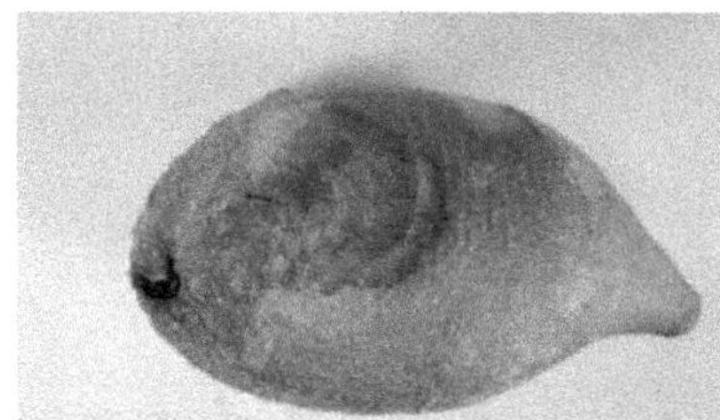

Management:

- Disease is generally not a problem if good sanitation is implemented.
- Select only disease-free roots for seed.
- Use cut transplants rather than slips.
- Practice crop rotation.
- Treat seed roots with an appropriate fungicide prior to planting.

4. Leaf and stem scab

Causal Organism: *Sphaceloma batatas*

Symptoms:

- Small brown lesions on leaf veins which become corky in texture and cause veins to shrink which in turn causes leaves to curl.
- Lesions on stem are slightly raised and have purple to brown centers with light brown margins.
- Scabby lesions form on stems when lesions coalesce.

 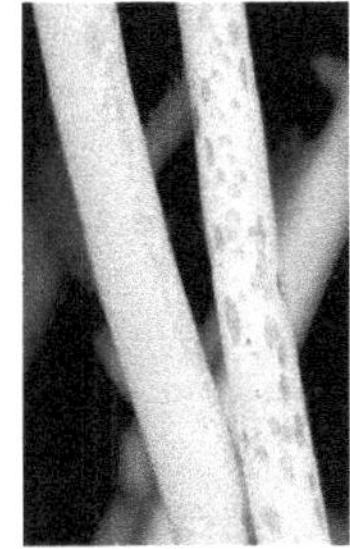 

Pathogen:
- The ascomata formed below the epidermis are dark brown to black and solitary to aggregate.
- They measure up to 150 μm in diameter, composed of pseudo parenchymatic tissues, and contain numerous monoascus locules.
- The asci are globose or ovoid, 8-spored, thick walled and measure 18-25 x 12-25 μm.
- The ascospores are hyaline, smooth, transversely 1-3 septate, constricted at the midseptum, and measure 12-18 x 4.5 μm.
- The acervulus is colourless, 12-16 μm in diameter.
- The conidiophores are short, simple to rarely branched and measure 10 x 3 μm; the conidia are hyaline, smooth, aseptate, oblong, and measure 4-9 x 2.5-3.5 μm.

Disease cycle & Epidemiology:
- The disease is transmitted by infected cuttings and through rain splash that carries masses of spores from infected to healthy plant parts of the same plant or to neighbouring plants.
- The disease is widespread in places with a high incidence of rain, mist and dew or in places where sprinkle irrigation is used.
- Under controlled conditions, a temperature range between 25 and 30°C is optimal for fungal growth.
- The fungus remains from one season to the next in crop refuse in the form of ascomata.
- When the temperature rises and there is enough moisture, the ascomata release asci and ascospores, which are the structures that initiate infection of young leaves and stems.
- Once in the plant tissue, the fungus grows and produces conidia, which are the secondary inoculum that spreads the disease in a field.

Management:
- Avoid the use of overhead irrigation.
- Rotate sweet potato with other crops.
- Use only disease-free planting material.
- Destroy sweet potato crop residue immediately after harvest.
- Application of appropriate fungicides can help to control the disease.
- Good control of the disease can be achieved with benomyl and chlorothalonil where licensed for use.
- The cultivars **Centennial** and **Beerwah Gold** were found highly resistant and moderately resistant, respectively.

- Philippine cultivars V2-1, V2-3 and V2-30 and a number of AVRDC cultivars were also found to be highly resistant in Taiwan.
- It has been found that varieties with a thicker cuticle and fewer stomata are more resistant to fungus invasion.

5. White rust

Causal Organism: *Albugo ipomoea-panduratae*

Economic importance:

- White rust is a minor disease of sweet potato, present only on certain cultivars.
- There are no records about the importance of the disease on yield.

Symptoms:

- The most obvious symptom is the presence of chlorotic or yellowish blotches, initially roundish to angular where they are limited by veins, on the upper surface of leaves.
- On the lower surface, small pustules develop which later open and expose whitish masses of sporangial pustules.
- After sporulation, the infected tissue dies, forming irregular-shaped brown lesions.
- In some cultivars or growing conditions, infection induces the development of galls of raised, thickened tissue.
- Galls may develop on leaves, petioles, stems and flowers.
- When pustules erupt, the galls become covered in the white spores.
- Diseased plants can also present general distortion, defoliation and flower abortion.
- Distortion may occur where galls form on any part of the stem.
- The disease may cause twining while twining species may assume an upright habit.
- In some very sensitive cultivars, symptoms resembling witches' broom, with shortening of internodes and bunchy growth habit, have been observed.

Pathogen:

- The mycelium is intracellular with typical knob-like haustoria.
- The sori are amphigenous or caulicolous, white or light yellow, prominent, superficial, measure 0.5-2.0 mm, rounded, often confluent and frequently producing marked distortion of the host.
- The sporangiophores are hyaline, club shaped, unequally curved at the base and measure 15 x 30 μm.
- The sporangia are produced in chains.

- They are short, cylindrical, with more rounded terminal, hyaline, and smooth; the membrane with an equatorial thickening, is usually very pronounced, measuring 14-20 x 12-18 µm.
- The oosporic sori are separated from the sporangial caulicolous, rarely on the petioles, measure 1-2 x 5-6 cm or even more causing marked distortion of the host.
- The oospores are light yellowish brown, 25-55 µm in size, and are epispore papillate or with irregular, more or less curved ridges.

Disease cycle and Epidemiology:

- During the growing season, the disease is spread by air borne sporangia after landing on the plant surface.
- Germination can be direct such that the sporangia produce an infecting hypha which penetrates the plant tissue, develops intercellulary and sends round haustoria inside the cells.
- There is indirect germination when the sporangium liberates biflagellate zoospores that swim in a film of water and invade the cells.
- Oospores overwinter in crop refuse (leaves and stems) in the field and are responsible for primary infection of sweet potato plants the following growing season.
- There is no information about the environmental factors that favour white rust development in sweet potato.
- The only factor mentioned was rainfall. In other Oomycetes, the free water on plant surfaces determines the way in which the sporangia will germinate.
- Hence, with direct germination one sporangium is one infection point but if germination is through indirect germination, each zoospore is one infection point and every sporangium contains several zoospores.
- In the case of *A. ipomoeae-panduratae,* germination directly or indirectly occurs optimally at 12-18°C.
- Infection occurs through stomata during periods of rain and cool temperatures.

Management:

- No control methods are mentioned in the literature, apparently because infections are not serious enough.
- In extreme cases copper fungicides can be used, as for other fungi of the same group.

6. Bacterial soft rot

Causal Organism: *Erwinia chrysanthemi*

Symptoms:

- Brown to black water-soaked lesions on stems and petioles which expand rapidly and and cause large areas of soft rot on the stem.
- Stem may collapse causing several vines to wilt; entire plant may die.
- Storage roots may develop areas of soft rot which is initially colourless, but eventually turns brown with a black margin.

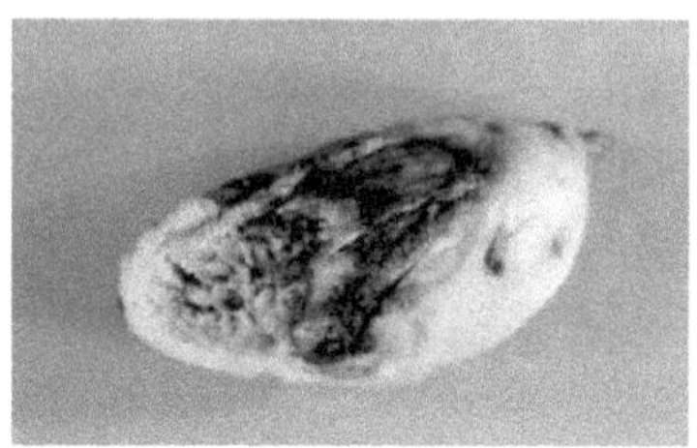

Management:

- Avoid wounding storage roots at all stages of growth.
- Plant only disease-free seed material.
- Discard any stored roots which become infected with the disease.
- Vines for transplanting should be cut above the soil surface.
- Plant sweet potato varieties which are resistant to the disease.

7. Bacterial wilt

Causal Organism: *Ralstonia solanacearum*

Symptoms:

- New sprouts wilting and have water-soaked bases which turn yellow-brown to dark brown in colour.
- Vascular system of the sprouts is discoloured brown.
- Infection of healthy transplants causes the lower portions of the stems to become water-soaked and turn a similar colour to infected sprouts.
- Yellow-brown streaks may develop inside storage roots and, if infection is severe, gray-brown water-soaked lesions may be present on the root surface.

Management:

- Quarantine procedures have been put in place in regions of China where the disease is severe.
- Only disease-free storage roots should be used for planting and planting should only be done in sites free of the disease.
- Rotating sweet potato with a flood crop such as paddy rice or a non-host such as corn or wheat can be beneficial.
- Growing sweet potato during cooler periods of the year allows some avoidance of the disease.

8. Pox

Causal Organism: *Streptomyces ipomoea*

Symptoms:

- Poor growth of plants.
- Reduced yield.
- Circular dark brown, corky lesions on tubers which are V-shaped in cross section.
- Cracked and distorted tubers which resemble dumbbells.
- Rotting of feeder roots.

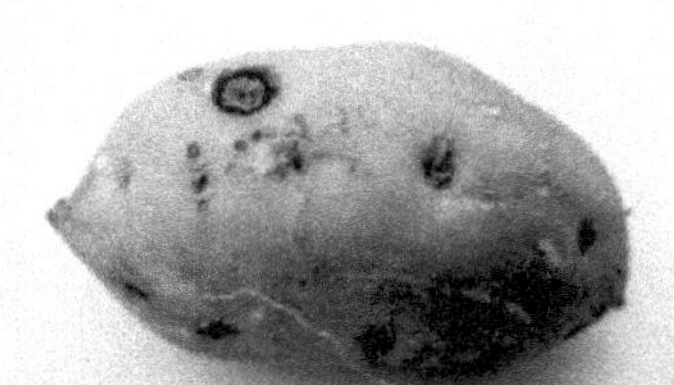

Management:

- The most effective method of controlling the disease is through the use of resistant varieties of sweet potato.
- If resistant varieties are not being used then the soil should be maintained at a low p^H which is unfavourable to the pathogen.
- Sweet potato should be rotated with other crops which are non-hosts to prevent build up of the pathogen in the soil.
- Fumigation of the soil prior to planting can be an effective method of reducing the severity of the disease.

9. Sweet potato virus disease (SPVD)

Causal Organism: *Sweet potato feathery mottle virus (SPFMV) and Sweet potato chlorotic stunt virus (SPCSV)*

Symptoms:

- Sweet potato virus disease is a disease complex caused by two viruses; sweet potato chlorotic stunt virus (SPCSV) and sweet potato feathery mottle virus (SPFMV).
- The symptoms are severe stunting of infected plants, stunting, distorted and chlorotic mottle or vein clearing of the leaves.
- It is confirmed that SPCSV enhances the accumulation of SPFMV.
- The symptom caused by SPCSV alone is negligible.
- Whereas symptoms caused by SPFMV is localized, mild and often asymptomatic and won't cause significant damage to the plant.
- Common symptoms include appearance of feathery, purple patterns on the leaves.

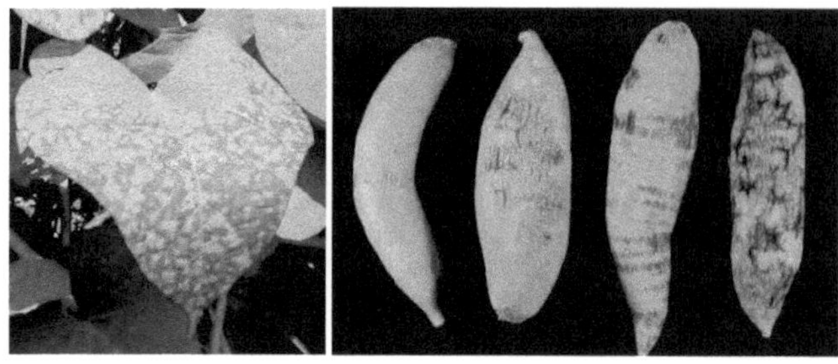

Mode of spread and survival:

- It is estimated that SPVD causes yield loss up to 80-90%.
- The disease was first reported in 1939 from eastern Belgian Congo (present Democratic Republic of Congo).
- SPCSV is crinivirus of Closteroviridae and SPFMV is potyvirus belong to Potyviridae.
- SPFMV is transmitted by a wide range of aphid species.
- **SPCSV is transmitted by white flies (*Bemisia tabaci*).**

Management:

- Use healthy cuttings for planting.
- Remove the infected plants and burn them.
- Follow crop rotation.
- Spray suitable insecticides to control aphids and white flies.

Physiological Disorder:

1. Chilling injury:

- Sweet potato roots are very sensitive to chilling injury at temperatures of 12.5°C (55°F) or below.
- Symptoms of chilling injury include fungal decay, internal pulp browning, and root shriveling.
- Chilled roots that have been cooked can have "hardcore" defect and a darker colour than non-chilled roots.

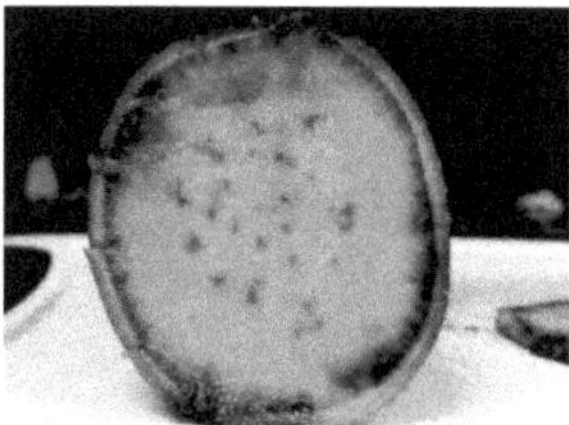

References:

Walker, J.C. 1952. *Diseases of vegetable crops,* 1st edn. MacGraw-Hill, New York.

COLOCASIA

Introduction:

- Taro (*Colocasia esculenta*) a clonally propagated aroid, is grown largely in humid tropical areas of the world.
- The crop, first domesticated in South-east Asia, has continued to spread throughout the world and is now an important crop in Asia, the Pacific, Africa and the Caribbean (Ravi *et al.,* 2009).
- It is the most important edible species of the monocotyledonous family Araceae.
- Almost all parts of a taro plant are utilized.
- Corms are baked, roasted, or boiled as a source of carbohydrates, leaves are frequently consumed as a vegetable representing an important source of vitamins, and even petioles and flowers are consumed in certain parts of the world.
- Worldwide, taro ranks fourteenth among staple vegetable crops.
- Most of the global taro production comes from developing countries, characterized by smallholder production systems relying on minimum external resource inputs.
- This makes this food crop very important for food security, especially among subsistence farmers in developing countries.
- Diseases of colocasia significantly reduce the number of functional leaves and have led to a yield reduction of about 50% worldwide (Jackson, 1999).
- This crop is attacked by bacteria, fungus, virus, nematode, etc. So it is important to know about common diseases of elephant foot yam and their management.

Diseases:

S. No.	Disease Name	Causal Organism
Fungal diseases		
1.	Phytophthora leaf blight	*Phytophthora colocasiae*
2.	Pythium root rot	*Pythium* sp.
Physiological Disorders		
3.	Metsubre	

1. Leaf blight

Causal Organism: *Phytophthora colocasiae*

Symptoms:

- *Phytophthora colocasiae*, foliar oomyceteous diseases agent, is a major limiting factor in taro production worldwide (Brooks, 2008).
- Reduction in corm yield may be up to 50% due to this disease.
- In its early stages, Phytophthora leaf blight occurs as small dark brown or purple lesions with amber ooze in the center.
- Older lesions are zonate with white fuzz of sporangia on the outer edge (Misra *et al.,* 2008).

Management:

- Hot Water Disinfestations.
- Fallows for Disease Suppression.
- Isolate plantings (e.g., three small, separate patches instead of one large patch).
- Prepare the soil well and amend it before planting if calcium, magnesium, or phosphorus is needed.
- Monitor plant calcium levels by leaf analysis, and maintain calcium at recommended concentrations to prevent development of *Pythium* corm rot. Add lime material before planting to raise soil pH to 6.0-6.8 (Narula and Mehrotra, 1987).
- Rotate taro with other crops.
- Incorporate compost and apply surface mulch.
- Rogue (kill and remove) diseased plants, taking them far from the planting area and destroying them by burying, burning (if allowed), or composting.

2. Root rot

Causal Organism: *Pythium myriotylum*

Symptoms:

- The pathogen cause stunting.
- Infected taro plants have a fringe of roots at the base of the petioles.
- They are easy to pull out or knock over and usually smell bad.
- Corm rots may be present, but this is a late symptom.

Management:

- The severity of the disease may be reduced by soil drenching with fungicide Captan @ 0.2%.

- Seed should be selected carefully to avoid those showing any disease symptoms.
- The selected seed should be dipped into Captan suspension to provide them protection for a few days after planting (Trujillo, 1967).
- Summer deep plowing, soil solarization, and crop rotation practices must be followed to reduce the infection.

Physiological Disorder:
- The plant requires all essential nutrients in balanced proportion, and deviation from this may result in physiological disorders.
- This may be due to deficiency or toxicity of nutrients.

1. Metsubre:

Symptoms:
- Effected corms have smooth or concave top, slightly brownish in colour and are of varying size (Bhat, 2016).

Cause:
- It is a nutritional disorder of colocasia and is supposed to be due to calcium deficiency.

Management:
- The Application of calcium will control this problem.
- Balanced use of fertilizer will also helpful.

References:

Bhat, K. L., (2016). *Physiological Disorders of Vegetable Crops* (p. 258). Daya Publishing house, New Delhi. Brooks, F. E., (2008). Detached-leaf bioass.

Brooks, F. E., (2008). Detached-leaf bioassay for evaluating taro resistance to *Phytophthora colocasiae. Plant Disease*, 92, 126–131.

Jackson, G. V. H., (1999). Taro leaf blight. Published by the plant protection service of the secretariat of the pacific community. *Pest Advisory Leaflet.,* 3, 2.

Misra, R. S., Sharma, K and Mishra, A. K., (2008). Phytophthora leaf blight of taro (*Colocasia esculenta*): A review. *The Asian and Australian Journal of Plant Science and Biotechnology,* 2(2), 55–63.

Narula, K. L. and Mehrotra, R. S., (1987). Bio-control potential of phytophthora leaf blight of colocasia by phyllosphere microflora. *Indian Phytopath.,* 40, 384–389.

Opara, E., Theresa, C. N. and Isaiah, C., (2013). Potency of some plant extracts and pesticides on bacterial leaf blight disease of cocoyam (*Colocasia esculanta)* in Umudike, South eastern Nigeria. *Greener J. of Agricultural Sciences,* 3(5), 312– 319.

Ravi, V., Ravindran, C. S. and Suja, G., (2009). Growth and productivity of elephant foot yam (*Amorphophallus paeonifolius*) (Dennst. Nicolson): *An overview. J. Root Crops.,* 35, 131–142.

Trujillo, E. E., (1967). *Diseases of genus colocasia in the Pacific area and their control.* In: Proceedings of the International Symposium on Tropical Root Crops (Vol. 2, pp. 13–19). University of West Indies, St. Angustine, Trinidad.

<h1 style="text-align:center">MORINGA</h1>

Introduction:

- The mineral packed, vitamin rich, nutritious vegetable called the Miracle tree or drumstick or horse radish tree or West Indian Ben is botanically *Moringa oleifera*.
- This is the most economically important species among the 12 species that belongs to the family Moringaceae.
- The name drumstick derives from the shape of the pod, resembling the slender and curved stick used for beating the drum.
- Probably the name radish tree originates from the pendulous, slender and thin shape of the immature fruits of the tree resembling very much the siliqua of the radish.
- India is the prime producer of Drumstick with an annual production of 2.2 to 2.4 million tonnes of tender fruits from an area of 43,600 ha leading to the productivity of around 50 tonnes per ha (Robiansyah *et al.,* 2014; Sharma *et al.,* 2011).
- Among the different states, Andhra Pradesh leads in both area and production followed by Karnataka and Tamil Nadu. Tamil Nadu is the pioneering state as it has varied genotypes from diversified geographical areas.
- Moringa is resistant to most pests and diseases. But different minor diseases and many pests are recorded from various moringa growing countries.
- Root rot caused by *Diplodia* sp., twig canker caused by *Fusarium pallidoroseum,* and fruit rot caused by *Cochliobolus hawaiiensis* are some of the reported diseases (Patricio and Palada, 2017; Carbungco *et al.,* 2017; Rajangam *et al.,* 2001).

Diseases:

S. No.	Disease Name	Causal Organism
Fungal diseases		
1.	Damping off	*Pythium aphanidermatum, Rhizoctonia solani*
2.	Twig canker	*Fusarium pallidoroseum*

1. Damping off

Causal Organism: *Pythium aphanidermatum, Rhizoctonia solani*

Economic Importance:

- Disease of nursery beds and young seedlings resulting in reduced seed germination and poor stand of seedlings.
- Very high seedling mortality of 25-75%.

Symptoms:

- **Pre-emergence damping off**: Seedlings disintegrate before they come out of soil surface leading to poor seed germination.

- **Post-emergence damping off** is characterized by development of disease after seedlings have emerged out of soil but before the stems are lignified.
- Water soaked lesion formation at collar region.
- Infected areas turn brown and rot.
- Plants shrivel and collapse as a result of softening of tissues.
- In *Rhizoctonia solani* attack infected stems become hard, thin (**wire stem** symptoms) and infected seedlings topple.
- Disease appears in patches both in nursery and field beds.

Mode of spread and survival:
- **Primary:** Oospores in soil in case of *Pythium.* Sclerotia in soil in case of *Rhizoctonia.*
- **Secondary:** Zoospores through irrigation water in case of Pythium. Mycelial growth in soil and sclerotia through irrigation water in case of *Rhizoctonia.*

Favourable conditions:

For Pythium
- Heavy rainfall
- Excessive and frequent irrigation
- Poorly drained soil and close spacing and
- High soil moisture with temperature around 25-30°C favours the disease development.

For Rhizoctonia
- High soil moisture with temperature around 30–35°C.

Management:
- Seedlings should be raised in well drained nursery area.
- Uproot the diseased seedlings and burn.
- Seed treatment with captan @ 4g/kg seed or chlorothalonil @ 2g/kg seed (*R. solani*).
- Drench the base of stem with COC @ 0.25% or metalaxyl @ 0.1% or Bordeaux mixture @ 1.2%.

2. Twig canker

Causal Organism: *Fusarium pallidoroseum*

Disease symptoms:
- The first symptom of the disease is clearing of the veinlets and chlorosis of the leaves.
- The younger leaves may die in succession and the entire may wilt and die in a course of few days.
- Soon the petiole and the leaves droop and wilt.
- In young plants, symptom consists of clearing of veinlet and dropping of petioles.

- The symptoms continue in subsequent leaves.
- At later stage, browning of vascular system occurs. Plants become stunted and die.

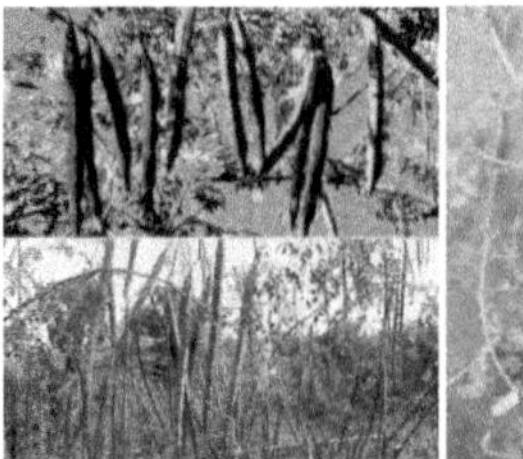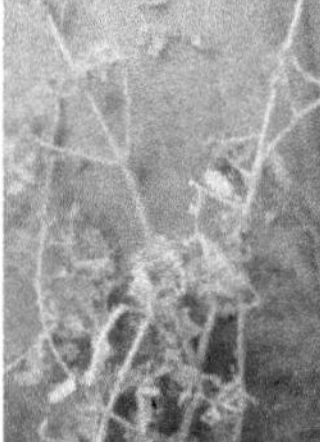

Mode of spread and survival:
- Soil and implements.

Favourable conditions:
- Relatively high soil moisture and soil temperature.

Management:
- The use of varieties adapted to the area and site selection is one of the best measures to avoid incidence of canker.
- Pathogen's main entry is through wounds thus, avoid all unnecessary bark wounds.
- If a callus formed around a canker, refrain from cutting into the infected area to avoid further fungal activity and damage.

References:

Anwar, F., Latif, S., Ashraf, M., and Gilani, A.H. (2007). *Moringa oleifera*: a food plant with multiple medicinal uses. *Phytother Res.* 21 (1), 17–25. PubMed http://dx.doi.org/10.1002/ptr.2023

Butani, D.K., and Verma, S. (1981). Insect pests of vegetables and their control-drumsticks. *Pesticides.* 15 (10), 29–32.

Butani, D.K., and Verma, S. (1984). *Insects in Vegetables* (Delhi, India: Periodical Expert Book Agency), pp.356.

Carbungco, E.S., Pedroche, N.B., Panes, V.A., and De la Cruz, T.E. (2017). Identification and characterization of endophytic fungi associated with the leaves of *Moringa oleifera Lam. Acta Hortic.* 1158, 373–380 10.17660/ActaHortic.2017.1158.42.

LEAFY VEGETABLES

Introduction:
- This group of vegetables includes sorrel, spinach, lettuce, amaranth, fenugreek and basella.
- Leafy vegetables also referred to as greens or potherbs, are popular around the world, especially in Asia.
- They are quick growing crops that are harvested 4-6 weeks after sowing.
- These vegetables are very perishable and are therefore grown in peri-urban areas.

- Leafy vegetables are rich source of protein, vitamins A and C; and minerals like iron, calcium and phosphorous.
- These vegetables provide roughage and have an important place in balanced diet.
- Dieticians recommend daily consumption of at least 116g of leafy vegetables in a balanced diet (Mehrotra and Narain, 1969).

Diseases:

S. No.	Disease Name	Causal Organism
Fungal diseases		
1.	White rust	*Albugo occidentalis*
2.	Downy mildew	*Peronospora effuse, Bremia lactucae*
3.	Powdery mildew	*Leveillula taurica , Erysiphe cichoracearum*
4.	Damping off	*Fusarium* sp., *Pythium* sp., *Rhizoctonia* sp.
5.	Anthracnose	*Colletotrichum dematium, Microdochium panattonianum*
6.	Cercospora leaf spot	*Cercospora beticola, Cercospora longissima*
7.	Septoria leaf spot	*Septoria lactucae*
8.	Stemphylium leaf spot	*Stemphylium botryosum*
9.	Phyllosticta leaf spot	*Phyllosticta spinacea*
10.	Wilt	*F. oxysporum* f. sp. *lactucae, F. oxysporum* f. sp. *spinaciae*
11.	Rust	*Puccinia aristidae, Puccinia dioicae*
Bacterial diseases		
12.	Bacterial leaf spot and head rot	*Xanthomonas campestris* pv. *Vitians*
13.	Bacterial soft rot	*Erwinia carotovora* sub sp. *Carotovora, Pseudomonas marginalis* pv. *marginalis*
Viral diseases		
14.	Mosaic	*Lettuce Mosaic Virus*
Physiological Disorders		
15.	Tip Burn	
16.	Russet Sprouting	
17.	Pink Rib	
18.	Brown Stain	

Diseases:

1. Damping off

Causal Organism: *Fusarium* sp., *Pythium* sp., *Rhizoctonia* sp.

Symptoms:

- Pathogens associated with damping-off are soil borne.

- The disease is more serious in warm and wet soils resulting in both pre- and post-emergence death of seedlings.
- Pre emergence damping-off results in a brown, gelatinous rotting within the seed coat.
- Radicles and cotyledons may become brown and soft after germination but fail to emerge.
- In post emergence damping-off, water soaked lesions appear on hypocotyls and roots resulting in collapse of seedlings.

Management:
- Sterilize the soil with 1.0-1.5 percent solution of Formalin.
- Soak seed in hot water at 50°C for 25 minutes followed by seed treatment with one per cent sodium hypochloride solution for 10 minutes.
- Before sowing, treat the seed with Captan or Thiram @ 2-3 g per kg of seed.
- Drench the soil with 0.2 percent solution of Captan or Thiram.
- Follow crop rotation and avoid planting in sick soils.

2. White rust

Causal Organism: *Albugo occidentalis*

Symptoms:
- It is a major foliar disease of spinach.
- Symptoms appear as small chlorotic areas on upper surface of leaves.
- As the disease progresses, small white and shiny blister like pustules appear on lower side of leaves.
- Severely affected leaves give blighted appearance.

Etiology:
- The pathogen survives in crop debris in the form of resting spores.

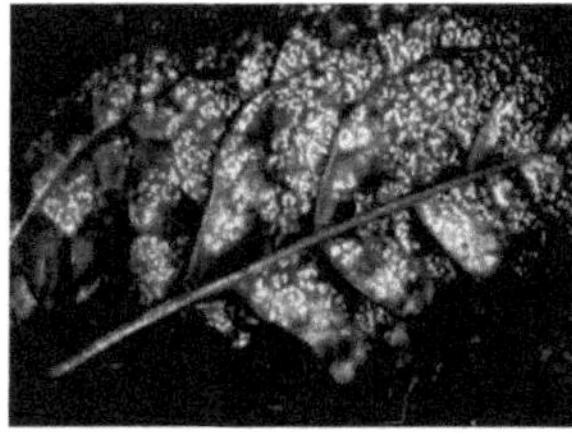

Management:
- Grow resistant varieties and follow long crop rotations.
- Sow the crop in lines and avoid flooding of fields.
- Spray the crop with Ridomil MZ @ 2 g per litre of water.

3. Downy mildew

Causal Organism: *Peronospora effusa*

Symptoms:

- It is one of the important diseases of spinach and appears in cool and moist weather.
- The symptoms first appear as yellowish, irregular spots on upper surface of leaves.
- These lesions enlarge in size and coalesce.
- Greyish downy growth of the pathogen consisting of sporangiophores and sporangia appear on lower surface of leaves.
- Affected leaves show curling and distortions.

Etiology:

- The pathogen is seed borne and also survives as oospores on diseased plant debris.

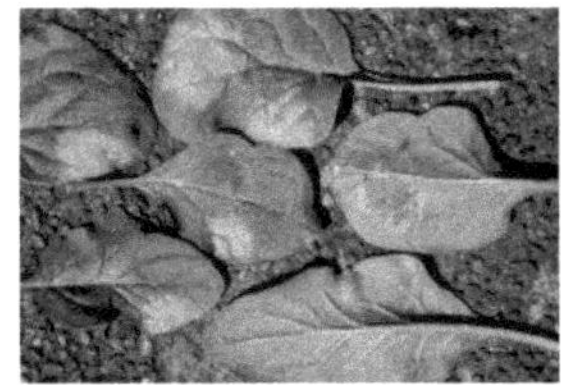 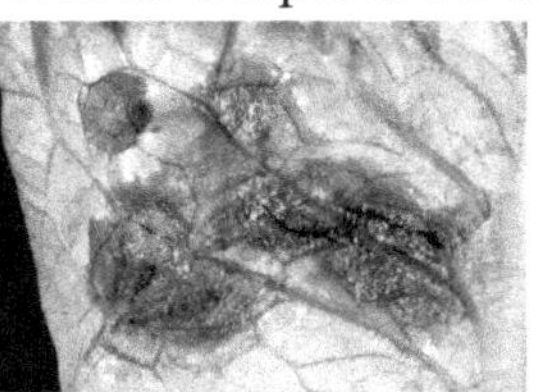

- Downy mildew of lettuce is a disease caused by a fungus-like Oomycete (*Bremia lactucae*) organism, producing yellow patches on upper leaf surfaces, often angular because they are limited by the veins and fuzzy white mould on the corresponding underside.
- These patches turn brown as the leaf tissue dies.
- It affects seedlings and mature plants.

Management:

- Use disease free seed, destroy the diseased plant debris and follow crop rotation.
- Grow resistant varieties.
- Spray the crop with Mancozeb (Indofil M-45) @ 2 g per litre of water or Fosetyl Al (Alliete) @ 2-3 kg per hectare.

4. Cercospora leaf spot

Causal Organism: *Cercospora beticola*

Symptoms:

- It is an important disease of spinach beet.
- Symptoms appear as small, brown lesions on leaves.
- Under favourably environmental conditions, the lesions enlarge in size and coalesce and may extend up to petioles.
- The pathogen survives on diseased plant debris, which serves as a primary source of inoculum.
- On lettuce, leaf spots tan to brown, circular or oval, up to 1 cm diameter, with small (0.5-1 mm) whitish centres, sometimes with yellow halos, and joining together to cover large areas of the leaf.
- The older leaves are infected first.

Disease cycle & Epidemiology:

- Spread is by spores produced on both sides of the leaf spots, splashed by rain, and blown in wind-driven rain. Survival is in crop debris, and also on weeds.
- High temperatures (25-35°C) and high humidity or rain favour outbreaks of the disease.

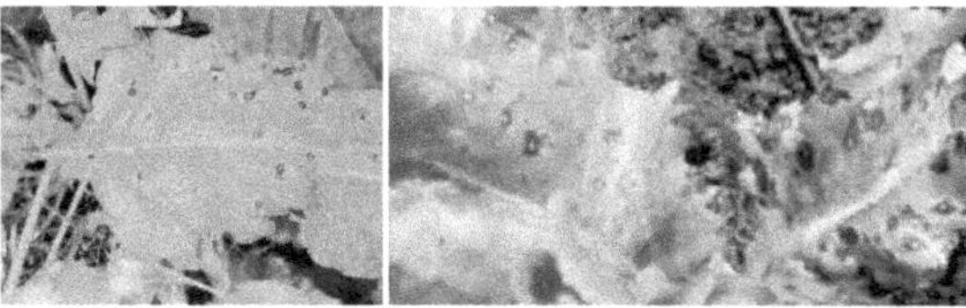

Management:
- Grow resistant varieties.
- Spray the crop with Blitox @ 0.2 percent. If required, repeat the spray after fifteen days.

5. Wilt

Causal Organism: *F. oxysporum* f. sp. *lactucae, F. oxysporum* f. sp. *spinaciae*

Economic Importance:
- Reported in Europe (Italy) in 2002, this seed and soil-borne disease was first confirmed in the UK (Lancashire) and Ireland in summer 2017, where it caused serious losses in several glasshouse crops.

Symptoms:
- Infection in seedlings causes wilt, and in older plants it causes leaves to yellow, wilt and turns brown.
- The vascular system in the stem turns reddish-brown.
- Plants are usually stunted and may fail to heart.

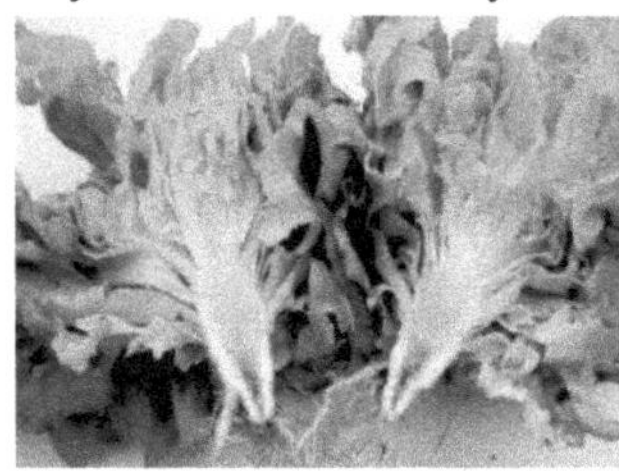

Management:
- Avoid planting lettuce in soils known to be infested with FOL, or plant lettuce in these locations only in the winter when symptoms are likely to be less severe.
- If available, plant tolerant or resistant varieties. Partial resistance to race 4 is available in some outdoor butterhead, Lolla Bionda, Lolla Rossa, Multileaf, Oakleaf, Romaine, Batavian and Crunchy types.
- Resistant butterhead types for protected cropping are not yet commercially available although on-farm testing of promising new varieties is underway.
- Note that infection can still occur in hydroponic crops, but disinfestation between crops is generally easier than for soil-grown crops.
- Crop rotation with non-hosts (e.g. Pak Choi) or leaving the soil fallow will help reduce build-up of FOL race 4 in soil.

- Plant disease-resistant spinach varieties such as Jade, St. Helens, Chinook II, and Spookum. The plants may still be affected but are less susceptible to fusarium spinach decline.

6. Anthracnose

Causal Organism: *Colletotrichum dematium, Microdochium panattonianum*

Disease symptoms:
- **In initial stage:** Small, circular, water - soaked lesions on both young and old leaves.
- **In late stage:** Lesion turns brown to brownish in color, and become thin and papery. Tiny black fruiting bodies (acervuli) form profusely in diseased tissue and are a characteristic feature of the disease.
- **Host range:** Cowpea *(Vigna unguiculata),* bean *(Phaseolus vulgaris)* and betel vine *(Piper* sp)

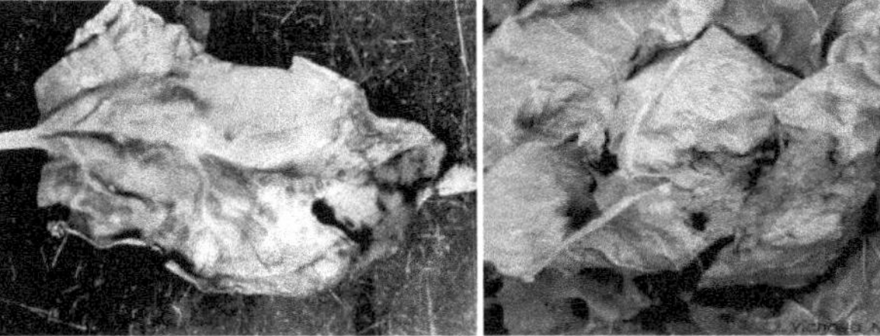

Mode of spread and survival:
- Fungus survives in plant debris or soil.
- **Primary:** Seed borne inoculum and dormant mycelium in infected plant debris.
- **Secondary Infection:** Spores are spread from plant-to-plants by splashing water from rains or sprinklers.

Favourable conditions:
- Relative humidity > 90%, High soil moisture and frequent rains favour the development of disease.

Management:
- Reduce crop refuse.
- Practice crop rotation, ensuring that fields are out of lettuce production for 4 to 5 years.
- Avoid cultivating in wet weather.
- Prevent moving infested soil to lettuce fields by washing equipment between fields.
- If infections are few, remove affected plants and any old, dead leaves as soon as spots are visible.
- Control prickly lettuce and other weed hosts.
- Plant lettuce types that are more resistant.
- Dithane M-45 at 2 lb/A on 7- to 10-day intervals can be used on seed crops only.

7. Stemphylium leaf spot

Causal Organism: *Stemphylium botryosum*

Disease symptoms:
- **Initial stage:** Small (0.1 to 0.2 inch diameter), circular to oval, gray-green leaf spots.

- **Late stage:** Leaf spots enlarge, remain circular to oval in shape, and turn brownish in color. Older spots coalesce, dry up, and become papery in texture.
- Visual signs of fungal growth are generally absent from the spots; hence this symptoms is readily differentiated from foliar diseases in which purple growth (downy mildew), green spores (Cladosporium leaf spot), or acervuli (anthracnose) develop within circular lesions.
- Overall, symptoms resemble the brownish, circular spots caused by pesticide or fertilizer toxicity.

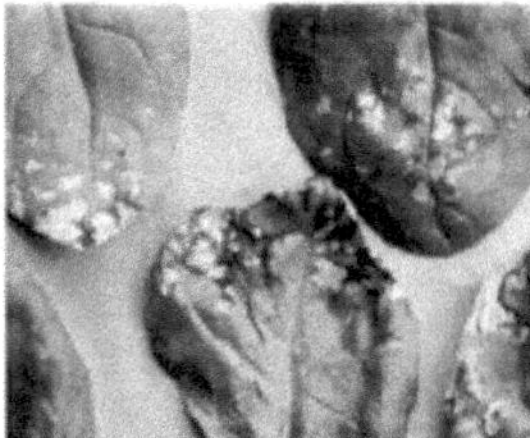

Mode of spread and survival:
- Fungus survives in seeds and infected seeds are the source of primary inoculums.
- Secondary infection occurs by means of conidia.

Favourable conditions:
- High humidity and moisture conditions favour the development of disease.

Management:
- This disease appears to be of minor importance and no spray controls are recommended.

8. Septoria leaf spot

Causal Organism: *Septoria lactucae*

Symptoms:
- Small, irregularly shaped chlorotic spots on oldest plant leaves which enlarge and turn brown and dry out.
- Lesions may fall out of leaves creating holes.
- Leaf spots may have chlorotic halos.
- If plant is severely infected, lesions may coalesce forming large necrotic patches, wilting leaves and plant death.

Mode of spread and survival:
- Fungus survives in infected seed and in crop debris.
- Disease spreads in humid or wet conditions.
- It can be spread by splashing water.
- Wild lettuce is an important overwintering site for the fungus.

Management:

- Plant pathogen free seed.
- Plant in areas where *Septoria* is uncommon.
- Ideal planting sites are in regions with low rainfall.
- Hot water treatment of seeds prior to planting may help reduce levels of disease.

9. Rust

Causal Organism: *Puccinia aristidae*

Symptoms:

- It attacks sugarbeet also.
- This is heteroecious rust.
- Light yellow, green colour spots less than 2.5 mm in diameter appear.
- These enlarge and turn yellow as the pustule forms and they turn orange as a rust crop opens.

Mode of spread and survival:

- The fungus can attack spinach where the alternate host *Distichlis spicata* (Salt grass) is nearby to serve as a source of sporidia.

Management:

Eradication of salt grass by late fall burning or by ploughing it down.

Spraying Maneb or Zineb @0.2%.

10. Bacterial Leaf Spot

Causal Organism: *Xanthomonas oxonopodis* pv. *Vitians*

Economic Importance:

- It was first described in the United States by Nellie Brown in 1918 from diseased lettuce in South Carolina and Virginia.
- The disease was first reported in California in 1964.
- It has since been reported from the major lettuce growing regions worldwide probably due to contamination of seed.

Symptoms:

- An early symptom of bacterial leaf spot is small (less than 0.25 inch in diameter), water-soaked leaf spots on the older leaves of the plant.
- These lesions are typically bordered by leaf veins and angular in shape.
- Lesions quickly turn black (a diagnostic characteristic of this disease).
- If the disease is severe, numerous lesions may coalesce, resulting in the collapse of the leaf.
- Older lesions dry up and become papery in texture, but retain the black colour.

- Lesions rarely develop on newly developing leaves.
- Bacterial leaf spot can occur on both leaf and head lettuce varieties.
- As with most bacterial diseases, the pathogen, *Xanthomonas campestris* pv. *vitians,* is highly dependent on wet, cool conditions for infection and disease development.

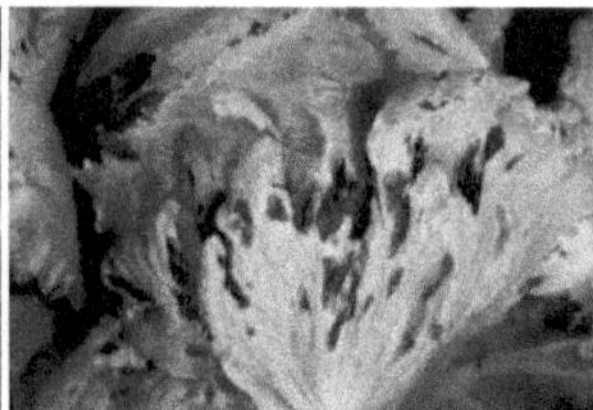

Epidemiology:
- Symptoms develop only if rain or sprinkler irrigation is present.
- Splashing water from these sources moves the bacteria from plant to plant.
- The pathogen is seedborne.
- In the case of lettuce seedlings grown as transplants, the pathogen may become established on plants during the greenhouse phase of growth.
- It has also been found growing epiphytically on weed plants, but the significance of this in disease development in lettuce is not known.

Management:
- Use pathogen-free seed as the first step in disease management.
- However, reliable seed assays and established threshold levels are not yet available.
- Avoid sprinkler irrigation when possible.
- Avoid planting back-to-back lettuce crops if the first crop was diseased and infected lettuce residue is present because the bacterium can survive on un-decomposed lettuce residue and be spread to subsequent lettuce crops.
- Copper fungicides can be used, but are not very effective; they must be applied before infection occurs.

11. bacterial soft rot

Causal Organism: *Pectobacterium carotovorum* subsp. *Carotovorum*

Symptoms:
- Bacterial soft rots affect the leaves and stems.
- Water-soaked spots occur on the outer leaves and form large brown slimy areas which progress to the inner leaves of the "head".
- The rot in the outer leaves cause the leaves to wilt, and eventually the stem, which results in collapse of the plant.
- Soft rot is important in the field during warm wet weather, and also important in transit and storage.
- The bacteria that cause soft rots occur in the soil; they infect through wounds made by insects, and those made when planting, weeding, harvesting, and transport.
- Infection also occurs through natural openings when water is present.

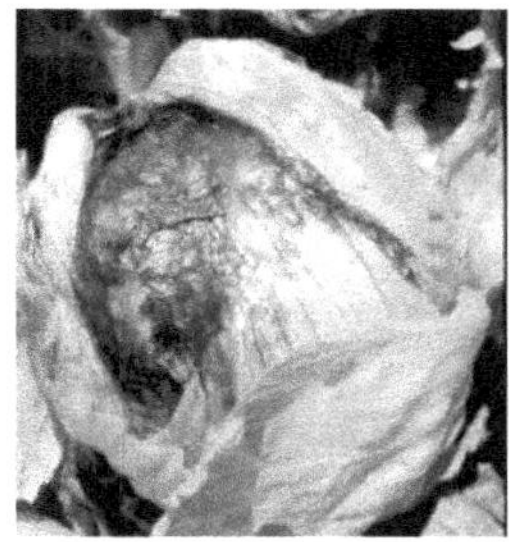

Mode of spread and survival:

- Spread is by rain splash, knives used for cutting (rots occur later in storage), and insects.
- In storage, rots also occur when infected leaves are in contact with those that are healthy.
- Survival is in the decaying remains of crop debris in the soil.

Management:

- Avoid planting in soil that becomes waterlogged.
- Plant lettuce on raised beds.
- To minimize soft rot losses, control insects, try to avoid mechanical injury during harvest, packing and shipping, and do not pack produce when wet.
- Additionally, store and ship produce at temperatures near 4°C (39°F).

12. Lettuce mosaic disease

Causal Organism: *Lettuce mosaic virus*

Economic Importance:

- Lettuce mosaic is one of the most common and potentially devastating diseases of lettuce.
- Caused by the Lettuce mosaic potyvirus (LMV), the disease was first reported in Florida, but has since been reported worldwide.
- LMV is the most important viral disease in California, the world's foremost lettuce growing region.

Symptoms:

- The disease is characterized by light and dark green patches and mosaic mottling of infected leaves.
- The leaves remain under-sized and are deformed.
- The plants remain stunted in growth.
- Infected heads may appear dull green, with outer leaves developing a characteristic downward curling.

Mode of spread and survival:

- The virus is transmitted in a non-persistent manner by a number of aphid species, including the green peach (*Myzus persicae*) and the cotton aphid (*Aphis gossypii*).

- LMV may also be mechanically transmitted in sap, and is the only economically important virus of lettuce that is seed transmitted.

Management:
- Control the insect-vector by using systemic insecticides like Rogor 30EC or Malathion.
- Remove and destroy the diseased plants and grow resistant varieties.

Physiological disorders of lettuce:

1. Tipburn:

Symptoms:
- Small brown spots first appear along the outer margins of outer leaves, then coalesce and form a brown fringe around the leaves-infection by brown soft rot may occur.

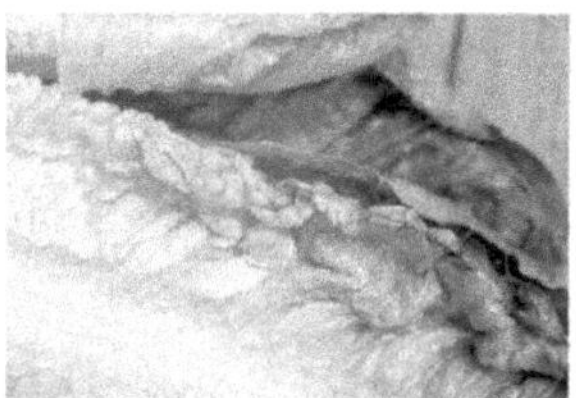

Cause:
- Uneven distribution of water and calcium within the plant.

Management:
- Maintain a pH of 5.5-6.5, calcium sprays and good water management.

2. Russet spotting:

Symptoms:
- Numerous small tan to brown spots on the midribs of leaves which increases in number with storage periods.

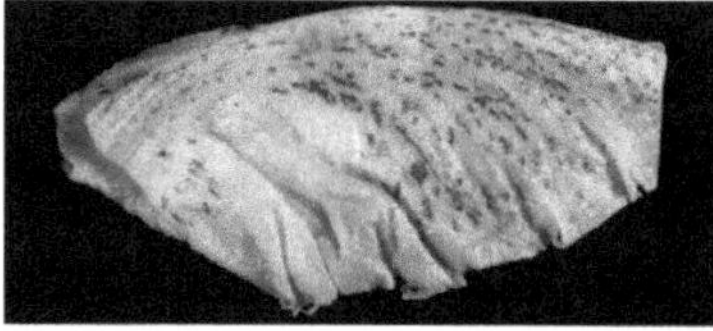

Cause:
- Induced by ethylene and temperatures above 3°C during storage.

Management:
- Maintain temperature near 0°C, holding in low O2 atmosphere and not storing in same room with ethylene producing products reduces russest spotting development.

3. Brown stain:

Symptoms:

- Characterised by lesions that are about 1cm long.
- Their margins are darker than their centers, giving a halo effect.

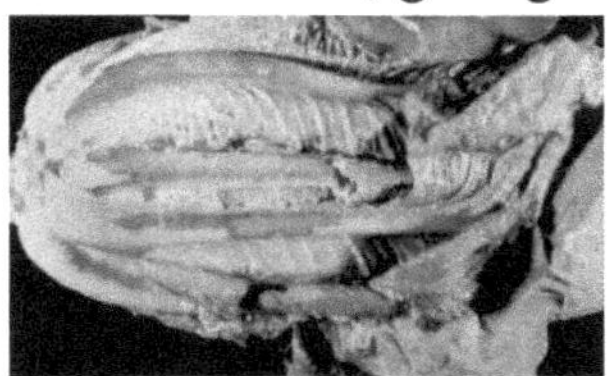

Cause:
- It is caused by CO_2 and aggravated by low O_2 and added CO.

Management:
- Don't hold intact lettuce heads where CO_2 concentrations might exceed 2%.
- Shred and cut lettuce because it is less sensitive to CO_2 injury.

4. Pink rib:

Symptoms:
- Characterised by light to dark pink discolouration of larger midribs.

Cause:
- Over storage.

Management:
- Keep temperature near 0°C and avoid prolonged storage (> 2 weeks).

References:

Mehrotra, B. S. and Narain, U., (1969). Studies on the genus Alternaria I. Some new records and a new species. *Indian Phytopath. Soc. Bull.,* 5, 1–7.

Meier, F. C., Drechsler, C. and Eddy, E. D., (1922). Black rot of carrots caused by *Alternaria radicina n. sp. Phytopathology,* 12, 157–168.

Mitter, J. H. and Tandon, R. N., (1930). Fungus flora of Allahabad. *J. Indian Bot. Soc.,* 9, 190–198.

Mohanty, N. N., (1961). *Alternaria blight of carrot. Proc. Indian Sci. Congr.* Part III, 256–257.

Narain, A., Swain, N. C., Sahoo, K. S., Das, S. K., & Shukla, V. D., (1985). A new leaf blight and fruit rot of water melon. *Indian Phytopath.,* 38, 149–15.

www.ingramcontent.com/pod-product-compliance
Lightning Source LLC
Chambersburg PA
CBHW040205110726
48005CB00019B/2902